Hill-Stream Ecology

Hill-Stream Ecology

Dr. Pawan Kumar 'Bharti',
(M.Sc., Ph.D., FASEA)

Founder Member
Centre for Agro-Rural Technologies,
RIIT Campus, Barwala, Panchkula, Haryana

BIOTECH

2012

BIOTECH BOOKS®

ISBN 978-81-7622-241-9

Published by: **BIOTECH BOOKS®**
4762-63/23, Ansari Road, Darya Ganj,
New Delhi - 110 002
Phone: +91-011-23262132
E-mail: biotechbooks@yahoo.co.in

Printed at: **Chawla Offset Printers**
Delhi - 110 052

PRINTED IN INDIA

Preface

The main sources of water in Himalayas are glaciers. The glaciers are an important resource of freshwater stored in the solid state. The Himalayas are the cradle of a large number of streams and mighty rivers. These hill-streams and rivers ensure all the year round availability of water for irrigating crops as well as for meeting domestic and other needs. Agriculture being the main source of livelihood, water resources generated in the Himalayas are therefore, their greatest gift to this country particularly so far the vast areas in the Indo-gangetic plains in the north. Everything originated in the water and everything is sustained by water. All life on earth depends on water. Man uses water for many purposes drinking, irrigation, fisheries, industrial purposes, transportation and recreations. Water is the most Essential commodity for all living creatures. Man needs it for his physiological existence water is the elixir of life It is the source of energy and govern the evaluation and function of the universe on the earth 97.3% of the worlds water *i.e.* 1.4 billion cubic kilometer ocean salty water cannot be used for agriculture domestic and industries purposes. Out of it 2.7% freshwater *i.e.* 73×10^6 cubic in the form of streams, lakes and wells.

Water quality characteristic of aquatic environment arise from a multitude of physical, biological and chemical interactions. The water bodies, lakes, rivers, dams and estuaries are continuously subject to a dynamic state of change with respect to the geological age and geochemical characteristics. Water pollution is a serious problem as almost 70% of India's surface water resources and a growing number of its groundwater reserves have been contaminated by biological, organic and inorganic pollutants.

A healthy ecosystem has a variety of organisms that play different roles in various food chains. If the ecosystem loses one of its members, it can be crippled. Ecological study of hill-stream describes the distribution and abundance of aquatic living organisms and also their contribution into environment. Biological diversity mainly influenced by the physicochemical characteristics of the aquatic ecosystem through the food chain. The biotic community in the stream exhibited the quantitative and qualitative fluctuations due to varied nutrient dynamics and ultimately changed the different trophic status of species community and limnological status of aquatic ecosystem. Heavy Metals are the hot topic of the present era, so the quantification and role of Heavy Metals in an aquatic ecosystem is described in the book.

This book gives an outline about hill-stream ecology, pollution; water quality; nutrients and ions; planktonic diversity; primary productivity; benthic diversity; heavy metals; various human activities; interlinking of rivers; Vedic significance of rivers and chants; National water policy; water quality index and water quality standards and related aspects are described in separate chapters. The present book mainly deals with biological diversity, primary productivity, Heavy Metals and physico-chemical characteristics of Sahastradhara stream, which gives a baseline data about the biological status of hill-stream. After references, a glossary is given to describe the definitions of selected terms and words. The glossary will be beneficial for the researchers, students of stream ecology and Environmental Science.

Pawan Kumar 'Bharti'

Contents

Chapter 1
Introduction

Contents

1.1 Water

In Vedic Literature water is mainly called, as Apha we all know that waters is the elixir of life. All living organisms, plants and animals are structurally 30-98% water. Besides being a structural component of body water is essential environmentally too.

Water is the medium through which nutrients of soil underneath and above on the surface move horizontally as well as vertically water has great power of dissolving most of the inorganic components in mixture form and in the pure elemental and ionic form. Water provides a medium for interaction among different compounds water is a great nurture for plants as well as for animals water helps in conducting of energy the form of heat helps in maintaining a soothing climate, water acts as a rejuvenator and medicament it self (Rig 1.23.19).

1.1.1 Origin of Water

The origin of water on earth is not clear so far. However, the current presumption is that the primordial earth had no oceans and perhaps very little atmosphere. It is believed that the volatile constituents bound in the earth crust, oozing to the surface through volcanoes, rock movements and hot springs, condensed to form the ocean, atmosphere and mountains. This way perhaps this remarkable combination of hydrogen and oxygen called water come into being and eventually became an indispensable component of earth's environments. No body can imagine life without water. Water is our basic requirement even animal and plant can't survive without water. It is common statement that *"Life is not possible without water"*. Thus life and water are inseparable faces of the same coin.

Water is the most Essential commodity for all living creatures. Man needs it for his physiological existence water is the elixir of life It is the source of energy and govern the evaluation and function of the universe on the earth 97.3% of the worlds water *i.e.* 1.4 billion cubic kilometer ocean salty water cannot be used for agriculture domestic and industries purposes. Out of it 2.7% freshwater *i.e.* 73 x 10^6 cubic in the form of streams, lakes, wells and tube wells *i.e.* 0.6% 8.5 x $10^{15}m^3$ is groundwater which oceans at the depth of 80 meter below the ground surface (Kataria, 1994).

Chemically, water is the mono-oxide of Hydrogen *i.e.* (H.O.H). It freely disassociated into hydrogen and hydroxyl ions. The ionization product (H^+) and (OH^-) is about 10^{-14}. Water is a colourless liquid and possesses a high dielectric constant (81), and there for salts gets highly ionized when dissolved in water but not so in the other solvents. Due to this property, water is known as universal solvent present on the earth that is why the natural water contains many salts in dissolved form. On the basis of amount these slats dissolved in the earth only 3% of the total water (approximately 1.4 billion cubic kilometer) is fresh and suitable for human consumption of this, less than 0.01% is associated with rivers and streams (Bharti, 2004).

1.1.2 Phases of Water

These are the main phases of water:

1. Permafrost
2. Hail
3. Fog
4. Water vapour
5. Dew
6. Ice
7. Aquifer
8. Sleet
9. Frost

Water is not only essential for life but predominant inorganic constituent of living matter forming in general nearly three quarters of the weight of living cells. It makes some 5 percent of the body weight of an adult human and can forms as 98% of the mass of certain jellyfish. Organisms that contain relatively small amounts of water are generally in dormant state or show very slow development; seeds and certain invertebrates that live in arid environments are examples. On the other hand high rainfall over a landmass in variably means a large biomass per unit area.

Every thing originated in the water and every thing is sustained by water all life on earth depends on water. Water is very essential for the survival of all living organism there is a wide variety of beneficial uses of water. Man uses water for many purposes, drinking, irrigation, fisheries, industrial purposes, transportation and waste disposal. The origin of water on the earth is not clear so far. However, the current presumption is that the primordial earth had no oceans and perhaps volatile constituents bound in the earth crust oozing to the surface through volcanoes rock movements and hot springs, condensed to form the ocean and the atmosphere. This way come into being and eventually become an indispensable component of earth's environment.

1.2 Source of Water

The main sources of water in Himalayas are glaciers. The glacier resources in the Himalayas are vast. The glaciers have their usefulness as water resources, modify the climate in the region, and influence the production and the transport of debris, cause flood and siltation of reservoirs. The total number of glaciers in the Himalayas is not known, but may be estimated provisionally from the figures of ice cover given by *VON WISSMAN* and the average area of glaciers the estimated figure for the total number of glaciers in the Himalayas is thus around 15,000.

The glaciers are an important resource of freshwater stored in the solid state. The size of these reservoirs in the Himalayas is not known in detail at present, but it is considered to be very large. A single large glacier, e.g. the *Gangotri glacier,* has an estimated total volume of well over 20 km^3 of ice. The reservoir is regulated by climate and especially by the prevalent summer air temperature the number of cloudy days and the amount of solid precipitation the annual balance between the input as snow and the output as melt water is rarely maintained. Imbalances often exist and seem to persist, as generalized trends of either positive balance or negative balance for decades (Bharti, 2004).

The Himalayas are the cradle of a large number of streams and mighty rivers. These hill-streams and rivers ensure all the year round availability of water for irrigating crops as well as for meeting domestic and other needs. Agriculture being the main source of livelihood, water resources generated in the Himalayas are therefore, their greatest gift to this country particularly so far the vast areas in the Indo-gangetic plains in the north. Everything originated in the water and everything is sustained by water. All life on earth depends on water. Man uses water for many purposes drinking, irrigation, fisheries, industrial purposes, transportation and recreations.

1.2.1 Main Sources of Water on Earth

Basically these are the main sources of water on earth planet:

1. Rainfall
2. Groundwater
   - ☆ Dug wells
   - ☆ Bore wells
   - ☆ Tube wells
   - ☆ Hand pumps
3. Surface water
   - (*a*) Freshwater:
     - (*i*) Lentic (still water)
       - ☆ Ponds
       - ☆ Lakes.
       - ☆ Wetlands
     - (*ii*) Lotic water (running water)-
       - ☆ Rivers
       - ☆ Springs
       - ☆ Streams
       - ☆ Brooks
   - (*b*) Marine water
     - ☆ Ocean
     - ☆ Sea.

1.3 Origin and Regulation of River

There is a main source of water in India by the rivers. In India fourteen major river systems share about 83% of the drainage basis *i.e.* Indian rivers carry about 16,45,000 million cubic meter of water annually (Rao, 1975). In India all 14 major rivers including Coocum, Ganga, Gomti, Kaveri, Damodar and Mini-Mahi have become polluted due to various anthropogenic factors especially for the development activities. The river Damodar is perhaps the most heavily polluted river. Many parts of river do not seem to have any dissolved oxygen and no wonder that they fail to support the growth of desirable aquatic fauna and flora.

1.3.1 Origin of River

The Ganga is a holy river of India. Many Indians mainly Hindus worship it like a Goddess. Ganga is also known as Bhagarithi Ganga. Ganga is one of the four mighty rivers of world with its tributaries, and it is a symbol of purity. There are more than 50 big cities situated along with 12,500 km long bank of river Ganga. According to Deming (1975) if the entire ice over of the world would keep flow for 830 years. But now a day due to the various natural and human activities including burning of fossil fuels, natural activities like volcanic eruption, deforestation etc. the earth atmosphere is warming regularly due to the increase in the Co_2 level in the atmosphere.

The Water of dozens of rivers is rivulets and lakes enhance the rich heritage of this Himalayan State, Among the numerous rivers and streams the Ganga, Yaumna, Alaknanda and Kali are of great religions significance in India the rivers are veritable gifts form mother India it self like her they too are all women and again like her they bear a touch of divinity. Rivers have always been an inseparable part of Hinduism. For Hindus Ganga is not only the river of life but also at the same time the river of Death for he longs to die beside it or at the very least to have wish ashes after cremation on cash in its water. It is believed that the Holy waters of this rivers washes away the sins and cleanness the soul of lesser mortals same of the facts about the quality of Ganges's water cannot be lightly diseased scientist heaver say they have established how the water will keep for a year in bottles and that cholera grams die in it with in a few hours or even that a tank reputed to be fed from the Ganga has the power of dissolving human bones within there days. Geologists firmly believe that the mineral contents of the water. Also makes the difference a Sanskrit verse that a Hindu recites at the time of taking the dip.

"O Ganga, O Yamuna, and also Godavari and Saraswati and Narmada and Sindhu and Kaveri by your water I purify myself. This hymn to the rivers is also a hymn to the nation".

The Ganga is a holy river of India. Many Indians, mainly 'Hindus' warship it like a Goddess. Ganga is known by many names like Bhagarathi Ganga etc. Ganga is one of the four mighty rivers of world. With its tributaries it is largest and very important rivers basin of the country. It is symbol of purity. Alaknanda and Bhagrathi to form the river Ganga. The two parents Strom are snow fed and own their origin to the Himalaya glaciers known as Gomukh. Ganga after traveling a distance of 2525 km falls into Ganga Sagar (West Bengal). The Ganga joins Ram Ganga at Kannauj and Yamuna at Allahabad. At Rishikesh the Ganga cuts across the Shivalik hills and for the first time enter the plains.

Ganga river has a great advantage in various ways to different living organisms. Haridwar is located at the bank of river Ganga. Haridwar has a great importance for the Ashrams and temples. We receive freshwater form the rivers but we also dump our wastes and other things in their water bodies, which has created the problem of water pollution. It is estimated that about 1200 million liters of waste are released in Ganga from about 27 major cities situated at its banks. At Haridwar thousand of pilgrims take bath on every 'Snanparv' like, Baishakhi, Sharad purnima, etc. and at the occasion of Kumbh many lacks of pilgrims take bath in the river Ganga.

The sustainable use of river water in agriculture resources is an essential component in the future development of Asian third world countries, especially those regions bordering or connecting the Himalayas, where population growth is rapid and predicted to continue. This population pressure results in an intensification of agriculture through the adoption of multiple annual crop solution and supported by large application of inorganic and organic fertilizers and the expansion of cultivated land on to steeper will stapes and previously forested areas (Schreier *et al.* 1994) continued and excessive application of mineral and organic fertilizers to increase crop field may however, lead to detrimental effects in the form of soil and water acidification as well as downstream eutrophication.

In India all 14 major rivers including Coocum, Ganga, Gomti, Kaveri, Damodar and Mini-Mahi have become polluted. The river Damodar is perhaps the most heavily polluted river. Many parts of river do not seem to have any dissolved oxygen and no wonder that they fail to support the growth of desirable aquatic fauna and flora.

The river Ganga form Haridwar to Calcutta is treated as one unending sewer fit only to carry urban liquid waste, half burnt dead bodies, carrion, pesticides and insecticides. All along Grange's nearly 1,550 miles journey to the sea, some 27 major towns and cities have identified among which hardly a third have any thing resembling a sewage treatment plant of about 312 industrial units dumping their wastes in to the water, only the dozen have effluent treatment facilities. These 27 cities contribute 902 million liters of water to the river each day. The biggest culprits are the cities of Hardwar, Kanpur, Varanasi, Patna and parts of Calcutta form Kanpur alone 270 million liters daily of untreated sewage including 30 x 106 liters daily of industrial effluents flow into the river. The water of Ganga affects the health of 250 million of people in northern India.

A hill-stream *Sahastradhara,* 15km far from Dehradun is the main assistant stream of river song, which ultimately joins to Ganga in lesser foothills of Shivalik Himalayas in Uttarakhand State. The hill-stream has a great ecological significance as well as a famous tourist place of north India.

Modern civilization is dependent on water for irrigation, industry, and domestic needs, shipping and of increasing importance for sanitation and disposal waste. Most of our water bodies such as ponds, lakes, streams and rivers have become polluted and a consequence of increasing industrialization, urbanization and other development activities. Today many of the rivers of the world revives millions of litter of sewage, domestic wastes and industrial and agriculture effluents containing substances varying form simple nutrients to highly toxic substances *viz.* nitrates, selenium, cadmium, mercury, chlorinated hydrocarbons etc. In U.S.A. every major river has become seriously polluted. The great lakes, which furnish the greatest single sources of water to America and Canada, have already been polluted. Massive pollution turned Rhine into a dead river in the heart of Western Europe.

1.3.1 Regulation of River

Glacier melts and the water pass through heavy and porous agents of erosion and transportation the Himalayan rivers Ganga and Brahmaputra together account for 3% the total flux of dissolved load to the world is ocean (Sarin *et al.* 1989). It has been estimated that the non-Himalayan rivers of peninsular India carry less than 5% of the total mass transport as compared to Himalayan rivers (Subramaniam 1979).

Thus a high altitude Himalayan river basin provides a natural unit within which one can examine natural weathering and agrochemical processes. However, even today the study and management of the Himalayan River is unfortunately constrained by a lock of reliable hydrological data. Although some work has been done in the last few decades (Hasnain *et al.* 1989, Hasnain, 1992 and 1996; Hasnain and Renoj 1996, Chauhan and Hasnain 1993, Sarin *et al.* 1992), It is either confined to a hear source region or is based on only few samples. Adequate understanding of the Himalayan proglacial streams is extremely important for the development of a realistic programme for utilizing the potential of water that exits in the form of snow and ice in this area. Several studies have been carried out in the lower part of the Ganga river system (Abbas and Subramaniam, 1984, Sarin *et al.* 1989 and Handa, 1972). But very little information is available on agrochemical and biological aspects of the Ganga headwater.

Water is a resource circulated throughout all ecosystems and is one of the most important factors of them (Odum 1971). From the point of view of ecohydrology, for the main elements of an ecosystem including inorganic and organic compound, producers and consumers both the quantity and the chemistry of water have a decisive impact on its biomass and biotic composition. Information obtained form current hydro-chemical analyses of water specimens is very important but it is sometimes difficult to Gauge the overall situation especially the occurrence of nutrient, which may be very important to an ecosystem.

Ecological, geo-chemical and hydrological research has been carried out in various ecosystems to understand the factors controlling the chemistry of natural water (Likens *et al.* 1977, Baro and Bricker, 1990). Many of such studies have been under taken during the last two decades to understand the processes that control the hydrochemistry of alpine and sub-alpine systems of North America and Europe (William *et al.* 1993 and Psenner, 1989). Similar studies were also done in China and central Asia (Xue and schnoor, 1994). Recently, some studies focused on the hydro-chemical processes of snow and ice in the Himalayan/Korakoram mountain systems (Hasnain and Thayyen, 1999 a,b., Sarin *et al.* 1989 and 1992). Snow and glacier fed stream in the Himalayan and Karkoram are the major source of water in the most of the Indian sub-continent river systems.

Atmospheric input to the Himalayan uplands is mainly contributed by the southwest monsoon during the summer, which is mostly dominated by high So_4^{2-} concentration of anthropogenic origin form the Indian subcontinent (Wake *et al.* 1992). However, during winter the waterlines bring snow and rain loaded with an unusually high content of No_3^- from central Asia and Europe (Wake, 1989). This type of precipitation may result in water acidification and down stream eutrophication (Galloway, 1986). In early spring, the increased sulphate and nitrate concentration in the early melt water fraction input into a stream can drop the pH of the stream to a harmful level for the aquatic life (Reuss and Johnson, 1986). Sulphate and nitrate loaded melt water pulses have been reported in North America and Europe (Bales, 1992). The rapid snow melting processes and monsoon rainfall over glaciers may affect the water chemistry in the Himalayan/Karakoram region very significantly.

The sustainable use of land water and agriculture resources is an essential component in the future development of Asian third world countries, especially those regions bordering or connecting the Himalayas, where population growth is rapid and predicted to continue. This population pressure results in an intensification of agriculture through the adoption of multiple annual crop solution and supported by large application of inorganic and organic fertilizers and the expansion of cultivated land on to steeper will stapes and previously forested areas (Schreier *et al.* 1994) continued and excessive application of mineral and organic fertilizers to increase crop field may however, lead to detrimental effects in the form of soil and water acidification as well as downstream eutrophication.

In the monsoon months, the Himalayas force up the rain bearing wind up the mountains to deposit most of their moisture on the Indian side. The rainfall in the Himalayas during the monsoon season feeds northern India with plentiful water and in winter the Himalayas store up the snow on the mountains to maintain the flow of the rivers in the dry seasons. Not only do the Himalayas cause rain in the hills, but also their influence on the rainfall in the plains immediately below the foothills is found to be marked the monsoon rainfall substantially increases from Manipur to Bareilly, which is still in the plains, as we approach the Shivaliks.

The ice melting, generally takes place between from the end of February to the beginning of October in the eastern Himalayas and between from the end of April to the beginning October in north- western Himalayas. The winter snow that falls and accumulates below the altitude of the glacier termini melts early in the summer season, the remainder passes as it were, through the cycle of the ice reservoir mentioned earlier and is a part of its annual balance.

The amount of suspended matter in river water depends on the hydraulic condition of the stream and the availability of suitable size fraction of sediment (Gurnell, 1982). The Himalayan rivers carry large sediment loads as they drain through the most active tectonic zones and easily erodible foothills of the Himalaya and streams, mass movement and human activities all contribute to the suspended load of the stream further the turbulent nature of the flow and the low temperature of the stream also enhance the suspended load. The turbulent water brings ever-coarser materials into suspension and the low temperature increases the viscosity of water thereby reducing the falling velocity of suspended sediments (Drewry, 1986).

1.4 Water Quality

The history of human civilization reveals that water supply and civilization are almost synonymous. Several towns, cities and communities have disappeared due to shortages originating from climatic changes. Millions of people all over the world, particularly in the developing countries are loosing their lives every year from water borne-disease (Dezuane, 1979). An understanding of water chemistry is the basis of the knowledge of the multidimensional aspect of aquatic environmental chemistry which involves the source, composition, reactions and transportation of water.

The quality of water is of vital concern for mankind since it is directly linked with human welfare. It is a matter of history that faecal pollution of drinking water caused water-borne diseases which wiped out entire populations of cities. At present the menace of water-borne diseases and epidemics still looms large on the horizon of developing countries. Polluted water has been the culprit or cause in all such cases in which the major sources of pollution are domestic wastes from urban and industrial wastes (Asaolu, 1998).

Water quality characteristic of aquatic environment arise from a multitude of physical, biological and chemical interactions. The water bodies, lakes, rivers, dams and estuaries are continuously subject to a dynamic state of change with respect to the geological age and geochemical characteristics. This is demonstrated by continuous circulation, transformation and accumulation of energy and matter through the medium of living thing and their activities (Adefemi, 2007).

The dynamic balance in the aquatic ecosystem is upset by human activities, resulting in pollution which meter, is manifested dramatically as fish kill, offensive taste, odour, colour and unchecked aquatic weeds. The over production of higher tropic levels biomass and the subsequent decay of dead plants could lead to oxygen depletion, death of aquatic organisms and development of anaerobic zone where bacteria action produce foul odours and bad tastes (Forstner and Wittman, 1979).

Water quality includes all physical, chemical and biological factor that influence the beneficial use of water, Lotic habitats are those exiting in relatively fast running streams, springs, river and brooks. The lakes represent lentic habitats; marshes and swamps represent ponds and wetland. The above classification of freshwater environment is based on currents and ratio of the depth of surface area.

A hill-stream consists of two major zones, Rithron and Potamon. Aquatic biodiversity is mainly occurring in potamon zone due to the slow velocity of running water. In potamon zone the community consists of the population of the following groups:

(A) Neuston

(B) Plankton

  (*i*) Phytoplankton

  (*ii*) Zooplankton

(C) Necton

(D) Benthos

(E) Macrophytes

The biotic community in the streams and rivers is quite different from that in the ponds, lakes and other stagnant water bodies. The differences in the community are largely due to differences in the physical and chemical conditions of their environments. The physiological changes, adaptations and other characteristics are also entirely different.

1.5 Pollution

Water pollution is a serious problem as almost 70% of India's surface water resources and a growing number of its groundwater reserves have been contaminated by biological, organic and inorganic pollutants. Pollution of surface and groundwater resources occurs through point and diffuse sources. Examples of point source pollution are effluents from industries and from sewage-treatment plants. Rapid population growth, urbanization and industrialization have led to a greater demand for an increasingly smaller supply of water resources in the country. Of the present water usage in the country, majority is consumed in agriculture (70–90%), and the remaining is consumed in industrial activities and for domestic purposes like drinking water and sanitation (Rao and Mamtha, 2004).

One of the important issues that impacts sustainable water management (SWM) practice in India is related to water quality. Problems with water quality are often as severe as problems with water availability, but less attention has been paid to them, particularly in India. Water pollution is a serious problem in India as almost 70% of its surface water resources and a growing number of its groundwater reserves are already contaminated by biological, organic and inorganic pollutants. In many cases, these sources have been rendered unsafe for human consumption as well as for other activities such as irrigation and industrial needs. This illustrates that water quality decline can in effect contribute to water scarcity as it limits the availability of water for both human use and the ecosystem.

1.5.1 Sources of Pollution

Pollution of surface and groundwater resources occurs through point and diffuses sources. Examples of point source pollution are effluents from industries, sewage-treatment plants and untreated domestic sewage. The main sources of diffuse pollution may be anthropogenic activities, such as agricultural applications of fertilizers and pesticides or of geo-chemical origin, such as natural contamination of groundwater sources by fluoride, arsenic and dissolved salts. Pollution from point sources can be controlled by disposal in engineered facilities, treatment and recycling of waste materials. Minimizing application of fertilizers and pesticides is a way to control pollution from agricultural activities. Natural contamination of groundwater sources by fluoride, arsenic and dissolved salts is dealt with by suitable treatment of extracted groundwater.

(*a*) Industrial Pollution

In case of industrial units, effluents in most of the cases are discharged into pits, open ground, or open unlined drains near the factories, thus allowing it to move to low-lying depressions resulting in groundwater pollution. The industries, which are burgeoning at a fast rate, produce about 55,000 million m^3 of wastewater per day, out of which 68.5 million m^3 is discharged into river and streams. Thus the magnitude of damage caused to our water resources can be estimated from the fact that about 70% of rivers and streams in India contain polluted water. The incidence of surface and groundwater pollution is highest in urban areas where large volumes of waste are concentrated and discharged into relatively small areas. The groundwater contamination is detected only some time after the subsurface contamination begins. Although the industrial sector accounts for only 3% of the annual water withdrawals in India, its contribution to water pollution, particularly in urban areas, is considerable (Rao and Mamtha, 2004).

(*b*) Pollution from Domestic Activities

Inadequate treatment of human and animal wastes contributes to the high incidence of water-related diseases in the country. To date, only 14% of rural and 70% of urban inhabitants have access to adequate sanitation facilities.

Therefore, water contaminated by human waste is often discharged directly into watercourses or seeps into the groundwater table from faulty septic tanks or pit latrines. The level of faecal coliform bacteria in most rivers often exceeds the WHO (World Health Organization) standards and is responsible for causing a number of gastrointestinal ailments among the population. All of India's 14 major river systems are heavily polluted, mostly from the 50 million cubic meters of untreated sewage discharged into them each year. The domestic sector is responsible for the majority of the wastewater generation in India. Combined, the 22 largest cities in the country produce over 7267 million litres of domestic wastewater per day, of which slightly over 80% is collected for treatment (Rao and Mamtha, 2004).

(*c*) Agricultural Activities

Use of fertilizers and pesticides to improve soil fertility and crop protection has created an environmental menace. Both these products find their way into the food chain and have implications on human health. Fertilizers and pesticides have entered the water supply through runoff and leaching to the groundwater table and pose a hazard to human, animal and plant populations. Some of these chemicals such as hexachlorocyclohexane (HCH), dichlorodiphenyltrichloroethane (DDT), endosulfan, methyl malathion, malathion dimethoate, and ethion are considered as extremely hazardous by the WHO and are banned or are under strict control in developed countries (Rao and Mamtha, 2004). Degradation of water quality creates water scarcity and limits its availability for human use and ecosystem and thereby impacts the optimum management of water resources. Pollution of surface and groundwater resources occurs through point and diffuses sources.

1.6 Effect on Ecology

Ecology is the study of the interactions between organisms and their environment. Various different species living in the same place, interacting amongst themselves and with their abiotic and biotic environment together form an ecosystem. Within an ecosystem there are several food chains and food webs. A food web is an overview of which species in an environment consume which species (plant, animal or both). A healthy ecosystem has a variety of organisms that play different roles in various food chains. If the ecosystem loses one of its members, it can be crippled. For instance, if owls in the forest food web would die out, rodents might start to multiply at an enormous speed, causing them to overrun the area and finish resources that other animals also use. Ecologists are people that study the interactions between organisms and their environment within food webs or other ecological relationships. Fieldwork is an essential component of this study. Laboratory experiments are also applied, under field conditions. Most of the time ecologists are involved in studying the natural environment and communities, but some are involved in applied ecology, using ecological knowledge in ecosystems directed by humans, commonly known as agro-ecosystems.

There are two kinds of aquatic environments, which can sustain life. These are saltwater life zones and freshwater life zones. The major types of organisms found in aquatic environments are determined by the salinity of the water. Salinity means the amounts of salts dissolved in a volume of water. That is why aquatic life zones are divided up between saltwater life zones and freshwater life zones. An example of a marine life zone is a coral reef. An example of a freshwater life zone is a lake or hill-stream.The largest saltwater life zones on earth are not very hard to find, as these are in the oceans. Oceans cover about 71% of the earth's surface and are very important for the preservation of all life on earth. Oceans play an important part in the hydrological cycle, because precipitation (rain) consists of evaporated oceanic water and in the regulation of the earth's climate. Oceans also participate in other matter cycles. Oceans are the living environment for about 250,000 species of marine plants and animals. Unfortunately, oceans are also dumps for human waste, because the (polluted) water of all inland water bodies eventually ends up in oceans.

Water is an important substance required by all living organisms and for all anthropogenic activities. The problem of environmental pollution due to toxic metals has begun to cause concern now in most major metropolitan cities (Bharti, 2007). Most of our water resources are gradually becoming polluted due to the addition of foreign materials from the surroundings. These include organic matter origin from plant and animal, land surface washing, and industrial and sewage effluents.

Metals that are naturally introduced into the water body come primarily from such sources as rock weathering, soil erosion, or the dissolution of water-soluble salts. Naturally occurring metals move through aquatic environments independently of human activities, usually without any detrimental effects. Humans consume metallic elements through both water and food. Some metals such as sodium, potassium, magnesium, calcium, and iron are found in living tissue and are essential to human life biological anomalies arise when they are depleted or removed. Probably less well known is that currently no less than six other heavy metals including molybdenum, manganese, cobalt, copper, and zinc, have been linked to human growth, development, achievement, and reproduction (Vahrenkamp, 1979; Friberg *et al.*, 1979). Even these metals, however, can become toxic or aesthetically undesirable when their concentrations are too great. Several heavy metals, like cadmium, lead, and mercury, are highly toxic at relatively low concentrations, can accumulate in body tissues over long periods of time, and are nonessential for human health.

The toxic heavy metals entering the ecosystem may lead to geo-accumulation, bioaccumulation and biomagnifications. Heavy metals like Fe, Cu, Zn, Ni and other trace elements are important for proper functioning of biological systems and their deficiency or excess could lead to a number of disorders. Food chain contamination by heavy metals has become a burning issue in recent years because of their potential accumulation in biosystems through contaminated water, soil and air. Therefore, a better understanding of heavy metal sources, their accumulation in the soil and the effect of their presence in water and soil on plant systems seem to be particularly important issues of present-day research on risk assessments (Lokeshwari and Chandrappa, 2006).

Natural events can occur that alter the river's ecology by changing these kinds of factors. Mudslides, heavy rainfall, and fires can make drastic changes. When Mt. St. Helens erupted in Washington State, it sent uncounted tons of fine ash in a torrent down through its river valleys. These events (though they seem extreme from our human point of view), are a very large and slow, but nevertheless integral, part of the river's ecosystem. While Mt. St. Helens's ash was destructive to the salmon that used its rivers, the mountain has erupted many times in the long history of the salmon, and they have adapted in their own mysterious ways. We are far from understanding everything about biological adaptation.

Rivers are closely connected with the atmosphere (the air above them). Gases from the air, like oxygen, carbon dioxide, and nitrogen dissolve into the water. The colder the water is, or the more it churns as it flows downhill, the more gases there will be in it. Rain scrubs molecules and other particles out of the air, and when the air is polluted by coal-burning power plants and automobile exhaust, the rain becomes acidic, and falls as acid rain. Acid rain can lead to the death of streams and lakes. Water that is too acidic falls on the earth and leaches minerals out of it, washing them into streams and lakes. Some of these minerals, like aluminium, are highly toxic to fish. Aluminium in water causes fishes' gills to become covered with thick mucus, and they are no longer able to breathe. Fish in acidic lakes simply suffocate to death.

The water bodies have a complex and fragile ecosystem; however they have self-cleaning ability but excess load always disturb the natural system and therefore readily accumulate pollutants. In some tourist hilly regions, there are not any more industrial pollution, but tourist's anthropogenic activities may alter the water quality of hill-streams and the physico-chemical characteristics of water of some tourist spot may affect the biological diversity of that water body.

When water rolls down the slopes of a watershed (or catchment area or drainage basin), it carries things with it. It dissolves chemicals and carries them. It carries particles of dirt. And it carries organic matter: tiny bits of leaves, bacteria, and a lot of other things too small to see. As it flows, it grows to rivulets, and carries larger bits of matter. By the time the water gets all the way down to the river, it is full of whatever was on (and in) the land around it. The river can carry sticks, leaves, logs, brush, and even sand, pebbles, rocks, and boulders. These heavier objects bounce along the bottom in a process called saltation. There are other ways that things can end up in a river. Winds can blow in sediment (particles of dirt) and bits of organic matter. A lot of living things like insects depend on flowing water to carry out their life cycles. Birds leave feathers, droppings, and urine. Other animals visit the river and often leave their waste in it. Many animals die in the river, adding their organic materials to the water.

Natural events can occur that alter the river's ecology by changing these kinds of factors. Heavy rainfall, mudslides and fires can make drastic changes in water ecology. These events (though they seem extreme from our human point of view), are a very large and slow, but nevertheless integral, part of the river's ecosystem.

Rivers are closely tied with the atmosphere (the air above them). Gases from the air, like oxygen, carbon dioxide, and nitrogen dissolve into the water. The colder the water is, or the more it churns as it flows downhill, the more gases there will be in it. Rain scrubs molecules and other particles out of the air, and when the air is polluted by coal-burning power plants and automobile exhaust, the rain becomes acidic, and falls as acid rain. Acid rain can lead to the death of streams and lakes. Water that is too acidic falls on the earth and leaches minerals out of it, washing them into streams and lakes. Some of these minerals, like aluminium, are highly toxic to fish. Aluminium in water causes fishes' gills to become covered with thick mucus, and they are no longer able to breathe. Fish in acidic lakes simply suffocate to death.

1.7 Objectives

Pollutants originating from the anthropogenic activities affect the water chemistry and there by the ability to predict the location and severity of potential impact can be achieved only through knowledge of hydro-chemical processes in pristine waters of similar physico-chemical characteristics (Bruns *et at.* 1991). If a sufficiently detailed knowledge has pristine, or baseline, water chemistry is available, the effects of local pollution, stemming form land use and atmospheric deposition of acidic oxides for example can be quantified.

The objectives characterized the water chemistry of these geologically young environments and to determine the nature and degree of anthropogenic impacts on stream ecology and chemistry of a hill-stream. The impact on water chemistry of anthropogenic pollution from industrial, agricultural, sources, quarrying and tourists activity has concerned environmentalists and scientists for the past three decades. In consequences, the chemistry of headwater streams, lakes and lowland rivers has been monitored widely in Europe and North America in an effort to define and quantifying these anthropogenic impacts.

1.8 Site Selection

Lesser Himalaya consists of a huge part of Uttarakhand, and Dehradun, Haridwar and Rishikesh are the main religious and beautiful cities, which are situated in the foothills of Himalaya. A hill-stream *Sahastradhara,* 15km far from Dehradun was selected the study site. Therefore, in the present study, an attempt has been made to understand the hydro-geochemical processes in Himalayan catchments, particularly in the Sahastradhara River headwater.

The purpose of this work is to provide preliminary observations of the geochemistry of natural water from Sahastradhara at Dehradun and to make geo-chemical comparison between 'Sahastradhara' water and water from other regions of the country. The present work is aimed towards developing baseline data for river water quality of *'Sahastradhara'* stream a major tributary of Song River and to understanding the weathering and geo-chemical processes active in Himalayan river basins.

Chapter 2
Overview of a Hill-stream

Contents

2.1 General

Sahastradhara stream originated basically from the hills of Mussoorie. Upstream of Sahastradhara is connected with river Badli near village *Karligarh*. River Badli is divided in to two branches *Jhandu Nala* and *Dhadola* at 840-1310 masl.

Sahastradhara is situated 15 km. Far Away from *Dehradun* in Northeast side. Site is connected by city bus service. This site is main attraction and interesting place for picnic tourist spot. The trickling waters from the nearly caves enhance the scenery; so many people go there to enjoy picnic. "Sahastradhara" is very well known for *sulfur springs* and streams of cold sulfur water gush out of mountain cavities in a spectacular way, tourist rest house and P.W.D.I/H are available for stay there.

Geologically, Sahastradhara hills are enriched with limestone. It is also famous for limestone quarrying, which is prohibited by Government after the appeals of M.C. Mehta (1985, *R.L.E case Dehradun Vs state of U.P*). Geographically, Sahastradhara is situated in the globe on Latitude 29.57°–31.20° E and Longitude 77.35°–79.20° N. The water of Sahastradhara is very beneficial for skin disease due to sulfur. Skin disease can be cure after bathing regularly in this water. The downstream of Sahastradhara meets with Kali Rao, which is mostly dry during study period and quarrying is running regularly in its basin. This stream meets with Song River, which is a tributary of River Ganga.

Geology

Sahastradhara hills are enriched with limestone. It is also famous for limestone quarrying, which is prohibited by government after the appeals of M.C. Mehta (1985, *R.L.E case Dehradun Vs state of U.P*).

The water of Sahastradhara is very beneficial for skin disease due to sulfur. Skin disease can be cure after bathing regularly in this water. The downstream of Sahastradhara meets with Kali Rao, which is mostly dry during study period and *quarrying was going on regularly in its basin*. This stream ultimately meets with Song River, which is a tributary of River Ganga.

Geography

The population of Dehradun is 12,79,083 (according 2001) and area 1,193 miles, has been surrounded by the natural beauties with lovely trees and cool climate, which is not only a pleasant place to live in but relaxing for holiday also.

This is not only a popular city but also valuable or important place for educational view in Uttarakhand, Dehradun is the capital of Uttarakhand state and also famous for *Forest Research Institute* (FRI), *Indian Military Academy* (IMA), *Oil and Natural Gases Corporation* (ONGC), *Zoological Survey of India* (ZSI) and other institute.

Sahastradhara stream originated from the hills of Mussoorie basically. Upstream of Sahastradhara is connected with river Badli near village *Karligarh*. River Badli is dividing in to two branches JhanduNala and Dhadola.

Sahastradhara is situated on the globe with the geo-coordinates:

- ✰ Latitude: 29.57°–31.20°
- ✰ Longitude: 77.35°–79.20°

Meteorology

Sahastradhara has a cool and pleasant climate. There are some data related to climatic condition of Sahastradhara valley regions.

Sea level: 840 – 1310 masl.

Rainfall (annually): 2911 mm (1984)
3198 mm (1985)
2601 mm (1986)

Maximum one-day Rain fall: 369 mm (12, 13 August 1986)

Temperature: 7– 38°C (Normal range).

Vegetation

Forest, vegetation, and other floral species of this area are normally similar to other sub- hilly region. Some species are given below:

- *Salix tetrasperma*
- *Arundo donex*
- *Epomoea carnea*
- *Vitex negundo*
- *Leucaena leucaena*
- *Lannea grandis*
- *Erythrina suberosa*
- *Bouhinia retusa*
- *Giant napier*
- *Eulaliopsis binata*

These plant species were planted in 5 big and 50 small size loose rock filled check dams constructed by *"Central soil and water conservation Research and training institute"* Dehradun under a project *"Mined area Rehabilitation Research project Sahastradhara* Dehradun.

2.2 Historical Resume

The importance of water reveals from the beginning of civilization always took place near the water sources. According to *Hippocrates* (460 B.C. – 345 B.C.), the father of medicine, "water contributes much to health" and averted the rain water should be used after boiling and filtering, otherwise it would smell bed and cause harshness (Borchart and Wotton, 1971).

Life can't exist without water it is an universal truths. Today we are going fast toward the way of success. Although man in touching the high of perfection yet on the other side he is the prime amuse for the explosion of the planet and its water resource. The very fast criteria, standard criteria for drinking water was reported in the literature in 1921 when United States published USPH standard for drinking water, But it specified only bacteriological parameters.

However, it is difficult to give the name of scientists, limnologists and hydrobiologists, who worked on the various aspects of water quality and aquatic ecology. This review includes some of the important contribution made from various parts of world. Various workers discussed the various aspects of water quality time to time from India and abroad nationally or internationally.

Clark (1924) analyzed the composition of river and lake water of United States. Galtsoff (1924) and Reinnard (1931) studied the limnology of upper Mississippi. Ghosuddin (1934) studied the algal flora of the river Moori. Ganpati (1940) studied the ecology of the temple tank containing a permanent bloom of *Microcystis aeruginousa*. Ganpati and Alikunni (1950) observed that water of river Ganga was heavily polluted which dangerous to the human health. Motiawant *et al.* (1956), Ganpati and Chacko (1957) and Daivid (1957-59) observed about the pollution of Ganga water. Chakraborty (1959) survey of the plankton and physico-chemical conditions of the Jamuna River at Allahabad.

Singh (1960) studied the chlorophyceae of Kumaon, Needham and Needham (1962), Macan (1974) and Petta (1984) indicated hydrologic conditions such as floods or low flows create habitats that may represent limiting conditions for flora and fauna, both vertebrates and invertebrates. As a consequence indicator species have been identified and are the subject of much of the limnological literature. Rao and Govind (1964) carried out the hydrobiology of Tungbhadra reservoir.

Verma (1964) carried out hydro-biological survey of Dalsagar tank. Baloni and Sarkar (1965) observed the pollution of Yamuna River at Okhla water intake out at Delhi. Saxena *et al.* (1966) observed pollution of the Ganga near Kanpur. Venkateswarlu (1969) investigated the role of algal in relation to pollution of river Moori of Hyderabad. Rai (1970) studied the ecology of algal community of river Ganga at Varanasi. Reynold and Johnson (1972), melt water demonstrates that chemical weathering takes place beneath the glacier.

Stround and Martin (1973) said reservoir releases might be made from either the surface or the bottom of the impoundment, with resultant opportunity to control downstream water temperature. Kand and Kachroo (1973) studied the limnology of Kashmir lakes. Edgington and Rolfe (1974) reporting on sampling. Agarwal *et al.* (1976) analyzed the hydrobiology of river Ganga at Varanasi. Kant and Anand (1978) investigated the interrelationship of phytoplankton and physical parameters in Mansar lake of Jammu. Goldberg *et al.* (1978) observed that nutrient pollution has been linked to eutrofication in the Chesa Peak Bay estuary for at least the several decades. Stalnakar (1979) attention in management of fish habitat is targeted on the floral composition of the stream.

Plummer and Back (1980); Christophersen and Wright (1981); Elder (1985) and Badola and Singh (1981) studied hydrobiology of Alaknanda. Gopal *et al.* (1981) studied the limnology of a freshwater reservoir of Jaipur. Meyback (1981), Stallard and Edmond (1983) concluded in tropical regions, erosion of silicates is more enhanced in response to both an increase in silica degradation rate with higher temperature and abundant rainfall and vegetation.

Hu *et al.* (1982), Sarin and Krishnaswami (1984), Sarin *et al.* (1989), Zhang *et al.* (1990 a) reported the chemistry of some large Asian rivers such as the Ganges/ Brahmaputra, Changjiang and Huanghe etc. have been of scientific interest for the last decade. Ferro (1982); Lohmunn *et al.* (1988), Jones *et al.* (1989) attention to the chemical quality of lakes and impoundments in the Himalayas has focused on the problems of eutrophication and salinity, in Nepal. Whitfield (1983) and Hall *et al.* (1991) have previously used E.C data in describing water quality within the Fraser basin. Raina *et al.* (1984) made pollution studied of river Jhelum. Chattopadhyay *et al.* (1984) made a study on the pollution status of river Ganga at Kanpur.

Telang (1985) observed form the Machenzie River, which drains into the Beauford Sea in the arctic, where the occurrence of carbonates in the drainage eosin accounts for the dominance of Ca^{+2} any Mg^{+2} in the river.

Sharma (1986) published a report on effect of physico-chemical factors and benthic fauna of Bhagirthi River in Garhwal Himalaya. Berner and Berner (1987) demonstrated the weathering of rock forming minerals with minor contribution from cyclic sea salt and pollution, is the major source of ions in river water.

Cooper *et al.* (1987) reported runoff decrease of the concentration of most ions to a minimum in melt water. Larson *et al.* (1988) studied the assessment of attainable surface water quality. Galloway (1989) observed the deposition of acidic oxide is likely to increase in the future in the developing areas of Asia. Sarin *et al.* (1989) indicate that the water chemistry of highland tributaries is dominated by carbonate weathering in the Ganges/Brahmaputra system. Paul and Verma (1990); Zhang *et al.* (1990a) studied the atmospheric input accounts for less than 5-10% of total river in dissolved fluxes for most of the major species.

Nautiyal (1990) explained the ecology of the Ganga River system in the upland of Garhwal Himalayan environment. Weinberg (1990) Coffey *et al.* (1992); Robillard *et al.* (1992) suggested that the importance of controlling water pollution at the agricultural watershed level is increasing day by day. Walcott *et al.* (1990) observed that in rural areas, nutrients and pesticides are released in surface and groundwater and may degrade the quality of water and cause various health problems to human. Round (1991) indicates diatoms are the most common and diverse primary producers in rivers.

Pathak (1991) studied some aspects of ecology of the river Sarju and Gomati of the Kumoan Himalaya. Tranter *et al.* (1992), found a sharp increase in the concentration of Cl^- is probably the result of selective Cl^- removal by rainwater over snow and ice. Bales (1992) also described sulphate and nitrate loaded meltwater pulses in North America and Europe. Jain (1992) reported the chemical characterizations of Kali River with special reference to disposal of municipal and industrial wastes.

Bhatt and Pathak (1992), Rundle *et al.* (1993) started a program of surveys on over 60 tributaries in the Annapurna, Lang tang, and Everest region. Chauhan and Hasnain (1993) reported the negative correlation between solute concentration and discharge near the source area. The TDS and EC values for the Samples of the lower Alaknanda are high during high flow in June. Karr, (1993) examined the river biota regarded as indicators of ecosystem healthy degradation and integrity. Tyler and Ormerod (1993), Wilkinson *et al.*(1995), Ormerod and Juttner (1996), Juttner *et al.* (in press) studies in 5-15 sub- catchments of the Likhu Khola and Kathmandu valley.

Callow and Petts, (1994), Norris *et al.* (1995) recognized that rivers integrate processes in whole catchments and their biota are regularly monitored to detect change on this scale. Aicha Ajakane, (1995) defined ecological characteristics of the benthic macro-invertebrates of high altitude streams (Morocco). Collins, R. (1995) studied the stream water acidification in response to anthropogenic pollution inputs at forested and cultivated catchments in the middle Hills, Nepal. Jenkins, A. (1995) studied the stream chemistry in the middle hills and high mountains of the Himalayas, Nepal.

Rasmussen (1996) measured higher levels of nitrate down stream of manure row crops than chemically fertilized row crops. Cameron (1996) studied the hydro-geochemistry and seasonal variation in major and minor components of the Fraser River, British Columbia. Jain (1996), Dolan and Elshearawi (1989), Berndtsson (1990) utilized the approach to determine the metallic load to the rivers.

Shyam sunder (1996) studied the biotic communities of a Kumoan Himalayan river. Srivastava *et al.* (1996) evaluated the phytoplankton productively and physico-chemical properties of Rapti river. Stolllemyer (1997) analyzed the stream water chemistry in water shads receiving different atmospheric inputs of H^+, NH_4^+, No^-_3 and So_4^{-}.

Dutta *et al.* (1997) evaluated the variation in physico-chemical characteristics of water and micro-benthic invertebrates in river Tawi near Nagrota bypass Jammu.

Khanna *et al.* (1998) studied phytoplanktonic communities in relation to certain physico-chemical parameters of Ganga canal at Hardwar. Joshi and Singh (1999) made a report on some physico-chemical values of River Ganga between Devprayag and Rishikesh. Jain (2000) described application of chemical mass balance approach to determine nutrient loading in the river Kali. Khanna and Singh (2000) evaluated seasonal fluctuations in the plankton of Suswa River at Raiwala, Dehradoon. Pande and Mishra (2000) studied water quality of freshwaters of Sahastradhara Lake and Mossoorie Lake, Dehradoon.

Ahamad and Hasnain (2001) described the snow and stream water chemistry of the Ganga headwater basin, Garhwal Himalayas, India. Fokmare and Musaddiq (2002) studied on physico-chemical characteristics of Kapsi Lake and Purna river waters in Akola District of Maharastra. Jhajhria (2002) made a report on limn biotic studies of Shekhawat pond at Jodhpur with special reference to plankton. Kumar *et al.* (2003) studied on water quality of the river Ambarampalayam, Coimbatore District, Tamilnadu.

Yeragi and Shaikh (2003) analyzed the primary productivity of Tansa River. Khanna and Bhutiani (2003) studied the limnological characteristics of the river Ganga at Haridwar. Khanna and Bhutiani (2003) also evaluated the limnological status of Satikund pond at Hardwar.. Graening and Brown (2003) observed ecosystem dynamics and pollution effects in an Ozark cave stream. Bharti (2004) described the limnological aspects and physico-chemical characteristics of Sahastradhara hill-stream in Doon velly. Iqbal *et al.* (2004) highlighted the Seasonal Variations of Physico-Chemical Characteristics of River Soan Water at Dhoak Pathan Bridge (Chakwal), in Pakistan. Sinha *et al.* (2004) calculated the water quality Index for Ram Ganga river at Mordabad.

Malik and Bharti (2005a, b and c) also described the planktonic population, nutrient dynamics and primary productivity in the water of stream Sahastradhara at Dehradun.

Otokunefor and Obiukwu (2005) analysed the impact of refinery effluent on the physicochemical properties of a water body in the Niger Delta. Bharti and Malik (2005) described the significance of rivers in Vedic literature.

CPCB (2006) reported the water quality status of Yamuna river (1999-2005). Sikoki and Zabbey (2006) described the environment gradients and benthic community of the middle reaches of Imo River, South Eastern Nigeria. Ghavzan *et al.* (2006) highlighted the limnological evaluation of an urban freshwater river with special reference to phytoplankton. Osibanjo and Adie (2007) identified the impact of effluent from Bodija abattoir on the physico-chemical parameters of Oshunkaye stream in Ibadan city, Nigeria. Alam *et al.* (2007) evaluated the different water quality parameters along rivers. Malik and Bharti (2007) described the ecology of Sahastradhara Hill-stream at Dehradun (Uttaranchal).

Ohimain *et al.* (2008) analysed the changes in Water Physico-Chemical Properties Following the Dredging of an Oil Well Access Canal in the Niger Delta. Zabbey *et al.* (2008) find out the plankton assemblages and environmental gradients in the middle reaches of the Imo River, Niger Delta, Nigeria. Prasad and Patil (2008) made a study of physico-chemical parameters of Krishna river water particularly in western Maharashtra. Saksena *et al.* (2008) evaluated the water quality and pollution status of Chambal river in National Chambal sanctuary, Madhya Pradesh. Karbassi *et al.* (2008) made a study on metal pollution assessment of sediment and water in the Shur river. Bharti *et al.* (2008) studied on the influence of Heavy Metals on Abundance of Cyanophyceae Members in Three Spring-fed Lake in Kempty, Dehradun.

Altin *et al.* (2009) made an assessment of seasonal variations of surface water quality charecteristics for Porsuk stream. Trivedi *et al.* (2009) made a study on the evaluation of Water Quality: Physico – Chemical Characteristics of Ganga River at Kanpur by using Correlation Study. Agbaire and Obi (2009) evaluated the seasonal Variations of Some Physico-Chemical Properties of River Ethiope Water in Abraka, Nigeria.

Varunprasath and Daniel (2010) analysed the physico-Chemical Parameters of River Bhavani in Three Stations, Tamilnadu, India. Prasanna and Ranjan (2010) find out the physico chemical properties of water collected from Dhamra Estuary. Fulazzaky *et al.* (2010) made an assessment of Water Quality Status for the Selangor River in Malaysia. Rani *et al.* (2011) made an assessment of temporal variations in water quality of some important rivers in middle Gangtic plains, India. Jindal and Sharma (2011) studied on water quality of Sutlej river around Ludhiana with reference to physic-chemical parameters. Kannel *et al.* (2011) pointed out the chemometrics in assessment of seasonal variation of water quality in freshwater systems. Kapsikar *et al.* (2011) evaluated the physico-chemical features of Kali river, Karwar,west coast of India.

2.3 Sampling Stations

The famous tourist spot of north India 'Sahastradhara' was selected for the study purpose. The sampling site is situated in Sahastradhara valley, 15 km far from Dehradun. We select five sampling stations along with this stream after significant distances, in which two stations were selected in upstream direction and two in downstream direction. All five stations can be finding in the following maps:

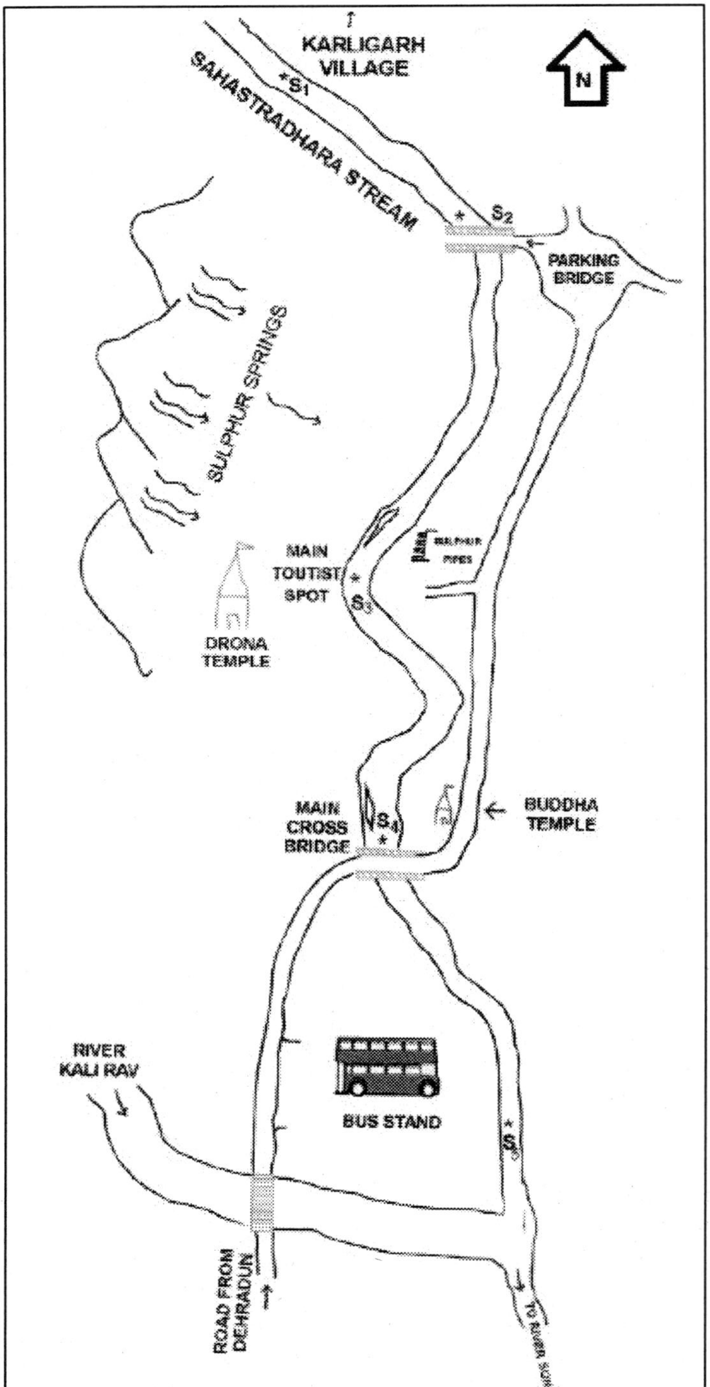

Figure 2.1: Outline Map of Sampling Stations at Sahastradhara Stream

Figure 2.2: Satellite Imagery of Sampling Stations at Sahastradhara Stream

The descriptions of selected five sapling locations are given below:

A) Sampling Station S$_1$ (Karligarh Village)

This site is situated just 1.5 km far away (towards upstream) from main tourists spot (Sulfur spring). This is the first upstream sampling site. This site is very close to village Karligarh.

B) Sampling Station S$_2$ (Parking Bridge)

This sampling site is just before 700 meter from S$_1$ site (downward). The velocity of water is more at this site than the other sites. This is the second upstream sampling station. The next sampling point is main tourist spot.

C) Sampling Station S$_3$ (Main Tourist Spot)

This site is main tourist spot of Sahastradhara due to the sulfur spring. People bath here and dump flower and food materials for fishes such as bread, rice and supplementary food. This site is just near the 'Drone temple'. Tourists visit here for recreational purpose through out the year and create anthropogenic activities.

Figure 2.3.1: First Upstream Sampling Station Near Karligarh Village

Figure 2.3.2: Second Upstream Sampling Station Near Parking Bridge

Figure 2.3.3: Central Sampling Station Near Main Tourist Spot

D) Sampling S_4 (Main Crossing Bridge)

This site is just 500-meter downward form main tourists spot. This is first downstream sampling station near 'God Buddha temple'. People and shopkeepers dump solid waste along with this site. Recently, a solid waste dumping site is developed here due to waste generated by local restaurants, dhabas, shops and hotels.

E) Sampling Station S_5 (Bus Stand)

This is the second downstream and last sampling station just 600-meter downward form crossing bridge or sampling station S_4. After this site, Sahastradhara stream immediately joins Kali Rao river, which is further connected with Song River.

Sampling Programme

Keeping in mind the water characteristics, and the water quality requirements, the following routine sampling and analysis programme was devised:

Collection of samples	:	Monthly [Between 21th -22nd of each month]
Time of sample collection	:	Between 9.00 A.M. to 11.00 A.M.
On site analysis	:	Temperature, pH, DO and free CO_2
Analysis within 24 hours	:	COD and physico-chemical parameters
Analysis within 15 days	:	Heavy metals
Calculation of data	:	After completion of analytical work

Figure 2.3.4: First Downstream Sampling Station Near Main Bridge

Figure 2.3.5: Second Downstream Sampling Station Near Bus Stand

The samples were collected from the selected sampling sites during the month of December 2003 to May 2004 in morning hours (from 9.00 am to 11.00 am). For the study of the status of water, samples were collected monthly from different sampling stations.

Chemicals and Glass Wares

The chemicals used in the present investigation were of analytical grade and were supplied by E. Merck India, S.D fine chemicals and B.D.H., India. All the glassware used was of corning grade, manufactured by Borosil India Ltd. All the glassware and Jeri canes were cleaned or washed with soda and chromic acid and rinsed with double distilled water 2-3 times.

Instruments

Following instruments were used during the study:

Sl.No.	*Name of Instruments*	*Manufacturer*
1.	BOD incubator	Tasco
2.	Spectrophotometer	Besto/Elico
3.	Electronic balance	Roy Electronic
4.	Conductivity meter	Tasco Chipset
5.	COD Assembly	–
6.	Atomic absorption spectrophotometer	Ecil
7.	Hot plate	Sunvic
8.	Hot air oven	Modern Scientifics
9.	Mantle heater	A.J., Enterprises
10.	pH meter	Hanna/Tasco
11.	Refrigerator	LG
12.	Distilled water assembly	–
13.	Computer system	IBM/HP

Sampling

Grab sampling was generally applied during the sampling. A grab sample is an ordinary sample which is taken from a particular place representing the whole water quality. This type of sample is valid only when it is certain that the water quality is not changing in a short time and effluent discharges, if any, are fairy regular. It is advisable to collect and analyze the grab samples separately at various timings, if the water quality is known to change with time. In such cases the schedule of timings shall be dependent on the frequency of discharge or change in water quality. This approach is used in studies to understand diurnal changes in pH, free CO_2, alkalinity, dissolved oxygen, etc. by collecting a 2 or 3 hour sample round the clock. In any kind of water, at least for dissolved oxygen, several grab samples spread over the whole day or even the night shall be important in limnological study.

The sampling of water from stream banks can be easily carried out using a wide mouthed polythene bottle but a sampler has to be used if the studies are to be undertaken at various strata of water. The sampling of sediments from the bottom of natural water bodies, stabilizing ponds or effluent drains is invariably carried out using special samplers. A large number of water and sediment samplers have been developed over the year with varying degree of sophistication. Most common of them and those which are readily available in India are Van Dron Water Sampler, Simple Laboratory Made Water sampler, Shallow Water sampler and Eckmen Dredge Sediment Sampler.

Stream water samples were analyzed by standard methods (APHA, 1995; Wetzel, 1975; Trivedi and Goel, 1984 and Santhanam *et al.*, 1989).

The trace heavy metals were analyzed in the laboratory by Atomic absorption spectrophotometer *AAS 4129 model* (APHA, 1995; ECIL Methods Manual, 2004; ITRC Manual, 1987).

The samples were taken in BOD bottles and plastic Jeri cane for physical, chemical and heavy metals analysis.

Materials

Following materials and accessories were used in sampling process:

(1) Sampling Bottles

300ml capacity BOD bottles were used for collecting the samples. These were washed with chromic acid and then rinse well with tap water followed by rinsing with distilled water. Then these were oven dried at 160°–180° for 3 hours.

(2) Pipettes

Pipettes were washed in same manner as in above. All the pipettes used were of borosil glass certified grade pipettes used were of 1ml capacity (micro pipettes), 5ml capacity and 10ml capacity.

(3) Reagents and Glassware

Some reagents were taken for on spot analysis and sample preservation. Glassware used in study *viz.* conical flask, beaker, burettes etc. were of Borosil glass certified grade. All the glassware were washed with chromic acid and then rinsed well with tap water and then with distilled water.

(4) Jeri Canes

Jeri cane used for carrying the samples from sampling sites to laboratories. Jeri cane made of plastic and washed well with water and then rinsed well with distilled water.

(5) Chemical Bottles

Some small chemical bottles were used for transporting some necessary chemical urgently required during the sampling for immediately analysis for selected parameters.

(6) Bag

A bag of large carrying capacity was taken during the sampling for the collection of all water, soil and sediment samples.

(7) Thermometer

Mercury thermometer was used for on spot measurement of the soil and water samples.

(8) pH meter

A handy pen pH meter was used for on spot evaluation of the pH of surface water, groundwater, soil and sediment samples.

Water Sample Collection

Samples were collected in Borosil BOD bottles and some Jeri canes for laboratory experiments. Some parameters were determined immediately on sampling sites, for rest parameters and heavy metals; samples were stored in refrigerator at 4°C. Heavy metals may be analyzed in the 6 months period from the preservation date.

Samples were taken in Jeri canes for determination of the parameters like conductivity, total solids, pH (hydrogen ion concentration), COD, free CO_2, total alkalinity, total hardness Ca/Mg, chlorides, lead, manganese, zinc, calcium and magnesium. Caps of cans were closed tightly after filling up of cane.

For dissolved oxygen/biochemical oxygen demand, samples were collected in sterilized 300 ml capacity BOD bottles. The bottles were filled completely with sample water up to the rim and stopper was placed only avoiding any kind of air bubble inside it. DO was immediately fixed by adding 2 ml each of alkaline potassium iodide and manganese sulphate ($MnSO_4$) at sampling spot. While the sample for BOD was incubated for 5 days in BOD incubator at 20°C.

2.4 Significance

Water provides a medium for interaction among different compounds water is a great nurture for plants as well as for animals water helps in conducting of energy the form of heat helps in maintaining a soothing climate, water acts as a rejuvenator and medicament it. Water is the medium through which nutrients of soil underneath and above on the surface move horizontally as well as vertically water has great power of dissolving most of the inorganic components in mixture form and in the pure elemental and ionic form.

Water quality characteristic of aquatic environment arise from a multitude of physical, biological and chemical interactions. The water bodies, lakes, rivers, dams and estuaries are continuously subject to a dynamic state of change with respect to the geological age and geochemical characteristics. This is demonstrated by continuous circulation, transformation and accumulation of energy and matter through the medium of living thing and their activities (Adefemi, 2007). The quality of water is of vital concern for mankind since it is directly linked with human welfare. It is a matter of history that faecal pollution of drinking water caused water-borne diseases which wiped out entire populations of cities. At present the menace of water-borne diseases and epidemics still looms large on the horizon of developing countries. Polluted water has been the culprit or cause in all such cases in which the major sources of pollution are domestic wastes from urban and industrial wastes (Asaolu, 1998). The dynamic balance in the aquatic ecosystem is upset by human activities, resulting in pollution which meter, is manifested dramatically as fish kill, offensive taste, odour, colour and unchecked aquatic weeds. The over production of higher tropic levels biomass and the subsequent decay of dead plants could lead to oxygen depletion, death of aquatic organisms and development of anaerobic zone where bacteria action produce foul odours and bad tastes (Forstner and Wittman, 1979).

The hill-streams have a complex and fragile ecosystem; however they have self-cleaning ability but excess load always disturb the natural system and therefore readily accumulate pollutants. In some tourist hilly regions, there are not any more industrial pollution, but tourist's anthropogenic activities may alter the water quality of hill-streams and the physico-chemical characteristics of water of some tourist spot may affect the biological diversity of that water body.

The preliminary observations of any proposed sampling station is quite important. The observations include the geo-cordinates, elevation, climate, geology, meteorology, vegetation structure, and other general information. Further investigations are the secondary data, which is generally originated with the help of primary observations directly or indirectly. Before the research work started, a preliminary survey should be conducted in the proposed location to be investigated. So, the overview of sampling site plays a significant role in the further research not only environmental research but also in every scientific stream.

Chapter 3
Assessment of Water Quality

Contents

Water is an important substance required by all living organisms and for all anthropogenic activities. The problem of environmental pollution due to toxic metals has begun to cause concern now in most major metropolitan cities (Bharti, 2007). Most of our water resources are gradually becoming polluted due to the addition of foreign materials from the surroundings. These include organic matter origin from plant and animal, land surface washing, and industrial and sewage effluents.

3.1 General

Ecological study of hill-stream describes the distribution and abundance of aquatic living organisms and also their contribution into environment. Biological diversity mainly influenced by the physico-chemical characteristics of the aquatic ecosystem through the food chain. The biotic community in the stream exhibited the quantitative and qualitative fluctuations due to varied nutrient dynamics and ultimately changed the different trophic status of species community and limnological status of aquatic ecosystem.

Physico-chemical and biological parameters play an important role in population dynamics of phytoplankton, zooplankton, benthos and fishes. Various parameters that affect the population dynamics of phytoplankton may be broadly classified as light intensity, photoperiod, chlorophyll content, nutrient availability, transparency, turbidity, temperature, velocity, water column depth. Light intensity, duration and water column depth are the basic parameters and others are the derived ones (Bharti, 2004)

3.2 Parameters

Following physico-chemical parameters of Sahastradhara water were selected for the assessment of water quality:

- ☆ Temperature
- ☆ pH
- ☆ Velocity
- ☆ Total solids
- ☆ Total suspended solids
- ☆ Total dissolved solids
- ☆ Electrical conductivity
- ☆ Dissolved oxygen
- ☆ Free CO_2
- ☆ Biochemical oxygen demand (BOD)
- ☆ Chemical oxygen demand (COD)
- ☆ Total alkalinity
- ☆ Total hardness

3.3 historical Resume

However, it is difficult to give the name of scientists, limnologists and hydrobiologists, who worked on the various aspects of water quality and aquatic ecology. This review includes some of the important contribution made from various parts of world. Various workers discussed the various aspects of water quality time to time from India and abroad nationally or internationally.

Clark (1924) analyzed the composition of river and lake water of United States. Galtsoff (1924) and Reinnard (1931) studied the limnology of upper Mississippi. Ghosuddin (1934) studied the algal flora of the river Moori. Ganpati (1940) studied the ecology of the temple tank containing a permanent bloom of *Microcystis aeruginousa*. Ganpati and Alikunni (1950) observed that water of river Ganga was heavily polluted which dangerous to the human health. Motiawant *et al.* (1956), Ganpati and Chacko (1957) and David (1957-59) observed about the pollution of Ganga water. Chakraborty (1959) survey of the plankton and physico-chemical conditions of the Jamuna River at Allahabad.

Singh (1960) studied the chlorophyceae of Kumaon, Needham and Needham (1962), Macan (1974) and Petta (1984) indicated hydrologic conditions such as floods or low flows create habitats that may represent limiting conditions for flora and fauna, both vertebrates and invertebrates. As a consequence indicator species have been identified and are the subject of much of the limnological literature. Rao and Govind (1964) carried out the hydrobiology of Tungbhadra reservoir. Verma (1964) carried out hydro-biological survey of Dalsagar tank. Baloni and Sarkar (1965) observed the pollution of Yamuna River at Okhla water intake out at Delhi. Saxena *et al.* (1966) observed pollution of the Ganga near Kanpur. Venkateswarlu (1969) investigated the role of algal in relation to pollution of river Moori of Hyderabad. Rai (1970) studied the ecology of algal community of river Ganga at Varanasi. Reynold and Johnson (1972), melt water demonstrates that chemical weathering takes place beneath the glacier. Stround and Martin (1973) said reservoir releases might be made from either the surface or the bottom of the impoundment, with resultant opportunity to control downstream water temperature. Kand and Kachroo (1973) studied the limnology of Kashmir lakes. Edgington and Rolfe (1974) reporting on sampling. Agarwal *et al.* (1976) analyzed the hydrobiology of river Ganga at Varanasi. Kant and Anand (1978) investigated the interrelationship of phytoplankton and physical parameters in Mansar lake of Jammu. Goldberg *et al.* (1978) observed that nutrient pollution has been linked to eutrofication in the Chesa Peak Bay estuary for at least the several decades. Stalnakar (1979) attention in management of fish habitat is targeted on the floral composition of the stream.

Plummer and Back (1980); Christophersen and Wright (1981); Elder (1985) and Badola and Singh (1981) studied hydrobiology of Alaknanda. Gopal *et al.* (1981) studied the limnology of a freshwater reservoir of Jaipur. Meyback (1981), Stallard and Edmond (1983) concluded in tropical regions, erosion of silicates is more enhanced in response to both an increase in silica degradation rate with higher temperature and abundant rainfall and vegetation. Hu *et al.* (1982), Sarin and Krishnaswami (1984), Sarin *et al.* (1989), Zhang *et al.* (1990 a) reported the chemistry of some large Asian rivers such as the Ganges/Brahmaputra, Changjiang and Huanghe etc. have been of scientific interest for the last decade. Ferro (1982); Lohmunn *et al.* (1988), Jones *et al.* (1989) attention to the chemical quality of lakes and impoundments in the Himalayas has focused on the problems of eutrophication and salinity, in Nepal. Whitfield (1983) and Hall *et al.* (1991) have previously used E.C data in describing water quality within the Fraser basin. Raina *et al.* (1984) made pollution studied of river Jhelum. Chattopadhyay *et al.* (1984) made a study on the pollution status of river Ganga at Kanpur.

Telang (1985) observed form the Machenzie River, which drains into the Beauford Sea in the arctic, where the occurrence of carbonates in the drainage eosin accounts for the dominance of Ca^{+2} any Mg^{+2} in the river. Sharma (1986) published a report on effect of physico-chemical factors and benthic fauna of Bhagirthi River in Garhwal Himalaya. Berner and Berner (1987) demonstrated the weathering of rock forming minerals with minor contribution from cyclic sea salt and pollution, is the major source of ions in river water.

Cooper *et al.* (1987) reported runoff decrease of the concentration of most ions to a minimum in melt water. Larson *et al.* (1988) studied the assessment of attainable surface water quality. Galloway (1989) observed the deposition of acidic oxide is likely to increase in the future in the developing areas of Asia. Sarin *et al.* (1989) indicate that the water chemistry of highland tributaries is dominated by carbonate weathering in the Ganges/Brahmaputra system. Paul and Verma (1990); Zhang *et al.* (1990a) studied the atmospheric input accounts for less than 5-10% of total river in dissolved fluxes for most of the major species.

Nautiyal (1990) explained the ecology of the Ganga River system in the upland of Garhwal Himalayan environment. Weinberg (1990) Coffey *et al.* (1992); Robillard *et al.* (1992) suggested that the importance of controlling water pollution at the agricultural watershed level is increasing day by day. Walcott *et al.* (1990) observed that in rural areas, nutrients and pesticides are released in surface and groundwater and may degrade the quality of water and cause various health problems to human. Round (1991) indicates diatoms are the most common and diverse primary producers in rivers. Pathak (1991) studied some aspects of ecology of the river Sarju and Gomati of the Kumoan Himalaya. Tranter *et al.* (1992), found a sharp increase in the concentration of Cl^- is probably the result of selective Cl^- removal by rainwater over snow and ice. Bales (1992) also described sulphate and nitrate loaded meltwater pulses in North America and Europe. Jain (1992) reported the chemical characterizations of Kali River with special reference to disposal of municipal and industrial wastes. Bhatt and Pathak (1992), Rundle *et al.* (1993) started a program of surveys on over 60 tributaries in the Annapurna, Lang tang, and Everest region. Chauhan and Hasnain (1993) reported the negative correlation between solute concentration and discharge near the source area. The TDS and EC values for the Samples of the lower Alaknanda are high during high flow in June. Karr, (1993) examined the river biota regarded as indicators of ecosystem healthy degradation and integrity. Tyler and Ormerod (1993), Wilkinson *et al.*(1995), Ormerod and Juttner (1996), Juttner *et al.* (in press) studies in 5-15 sub- catchments of the Likhu Khola and Kathmandu valley.

Callow and Petts, (1994), Norris *et al.* (1995) recognized that rivers integrate processes in whole catchments and their biota are regularly monitored to detect change on this scale. Aicha Ajakane, (1995) defined ecological characteristics of the benthic macro-invertebrates of high altitude streams (Morocco). Collins, R. (1995) studied the stream water acidification in response to anthropogenic pollution inputs at forested and cultivated catchments in the middle Hills, Nepal. Jenkins, A. (1995) studied the stream chemistry in the middle hills and high mountains of the Himalayas, Nepal. Rasmussen (1996) measured higher levels of nitrate down stream of manure row crops than chemically fertilized row crops. Cameron (1996) studied the hydro-geochemistry and seasonal variation in major and minor components of the Fraser River, British Columbia. Jain (1996), Dolan and Elshearawi (1989), Berndtsson (1990) utilized the approach to determine the metallic load to the rivers.

Shyam sunder (1996) studied the biotic communities of a Kumoan Himalayan river. Srivastava *et al.* (1996) evaluated the phytoplankton productively and physico-chemical properties of Rapti river. Stolllemyer (1997) analyzed the stream water chemistry in water shads receiving different atmospheric inputs of H^+, NH_4^+, NO_3^- and SO_4^{--}. Dutta *et al.* (1997) evaluated the variation in physico-chemical characteristics of water and micro-benthic invertebrates in river Tawi near Nagrota bypass Jammu.

Khanna *et al.* (1998) studied phytoplanktonic communities in relation to certain physico-chemical parameters of Ganga canal at Hardwar. Joshi and Singh (1999) made a report on some physico-chemical values of River Ganga between Devprayag and Rishikesh. Jain (2000) described application of chemical mass balance approach to determine nutrient loading in the river Kali. Khanna and Singh (2000) evaluated seasonal fluctuations in the plankton of Suswa River at Raiwala, Dehradoon. Pande and Mishra (2000) studied water quality of freshwaters of Sahastradhara Lake and Mossoorie Lake, Dehradoon. Ahamad and Hasnain (2001) described the snow and stream water chemistry of the Ganga headwater basin, Garhwal Himalayas, India. Fokmare and Musaddiq (2002) studied on physico-chemical characteristics of Kapsi Lake and Purna river waters in Akola District of Maharastra. Jhajhria (2002) made a report on limn biotic studies of Shekhawat pond at Jodhpur with special reference to plankton. Kumar *et al.* (2003) studied on water quality of the river Ambarampalayam, Coimbatore District, Tamilnadu. Yeragi and Shaikh (2003) analyzed the primary productivity of Tansa River. Khanna and Bhutiani (2003) studied the limnological characteristics of the river Ganga at Haridwar. Khanna and Bhutiani (2003) also evaluated the limnological status of Satikund pond at Hardwar.. Graening and Brown (2003) observed ecosystem dynamics and pollution effects in an Ozark cave stream. Bharti (2004) described the limnological aspects and physico-chemical characteristics of Sahastradhara hill-stream in Doon velly. Iqbal *et al.* (2004) highlighted the Seasonal Variations of Physico-Chemical Characteristics of River Soan Water at Dhoak Pathan Bridge (Chakwal), in Pakistan. Sinha *et al.* (2004) calculated the water quality Index for Ram Ganga river at Mordabad.

Otokunefor and Obiukwu (2005) analysed the impact of refinery effluent on the physicochemical properties of a water body in the Niger Delta. Bharti and Malik (2005) described the significance of rivers in Vedic literature,

CPCB (2006) reported the water quality status of Yamuna river (1999-2005). Sikoki and Zabbey (2006) described the environment gradients and benthic community of the middle reaches of Imo River, South Eastern Nigeria. Ghavzan *et al.* (2006) highlighted the limnological evaluation of an urban freshwater river with special reference to phytoplankton. Alam *et al.* (2007) evaluated the different water quality parameters along rivers. Malik and Bharti (2007) described the ecology of Sahastradhara Hill-stream at Dehradun (Uttaranchal). Prasad and Patil (2008) made a study of physico-chemical parameters of Krishna river water particularly in western Maharashtra. Saksena *et al.* (2008) evaluated the water quality and pollution status of Chambal river in National Chambal sanctuary, Madhya Pradesh. Karbassi *et al.* (2008) made a study on metal pollution assessment of sediment and water in the Shur river. Altin *et al.* (2009) made an assessment of seasonal variations of surface water quality charecteristics for Porsuk stream. Trivedi *et al.* (2009) made a study on the evaluation of Water Quality: Physico – Chemical Characteristics of Ganga River at Kanpur by using Correlation Study. Agbaire and Obi (2009) evaluated the seasonal Variations of Some Physico-Chemical Properties of River Ethiope Water in Abraka, Nigeria.

Varunprasath and Daniel (2010) analysed the physico-Chemical Parameters of River Bhavani in Three Stations, Tamilnadu, India. Prasanna and Ranjan (2010) find out the physico chemical properties of water collected from Dhamra Estuary. Fulazzaky *et al.* (2010) made an assessment of Water Quality Status for the Selangor River in Malaysia. Rani *et al.* (2011) made an assessment of temporal variations in water quality of some important rivers in middle Gangtic plains, India. Jindal and Sharma (2011) studied on water quality of Sutlej river around Ludhiana with reference to physic-chemical parameters. Kannel *et al.* (2011) pointed out the chemometrics in assessment of seasonal variation of water quality in freshwater systems.

3.4 Methodology

Temperature

Temperature measurements are usually made with mercury filled centigrade thermometer. The water temperature was recorded by dipping the thermometer into water. The unit of temperature is °C.

pH (Hydrogen Ion Concentration)

pH is the Hydrogen ion concentration in the given water sample. pH equals to negativity $\log_{10}$ of H^+ concentration.

$$pH = -\log_{10} (H^+)$$

The pH was measured by two methods-

1. By using pH strips.
2. By using electronic pH meter.

Velocity

Surface flow method was used to measure the speed of water. The rate of flow of uppermost stratum of water in the river was measured by throwing a light piece of wood in different segments of water.

The time taken by the wood piece to cover a known distance was calculated by the given formulate.

$$V = d/t$$

where,

V: Velocity (m/sec)

d: Distance covered

t: Time taken

Turbidity

Turbidity in water is caused by the substance, not present in the form of true solution. True solution have a particle size of less than 10^{-9} m. Any substance having more than this size will produce turbidity.

1. The turbidity of water was estimated by Jackson's turbiditimeter.

2. The water samples were collected from the river in plastic Jeri cane. Collected sample were shaked well and transferred in to the glass tube of Jackson's candle turbidity meter until the flame of candle disappears.
3. Noted the light path in centimeter (measured from inside the bottom of the glass tube) and the reading recorded in JTU.

Total Solids

Total solids or total residue is the term applied to material left in a beaker after evaporating a well mixed sample and subsequently evaporating and dried it in an oven.

- ☆ Take a 100ml washed and dried beaker and weight.
- ☆ Evaporate 100ml of unfiltered samples in the beaker, on water bath than dried it in an oven at 105 ± 1°C.
- ☆ Take final weight of the beaker after drying the sample.

Calculation

$$\text{Total Solids, mg/l} = \frac{A - B}{V} \times 10^6$$

where,

A: Final weight of beaker in gm.

B: Initial weight of beaker in gm.

V: Volume of sample.

Total Dissolved Solids

Total dissolved solids of filterable residue are those solids which left after evaporated of the filtered sample.

- ☆ Take a 100 ml washed and dried beaker and weight, immediately before used.
- ☆ Place filter paper what man no.42 in funnel.
- ☆ Pour 100 ml of well-mixed sample and filter through filter paper.
- ☆ Collect the filtrate in the 100 ml weighed beaker.
- ☆ Evaporate the sample after complete filtration and subsequently dry in an oven at 105°C ±1 for 4 to 6 hrs.
- ☆ Cool the beaker and weight.

Calculation

$$\text{TDS, mg/l} = \frac{A - B}{V} \times 10^6$$

where,

A: Final weight of beaker in gm.

B: Initial weight of beaker in gm.

V: Volume of sample.

Total Suspended Solids

Total suspended solids are the retained material on Whatman no. 42 filter paper after filtration TSS was determined by taking difference between the total solids and total dissolved solids.

Calculation

$$\text{TSS, mg/l} = \text{TS} - \text{TDS}$$

Electrical Conductivity

Electric conductance is the ability of a substance to conduct the electric current. In water, it is the property caused by the presence of various ionic species.

It is generally measure with the help of a conductivity meter having a conductance cell containing electrodes of platinum coated with Pt black or carbon. These electrodes are mounted rigidly and placed parallely at a fixed distance. Conductance, when measured between the electrodes having a surface area of 1 cm^3 and placed at a distance of 1 cm, is called electrical conductivity and is the property of water sample, rather then the measuring system. The term specific conductance is also used in place of electrical conductivity, but is an obsolete term. The unit of conductivity measurement is Siemens (S) per cm. The older unit mho per cm is now rarely used. The conductivity of most waters is generally low so the unit μ S/cm shall be much appropriate.

A simple whetstone bridge circuit is used to measure Electric conductivity by null method. The unit of specific conductivity is mhos/cm or millimhos/cm (mhos/ cm X 10^3) or micromhos/cm (mhos/cm X 10^6). The most common unit of Electric conductivity being followed is dS/m (deci Siemen/m) which is equal to the older unit of millimhos/cm. Electric conductivity was measured by digital conductivity meter.

As the ionization of the solutes depends on the temperature, conventionally the results are reported at 25°C.

Procedure

1. It is measured with the help of a conductivity meter. Follow the instructions supplied by the manufacturer.
2. Conductance depends on the area of the metallic electrodes and the distance between them. The factor used to convert the observed conductance into conductivity is called as the cell 'constant'. Cell constant of the 'conductance cell' is usually supplied by the manufacturer.
3. Note the temperature of the sample and find out the factor from conversion table to convert the values at 25°C.

Table 3.1: Conversion table for measurement of Electric conductivity

°C	Factor	°C	Factor	°C	Factor
32	0.89	22	1.06	12	1.30
31	0.90	21	1.08	11	1.33
30	0.92	20	1.10	10	1.36
29	0.93	19	1.12	9	1.39
28	0.95	18	1.14	8	1.42
27	0.97	17	1.16	7	1.46
26	0.98	16	1.19	6	1.50
25	1.00	15	1.21	5	1.54
24	1.02	14	1.24	4	1.58
23	1.04	13	1.27	3	1.62

Calculation

Conductivity = Observed conductance × Cell constant × Temperature factor at 25°C

Also the conductivity has a relation with total. It may be calculated (in mho/cm) by dividing the total dissolved solids by 640 (Mor *et al.*, 2003).

Free Carbon Dioxide

Determined free CO_2 by titration of the sample using a strong alkali to pH 8.3. At this pH all the free CO_2 is converted in to bicarbonates.

Reagents

(A) Sodium hydroxide (0.05N): Prepare 1.0 N NaOH by dissolving 40 gm of NaOH in Co_2 free distilled water diluted 50 ml of 1.0 N NaOH to 1 litter in Co_2 free distilled water.

(B) Phenolphthalein indicator: Dissolve 0.5 gm of phenolphthalein in 50 ml of 95% ethanol and 50 ml of distilled water.

Procedure

1. 100 ml of sample was taken in a conical flask. Add few drops of phenolphthalein indicator.
2. If the colour turns pink, free CO_2 declared to absent or if the sample remained colourless, titrate it against 0.05 N NaOH.
   (*a*) At the end point a pink colour will appear.

Calculation

$$\text{Carbon dioxide (mg/l)} = \frac{(\text{ml} \times \text{N}) \text{ of NaOH} \times 1000 \times 44}{\text{ml of sample}}$$

Dissolved Oxygen (DO)

Dissolved oxygen is the measure of oxygen concentration present in a given water sample. The concentration of oxygen reflects whether the process undergoing is aerobic or anaerobic.

Dissolved oxygen was measured by the Wrinkle's isometric method.

Reagents

(A) Sodium thio sulphate (0.025N): Dissolved 24.82 gm of $Na_2S_2O_3$. SH_2O in boiled distilled water and make up the volume to 1 liter. Add 0.4 g pallet of NaOH a stabilizer this is 0.1N stock solution. Diluted it to 4 times with boiled distilled water to prepare 0.025 N solution.

(B) Alkaline potassium iodine solution: Dissolve 100 gm of KOH and 50 gm of KI in 200 ml. of boiled distilled water.

(C) Manganous sulphate solution: Dissolved 100 gm of $MnSO_4$. $4H_2O$ in 200 ml. of boiled distilled water and filter.

(D) Starch solution: Dissolved 1 gm of starch in 100 ml. of warm distilled water and add a few drops of formaldehyde solution.

(E) Sulphuric acid: Conc. H_2SO_4

Procedure

300-ml. volume of the sample was taken in BOD bottle. Add 2 ml. of each $MnSO_4$ and alkaline KI solution by pipette. Stopper and mixed through let the precipitate settle, titrated the contents against, sodium thio-sulphate solution, using starch as an indicator. At change end point, initial dark blue colour changes into colourless.

Calculation

$$\text{Dissolved oxygen (mg/l)} = \frac{(\text{ml} \times \text{N})\text{ of titrant} \times 8 \times 1000}{\text{V2}\,(\text{V1} - \text{V/N})}$$

V_1: Volume of sample bottle after placing the stopper.

V_2: Volume of the part of the contents titrated.

V: Volume of $MnSO_4$ and KI added.

Biochemical Oxygen Demand

Biochemical oxygen demand is the measure of the degradable organic material present in a water sample, and can be defined as the amount of oxygen required by the microorganisms in stabilizing the biologically degradable organic matter under aerobic conditions.

The principle of the method involves measuring the difference of the oxygen concentration between the sample and after incubating it for 5 days at 20°C.

Apparatus and Reagents

(A) BOD bottle

(B) BOD incubator

(C) Sodium thiosulphate (0.025N)
(D) Alkaline KI
(E) $MnSO_4$
(F) Starch
(G) H_2SO_4 Conc.

Procedure

The samples were incubated for five days at 20°C and the dissolved oxygen was measured.

Calculation

$$BOD, (mg/l) = (D_1 - D_5)$$

where,

D_1: Initial DO in sample
D_5: DO after 5 days incubation.

Chemical Oxygen Demand

Chemical oxygen demand is the measure of oxygen consumed during the oxidation of the oxidizable organic matter by a strong oxidizing agent. Potassium dichromate in the presence of sulphuric acid is generally used as an oxidizing in determination of COD. Chemical oxygen demand test is widely used for the pollution strength of wastewater. All organic compounds with a few exceptions can be oxidized to carbon dioxide and water by the action of strong oxidizing agents regardless of biological assimilability of the substance.

Reagents

(A) Standard potassium dichromate (0.25N).
(B) Sulphuric acid (with 1 gm of silver sulphate in every 75-ml. acid).
(C) Ferrion indicator solution.
(D) Standard ferrous ammonium sulphate solution.

Procedure

(A) Place 50 ml or fraction diluted to 10 ml of sample with distilled water in hard glass bottle and add 25 ml standard potassium dichromate solution. Carefully add 75 ml conc. H_2SO_4 mixing after each addition. Digest the mixture in pressure cooker or autoclave for 30 minutes.

(B) Repeat the procedure with 100 ml distilled water and reagent as in (A).

(C) Transfer the contents to a 500 ml conical flask. The mixture to about 350 ml. Titrate the excess dichromate with standard ferrous ammonium sulphate using ferroin indicator. The end point is red. Designate the titration value for sample (a) as B and for distilled water (b) as A.

Calculation

$$\text{COD, mg/l} = \frac{(A - B)\,C \times 8}{\text{ml of sample}}$$

where,

A: ml. of $FeSO_4\,(NH_4)_2\,SO_4$ for blank.

B: ml. of $FeSO_4\,(NH_4)_2\,SO_4$ used for sample.

C: Normality of $FeSO_4\,(NH_4)_2\,SO_4$ solution determined above.

Total Hardness

Hardness is generally measured a concentration of only calcium and magnesium. Hardness is determined by EDTA titrimetric method.

Reagent

(A) EDTA Solution 0.01 m: Dissolved 3.723 gm of disodium salt of EDTA in distilled water to prepare 1 liter of solution.

(B) Eriochrome black T indicator: Mixed 100 gm NaCl and 0.5 gm of Eriochrome black T to prepare dry powder mixture.

(C) Buffer solution: Dissolved 16.9 gm. NH_4Cl in 143ml conc. NH_4OH, dissolved 1.79gm of disodium EDTA and 0.780 of $MgSO_4$ in distilled water. Mix both and dilute to 250 ml distilled water.

Procedure

50 ml. sample was taken in conical flask, added 1 ml buffer solution and 100-200 mg Eriochrome black T indicator. The solution turns wine red. Titrate against EDTA solution. At the end point colour changes from wine red to blue.

Calculation

$$\text{Hardness (mg/l)} = \frac{\text{ml of EDTA used}}{\text{ml of sample}} \times 1000$$

Alkalinity

Alkalinity is the measure of the capacity of the water to neutralize a strong acid. The alkalinity in the waters is generally imparted be the salts of carbonates, bicarbonates, phosphates, nitrates, borates, silicates, etc. together with the hydroxyl ions in free state. However, most of the waters are rich in carbonates and bicarbonates with little concentration of other alkalinity imparting ions. Total alkalinity, carbonates and bicarbonates can be estimated by titrating the sample with a strong acid (HCl or H_2SO_4), first to pH 8.3 using phenolphthalein indicator and then further to pH between 4.2 to 5.4 with methyl orange or mixed indicator. In first indicator, the value is called as phenolphthalein alkalinity (PA) and in second case, it is total alkalinity (TA). Values of carbonates, bicarbonates and hydroxyl ions can be computed from these two types of alkalinities.

Reagents

(A) Hydrochloric acid, 0.1 N: Dilute 12 N concentrated HCl to 12 times to prepare 1.0 N HCL. Dilute it further to make 0.1 N HCL.

(B) Methyl orange indicator: Dissolved 0.5 gm of methyl orange in 100 ml of distilled water.

(C) Phenolphthalein indicator: Dissolved 0.5 gm of phenolphthalein in 50 ml of 95% ethanol add 50 ml distilled water.

(D) Sodium carbonate: Dissolved 5.300 gm of Na_2Co_3, previously dried at 250°C for about 4 hours, in distilled water to prepare 1 later of solution.

Procedure

A sample of 50 ml was taken in a comical flask and adds 2 drops of phenolphthalein add now 2 or 3 drops of methyl orange indicator is added to the above sample and titrate against 0.1N HCL until a yellow colour changes to pink.

Calculation

$$\text{Total alkalinity (mg/l)} = \frac{V - N \times 1000 \times 50}{\text{ml of sample}}$$

where,

V: Volume of total HCl used with methyl orange,

N: Normality of HCL

3.5 Significance

Streams take their chemistry from the rocks and dirt beneath them as well as for a great distance around them. The area that a stream drains is called its drainage basin, or catchment area. We also often call it the river's watershed. Water flows downhill unless it evaporates, freezes, or is taken up by plants. So when it falls as rain, melts from snow or ice, or bubbles up from beneath the earth, it will either flow one direction or another, and always downhill. If you were to stand by a stream at the bottom of a valley, you might look up and see hills all around you. All the land you see that slopes downward toward your river is part of the river's drainage basin. Some drainage basins are so unbelievably huge that you can't even see where their downhill flows begin.

Water rolls down the slopes of a watershed or catchment area or drainage basin, it carries things with it. It dissolves chemicals and carries them. It carries particles of dirt. If it is meltwater from a glacier, it will carry glacial flour, which is sediment the glacier has made by grinding the rock beneath it very finely, making the water look almost milky white. And it carries organic matter; tiny bits of leaves, bacteria, and a lot of other things too small to see. As it flows, it grows to rivulets, and carries larger bits of matter. By the time the water gets all the way down to the river, it is full of whatever was on (and in) the land around it. The river can carry sticks, leaves, logs, brush, and even sand, pebbles, rocks, and boulders. These heavier objects bounce along the bottom in a process called saltation.

There are other ways that things can end up in a river. Winds can blow in sediment (particles of dirt) and bits of organic matter. A lot of living things like insects depend on flowing water to carry out their life cycles. Birds leave urine, droppings, and feathers. Other animals visit the river and often leave their waste in it. Many animals die in the river, adding their organic materials to the water.

Natural events can occur that alter the river's ecology by changing these kinds of factors. Mudslides, heavy rainfall, and fires can make drastic changes. When Mt. St. Helens erupted in Washington State, it sent uncounted tons of fine ash in a torrent down through its river valleys. These events (though they seem extreme from our human point of view), are a very large and slow, but nevertheless integral, part of the river's ecosystem. While Mt. St. Helens's ash was destructive to the salmon that used its rivers, the mountain has erupted many times in the long history of the salmon, and they have adapted in their own mysterious ways. We are far from understanding everything about biological adaptation.

Rivers are closely connected with the atmosphere (the air above them). Gases from the air, like oxygen, carbon dioxide, and nitrogen dissolve into the water. The colder the water is, or the more it churns as it flows downhill, the more gases there will be in it. Rain scrubs molecules and other particles out of the air, and when the air is polluted by coal-burning power plants and automobile exhaust, the rain becomes acidic, and falls as acid rain. Acid rain can lead to the death of streams and lakes. Water that is too acidic falls on the earth and leaches minerals out of it, washing them into streams and lakes. Some of these minerals, like aluminum, are highly toxic to fish. Aluminum in water causes fishes' gills to become covered with thick mucus, and they are no longer able to breathe. Fish in acidic lakes simply suffocate to death.

The narrow area alongside a stream that has its own special vegetation is called the riparian corridor. What plants you will find in a riparian corridor depend on where the river is: the continent, the climate, stream hydrology, geology, alkalinity of the soil, and many other factors. They contribute nutrients, shade, organic materials for small organisms to eat, soil stability, and habitat. They also contribute food for fish in the form of bugs dropping from branches.

Every stream also carries life-forms, and the habitats in which they live. Plants, visible and microscopic, fungi, larvae, crustaceans, molluscs, worms, fishes, mammals, and many other life-forms live in and utilize streams..

Diversity is key to the survival of a stream's life-forms. Genetic diversity must be present within each species. Species and biological diversity must be present as well—many different types of animals. None of these types of diversity can be created or fostered by humans. They are the products of millions of years of evolution by trial-and-error. Once they are lost, they cannot be re-fashioned by scientists. Finally, habitat diversity is essential. Each stream contains many different habitats and microhabitats. A single species may require several different habitats to carry out its life functions, and each habitat is inhabited by its own species that cannot live elsewhere. Keystone species are those species whose functions are so intertwined with the lives of other animals in a system that their disappearance will cause the system to become imbalanced or even collapse. The beaver is a perfect example of a keystone species. It dams rivers, creating ponds and wetlands that support an entire system of stream organisms. When beavers are removed from a stream, most of those stream organisms are displaced or die.

3.6 Case Study (Malik and Bharti, 2007d)*

Introduction

Himalayas are the cradle of a large number of streams and mighty rivers. Lesser Himalayas consists of a main part of Uttaranchal *i.e.* Kumaon and Garhwal Himalaya. Dehradun, Hardwar and Rishikesh are the main religious and beautiful cities, situated in the foothills of Garhwal Himalaya. A hill-stream Sahastradhara, a major tributary of river Song flows downward through Dehradun valley.

Dehradun valley rests in the arms of the Himalaya in the North and Shiwalik in the South and transversely bordered by Ganga in the South-East. Yamuna in the North-West forms an intermontane valley ecosystem extending from 29° 55′ to 30° 30′ N latitude and 77° 35′ to 78° 20′ E longitude with the area of about 2000 square kilometer ranging from 330 meter to 1800 m above msl (Valdiya, 1975).

The main sources of water in Himalayas are glaciers. The glaciers are an important resource of freshwater stored in the solid state and regulated by climate. Glacier melts and the water pass through heavy and porous sediment materials in the form of river. Water is the basic requirement of all living organisms. Lotic habitats are those exiting in relatively fast running streams, springs, river and brooks. The lentic habitats represent lakes, marshes, swamps, ponds and wetlands. A hill-stream consists of two major zones, Rhithron and Potamon. Aquatic biodiversity is mainly occurring in potamon zone due to the slow velocity of running water.

Ecological study of hill-stream describes the distribution and abundance of aquatic living organisms and also their contribution into environment. Biological diversity mainly influenced by the physicochemical characteristics of the aquatic ecosystem through the food chain. The biotic community in the stream exhibited the quantitative and qualitative fluctuations due to varied nutrient dynamics and ultimately changed the different trophic status of species community and limnological status of aquatic ecosystem.

Physico-chemical and biological parameters play an important role in population dynamics of phytoplankton, zooplankton, benthos and fishes. Various parameters that affect the population dynamics of phytoplankton may be broadly classified as light intensity, photoperiod, chlorophyll content, nutrient availability, transparency, turbidity, temperature, velocity, water column depth. Light intensity, duration and water column depth are the basic parameters and others are the derived ones (Khanna *et al.*, 2005)

---

* (***Reference:*** *Malik, D.S. and Bharti, P.K. (2007d): Ecology of Sahastradhara Hill-stream at Dehradun (Uttaranchal), In: 'Advances in Aquatic Ecology, Vol-I' ed. by V.B. Sakhare, Daya Publishing House, New Delhi, pp: 1-11.*)

The present paper deals with biological diversity, primary productivity and physico-chemical characteristics of Sahastradhara stream, which gives a baseline data about the biological status of stream. The purpose of this work is to provide preliminary observations of the ecology of natural water from Sahastradhara at Dehradun and to make geo-chemical comparison between 'Sahastradhara' water and water from other regions of the country. The present work is aimed towards developing baseline data for river water quality of *'Sahastradhara'* stream, a major tributary of Song River and to understanding the ecological processes active in Himalayan river basins.

Material and Methods

The sampling site is situated in Sahastradhara valley, 15 km far from Dehradoon, selected five sampling station along with stream for limnological study. The water samples were collected monthly from different sampling site s_1, s_2, s_3, s_4 and s_5 during 2003 to 2004 in morning period (from 9.00 am to 11.00 pm). First upstream S_1 (Karligarh village), second upstream S_2 (Parking bridge), main tourist spot S_3 (Sulphur Spring), first down steam S_4 (Crossing bridge) and second downstream S_5 (Bus stand) were the sampling stations with a distance of about 1 km for each. The samples were taken in BOD bottles and plastic Jeri cane for physical, chemical and biological parameters. The samples for different parameter were analyzed with the help of the procedure described by Mark (1977), APHA (1995), Mathur (1982), Trivadi and Goel (1984), Santhanam *et al.* (1989), Admondson (1992) and Khanna (1993).

Results and Discussion

The impact on water quality of anthropogenic pollution from industrial, agricultural, sources, quarrying and tourists activity has concerned environmentalists and scientists for the past two decades. Plankton is the primary producer of any aquatic ecosystem, which can be as an indicator of water quality. Dissolved oxygen is decreases or increases in an aquatic ecosystem due to the plankton. Plankton takes sunlight directly and makes food for the total ecosystem through the photosynthesis process. Plankton may vary at place-to-place and season-to-season.

Temperature plays a vital role in all physico-biochemical reactions and self-purification power of aquatic system. Organic matter, which is oxidized, is highly influenced by the temperature. Temperature fluctuation measurement is useful to determine the trends of biochemical and biological activities. The Sahastradhara stream has a difference in the fluctuation of water temperature was recorded maximum (17.7°C ± 0.4) in the month of May and minimum (13.1°C±0.66) in January. The temperature of water decreases form September and increases from January onward. Badola and Singh (1981) observed similar trend in the river Alaknanda in the Garhwal region. The maximum value of velocity of Sahastradhara stream was recorded in the month of May (0.64m/s ± 0.257) and minimum (0.58m/s ± 0.1315) in December. During the study period it has been observed that form January onward the velocity starts increasing up to April. Similar observation has been recorded by Joshi *et al.* (1995) in western Ganga canal at Hardwar.

Table 1: Physical Parameters (Mean values) of Sahastradhara Stream

Parameters	*Site–I*	*Site–II*	*Site–III*	*Site–IV*	*Site–V*
Temperature (°C) (Range)	15.75±1.14 (14–18)	15.37±1.63 (13–17.5)	15.0±1.41 (13–17)	15.75±1.6 (13.5–18)	15.75±2.277 (12–18)
Velocity (m/s) (Range)	0.3±0.14 (0.3–0.4)	0.9±0.1 (0.28–0.32)	0.35±0.05 (0.8–1.0)	0.8±0.02 (0.78–0.82)	0.65±0.05 (0.6–0.7)
Turbidity (JTU) (Range)	2.75±1.47 (1.0–5.0)	3.25±1.30 (2.0–5.0)	4.5±1.15 (3.0- 6.0)	3.75±1.48 (2.0–6.0)	4.75±1.48 (3.0- 7.0)
Total solids (mg/l) (Range)	1218±183.2 (955–1427)	1234.2±89.8 (1090–1332)	1277.25±122.6 (1115–1443)	1305.7±166.1 (1135–1520)	1290.75±146.1 (1148–1535)
TDS (mg/l) (Range)	1093.25±175 (840–1278)	1094.25±120.5 (895–1217)	1140.5±134.6 (1010–1322)	1189±158.01 (1039–1380)	1134.25±176.1 (965–1420)
TSS (mg/l) (Range)	124.75±14.39 (113–149)	140.0±28.16 (119–195)	136.75±40.95 (105–207)	116.75±13.8 (105–140)	156.5±41.69 (115–211)

Table 2: Chemical Parameters (Mean values) of Sahastradhara Stream

Parameters	*Site–I*	*Site–II*	*Site–III*	*Site–IV*	*Site–V*
pH (Range)	7.625±0.43 (7.2–8.1)	7.6±0.28 (7.3–8.1)	7.75±0.15 (7.5–7.9)	7.75±1.66 (7.6–8.0)	7.6±0.339 (7.2–8.1)
Free CO_2 (mg/l) (Range)	1.6525±0.39 (1.40–1.69)	1.75±0.017 (1.62–1.92)	1.825±0.25 (1.62–2.20)	1.74±0.09 (1.65–1.85)	1.87±0.21 (1.62–2.20)
D.O. (mg/l) (Range)	8.41±1.62 (7.04–11.08)	8.46±1.18 (6.84–10.07)	8.65±0.95 (7.04–9.47)	7.55±0.87 (6.04–9.06)	7.49±1.36 (6.04–9.47)
BOD (mg/l) (Range)	1.875±0.162 (1.60–2.0)	1.98±0.23 (1.7–2.2)	2.25±0.18 (2.0–2.5)	2.0±0.14 (1.8–2.2)	2.05±0.15 (1.9–2.3)
COD (mg/l) (Range)	2.55±0.32 (2.1–3.0)	2.6±0.25 (2.2–2.9)	2.9±0.22 (2.6–3.2)	2.68±0.22 (2.4–3.0)	2.7±0.18 (2.4–2.9)
Hardness (mg/l) (Range)	196.25±8.2 (190–210)	200.0±15.41 (185–220)	222.5±19.2 (200–250)	200.0±18.71 (180–230)	198.75±21.02 (185–235)
Alkalinity (mg/l) (Range)	250.0±134.7 (150–480)	262.5±140.8 (140–500)	305±172.1 (170–600)	292.5±168.8 (130–570)	317.5±175.2 (120–540)

The seasonal fluctuation of pH depends chiefly on amount of free carbon- dioxide, which is ultimately related to the rate of photosynthesis and also the decomposition of organic matter. The pH of natural water was controlled in a greater extent by the interaction of hydroxyl ions, resulting form the dissociation of carbonic acid and form hydroxyl ion arising from the hydrolysis of bicarbonate. In this study, it was recorded that the pH was always slightly alkaline. The pH of stream water was recorded highest (8.02 ± 0.1166) in December and lowest (7.4 ± 0.1414) in the month of April. Various workers in their studies have shown similar results in other rivers of Garhwal region. Sharma (1986) has also indicated the same trend of pH values on seasonal basis in the Bhagirathi River, Garhwal Himalayas.

The dissolved oxygen showed an inverse relationship with temperature as reposted by Das and Srivastava (1956) and Dobriyal (1985). The dissolved oxygen in

Table 3: Nutrients Parameters (Mean values) of Sahastradhara Stream

Parameters	*Site–I*	*Site–II*	*Site–III*	*Site–IV*	*Site–V*
Chloride (mg/l) (Range)	12.78±1.73 (11.36–15.62)	13.73±1.93 (11.36–16.58)	15.26±2.1 (12.78–18.46)	13.49±3.25 (9.94–18.46)	11.6±3.06 (8.52–16.58)
Calcium (mg/l) (Range)	84.67±3.58 (80.160–88.176)	85.67±4.28 (80.160–92.184)	91.68±10.13 (77.154–104.208)	89.18±8.26 (79.158–99.198)	88.43±6.19 (80.16–96.192)
Magnesium (mg/l) (Range)	48.66±3.09 (45–53)	57.33±3.29 (55–62)	64.66±2.36 (63.0–68.0)	55.33±2.49 (52.0–28.0)	51.0±5.29 (45.0–55.0)
Sodium (mg/l) (Range)	7.375±0.96 (6–8.5)	7.725±0.506 (7.0–8.2)	8.75±0.75 (8.0–9.5)	8.87±1.14 (7.0–10.0)	9.25±1.35 (7.5–11.0)
Potassium (mg/l) (Range)	15.13±0.74 (14–16)	15.75±0.901 (14.5–17.0)	16.62±0.65 (16.0–17.5)	16.5±0.79 (15.5–17.5)	17.0±1.35 (16.0–18.0)

Table 4: Planktonic Population (Mean values) of Sahastradhara Stream

Parameters	*Site–I*	*Site–II*	*Site–III*	*Site–IV*	*Site–V*
Total plankton (n/l) (Range)	1130.25±316.8 (700–1540)	1133±316 (725–1525)	1101.5±323.9 (693–1480)	1063.75±346.9 (700–1490)	1163.25±339.4 (730–1583)
Phytoplankton (n/l) (Range)	1018.25±286.1 (625–1380)	1023.75±291.5 (635–1380)	992.5±296.3 (615–1345)	951.25±318.2 (635–1340)	1037.5±259.5 (640–1410)
Zooplankton (n/l) (Range)	112±31.61 (75–160)	109.25±27.09 (77–145)	109±28.6 (78–140)	112.5±31.72 (65–150)	125.75±36.66 (90–173)
Total diatoms (n/l) (Range)	764.75±206.6 (492–1022)	784.5±218.5 (645–1015)	772.25±247.3 (480–1064)	732.5±236.5 (495–1035)	807±250.5 (495–1108)
Green algae (n/l) (Range)	190.5±59.86 (105–275)	179.5±64.96 (98–278)	161±40.72 (102–205)	164.5±57.21 (105–228)	157.5±50.13 (102–220)
Blue green algae (n/l) (Range)	63±24.53 (21–83)	57.25±21.57 (27–87)	59.25±17.72 (33–76)	54.25±25.86 (27–83)	58±32.04 (23–97)

water is often attributed to the fact that the oxygen is dissolved more during the period of active photosynthesis. Hutchinson (1957) reported that when the water has low temperature has greater capacity for holding dissolved gases. The highest value of dissolved oxygen was recorded (9.85 mg/l ± 0.776) in the month of January and the lowest value of dissolved oxygen was observed (6.68 mg/l ± 0.387) in the month of May. This trend was also stated by Khanna *et al.* (1992) in Ganga river at Hardwar. The higher value of dissolved oxygen during winter months can be attributed to increased solubility of oxygen at lower water temperature and high photosynthetic rate.

Table 5: Primary Productivity (Mean values) of Sahastradhara Stream

Parameters	*Site–I*	*Site–II*	*Site–III*	*Site–IV*	*Site–V*
Net primary productivity (mg/l)	0.271±0.069	0.220±0.0215	0.336±0.108	0.231±0.086	0.265±0.0522
(Range)	(0.200–0.355)	(0.200–0.255)	(0.140–0.500)	(0.105–0.320)	(0.200–0.330)
Gross primary productivity (mg/l)	0.6925±0.074	0.640±0.0776	0.716±0.1344	0.729±0.0975	0.676±0.0826
(Range)	(0.605–0.805)	(0.600– 0.705)	(0.550–1.01)	(0.505–0.900)	(0.580–0.810)
Community respiration (mg/l)	0.420±0.0184	0.420±0.0635	0.421±0.0394	0.498±0.156	0.411±0.0375
(Range)	(0.405–0.450)	(0.400–0.450)	(0.390–0.480)	(0.400–0.580)	(0.380–0.480)
Net production efficiency (%)	38.77±4.7	34.29±1.101	44.15±15.56	44.15±15.56	44.15±15.56
(Range)	(33.05–44.09)	(33.33–36.17)	(25.45–66.66)	(20.79–37.03)	(34.48–42.55)

Free carbon dioxide released during the decomposition of certain substances and respiration of living organism since higher temperature accelerate the decomposition of organic substances as well as the respiratory activity of the biota and shown direct relationship between the water temperature and free carbon dioxide (Hynes, 1970). The maximum value of free carbon dioxide was observed (2.2 mg/l ±0.155) in May and minimum value in January (1.70 mg/l ±0.066). Free carbon dioxide and dissolved oxygen showed a negative relationship to each other. The similar observations have also been reported by Quadri and Shah (1989) in some freshwater ecosystem. The highest rate of photosynthesis decreases free carbon-dioxide content and higher rate of decomposition increases free carbon dioxide. An inverse relationship between dissolved oxygen and free carbon- dioxide has been reported by Khan and Siddiqui (1971).

Chloride was found in form of chloride ion, and one of the major inorganic anions present in natural water. The maximum chloride concentration was recorded (17.14mg/l ± 1.33) in the month of May and minimum in the month of January (11.36 mg/l±2.008), chloride and hardness showed a positive relationship to one another. Chopra and Patrick (1994) also stated similar trend in aquatic ecosystem in the river Ganga at Rishikesh. The maximum calcium concentration was observed (15.99mg/ l ± 5.53) in the month of May while the minimum value of calcium was observed (80.336mg/l ± 2.64) in the month of January. Similar type of relationship of calcium was observed by Ahemad and Hasnain (2001) in freshwater bodies. Khanna and

Singh (2000) also reported similar trend of calcium distribution in river Suswa, Raiwala, Dehradun. Sahastradhara stream may be regarded as rich in calcium and other geochemical nutrients. Calcium is one of the essential nutrients, which plays an important role in biological system. In fact, Calcium content in water is responsible for bone growth of children.

Table 6: Correlation (=CORREL) Between Nutrients (Mean values) and Physico-chemical Parameters (Mean values) of Sahastradhara Stream

Parameters	*Chloride*	*Calcium*	*Magnesium*	*Sodium*	*Potassium*
Temperature (°C)	–0.86097	–0.51833	–0.92056	–0.01186	–0.14275
Velocity (m/s)	–0.17595	–0.12077	0.007842	0.179873	0.225839
Turbidity (JTU)	0.012697	0.818834	0.400371	0.92284	0.959357
Total solids (mg/l)	–0.00448	0.788427	0.273292	0.949891	0.906666
TDS (mg/l)	0.133154	0.71132	0.25802	0.764443	0.682478
TSS (mg/l)	–0.35586	0.096981	0.004271	0.35689	0.46296
pH (pH unit)	0.681329	0.761113	0.623067	0.395679	0.345766
Free CO_2 (mg/l)	–0.03224	0.686443	0.396104	0.833271	0.90927
DO (mg/l)	0.679888	–0.12231	0.471533	–0.65112	–0.55633
BOD (mg/l)	0.607899	0.912138	0.845587	0.615583	0.694262
COD (mg/l)	0.595229	0.954861	0.801927	0.654354	0.704159
Hardness (mg/l)	0.814816	0.795954	0.897315	0.312648	0.386789
Alkalinity (mg/l)	–0.04111	0.829565	0.331085	0.97707	0.985243

Magnesium is also an essential and beneficial element, but it is toxic at higher concentration. The recommended acceptable limit of magnesium for domestic purpose is 30mg/l in the river. The amount of magnesium in the river Sahastradhara was found maximum (57.2mg/l ± 7.24) in the month of May while the minimum value of magnesium was recorded (52.2mg/l ±6.55) in the month of January. Castante *et al.* (1985) in river Parana and Meybeck (1984) in river Zaire also reported similar trend of magnesium availability in natural water.

Sodium at lower concentration has no adverse effect on human health. The maximum sodium concentration was recorded (9.44 mg/l ± 1.016) in the month of May and minimum value of sodium was observed (7.1mg/l ± 0.663) in the month of January. Pande and Mishra (2000) observed similar results on Sahastradhara stream. Sodium is one of the most common cation present in the water bodies. Potassium is naturally occurring elements, like the sodium, however its concentration remains lower than sodium. The potassium is released by the clay mineral, weathering and leaching form the growing vegetation and decomposition of organic matter. Potassium concentration was observed highest in the month of May (17.2 mg/l±0.67) and lowest in the month of January (15.2 mg/l±0.812). Similar results were obtained by Sarin *et al.* (1989) and Subramanian (1989) observed the similar trend on the river Brahmaputra.

Table 7: Correlation (=CORREL) Between Plankton (Mean values) and Physico-chemical Parameters (Mean values) of Sahastradhara Stream

Parameters	*Total Plankton*	*Phytoplankton*	*Zooplankton*	*Total Diatom*	*Green Algae*	*Blue Green Algae*
Temperature °C	0.140144	0.040568	0.561048	–0.12814	0.203944	–0.06004
Velocity (m/s)	–0.09075	–0.11978	0.096464	–0.00984	–0.18658	–0.81972
Turbidity (JTU)	0.103772	0.005161	0.537763	0.394692	–0.95776	–0.35417
Total solids (mg/l)	–0.40534	–0.52983	0.405479	–0.18218	–0.91516	–0.73149
TDS (mg/l)	–0.70298	–0.80425	0.139674	–0.54607	–0.71164	–0.72652
TSS (mg/l)	0.823334	0.77943	0.635537	0.966082	–0.40829	0.080955
pH	–0.88664	–0.89145	–0.42828	–0.71618	–0.42595	–0.36483
Free CO_2 (mg/l)	0.27888	0.196314	0.548124	0.578174	–0.89315	–0.36232
DO (mg/l)	0.028383	0.184226	–0.75181	0.04589	0.505435	0.574037
BOD (mg/l)	–0.18081	–0.18513	–0.07095	0.161374	–0.74373	–0.20002
COD (mg/l)	–0.27454	–0.29116	–0.05821	0.047125	–0.75928	–0.19054
Hardness (mg/l)	–0.2978	–0.25029	–0.38539	–0.01229	–0.45865	0.023773
Alkalinity (mg/l)	–0.00781	–0.12433	0.568959	0.262619	–0.98348	–0.44697

The quantitative fluctuation of the planktonic diversity has shown a significant effect on the ecology of river. All natural water contains a variety of plankton as the natural flora and fauna. The phytoplankton community is a heterogeneous group of tiny plants adapted to suspension in the freshwater. The present study showed that the maximum number of total plankton were recorded (1523.6±26.56) in the month of January and minimum (718.6 ± 19.33) in the month of May.

Table 8: Correlation (=CORREL) Between Primary Productivity (Mean values) and Physico-chemical Parameters (Mean values) of Sahastradhara Stream

Parameters	*Net Primary Productivity*	*Gross Primary Productivity*	*Community Respiration*	*Net Production Efficiency*
Temperature °C	–0.59945	0.006189	0.311429	–0.57232
Velocity (m/s)	–0.82147	–0.40554	0.387568	–0.78591
Turbidity (JTU)	0.459379	0.237629	–0.09751	0.389256
Total solids (mg/l)	0.086601	0.565255	0.544701	–0.16675
TDS (mg/l)	0.01787	0.761621	0.801179	–0.33031
TSS (mg/l)	0.165469	–0.58282	–0.73453	0.444083
pH	0.409892	0.87509	0.647625	0.023325
Free CO_2 (mg/l)	0.335796	–0.03623	–0.24934	0.360837
DO (mg/l)	0.43596	–0.20694	–0.47748	0.522691
BOD (mg/l)	0.715985	0.330189	–0.11921	0.583037
COD (mg/l)	0.757185	0.484589	–0.01968	0.572202
Hardness (mg/l)	0.811178	0.38677	–0.13668	0.659382
Alkalinity (mg/l)	0.380434	0.349649	0.067672	0.259953

Phytoplankton was recorded maximum (1371 ± 25.77) in the month of January and minimum (633 ± 9.32) in the month of May. Eddy (1993) pointed out that plankton production is mainly influenced by temperature. Badola and Singh (1981) reported high values of plankton during January to March in freshwater of Kumaon Lake. According to Das and Pathani (1978) increment in turbidity will reduces the plankton production in a water body due to low light penetration and low rate of photosynthesis. According to Khanna (1993) the plankton were maximum in the month of winter probably due to low temperature, high content of dissolved oxygen low velocity and transparency of water and other suitable conditions. Allen (1920) stated that water currant is the chief factor influencing the plankton of stream San Joaquin River and its tributaries near Stockton in California.

Zooplankton were recorded maximum (152.6 ± 13.00) in the month of December and minimum (82 ± 13.02) in the month of May. Total diatoms were recorded maximum (1048.8 ± 34.02) in the month of January and minimum (495 ± 9.25) in the month of April. Green algae were recorded maximum (241.2 ± 29.77) in the month of January and minimum (106.4 ± 6.28) in the month of May. Blue Green algae was recorded maximum (81 ± 4.05) in the month of January and minimum (27.6 ± 3.98) in the month of May. Juttner *et al.* (1995) also reported the similar trend of diatom communities in Himalayan Hill-streams. Similar observations have been reported by Khanna *et al.* (1998) in relation to phytoplanktonic communities of Ganga canal at Haridwar. Khanna and Singh (2000) also reported the similar trend of planktonic diversity in Suswa River, Raiwala, Dehradun. Similar observations were also reported by Nautiyal (1982) in Alaknanda River and Khanna (1993) in river Ganga at Hardwar.

It is well established that the primary productivity is controlled by several physico-chemical and biotic interactions. The rate of production of organic mater per unit time is termed as productivity. There are two levels of production, primary and secondary. The amount of new organic matter resulting from photosynthesis is termed as primary productivity. The animal and plant communities inhabiting water bodies are considered as the direct manifestation of the productivity. The maximum net primary productivity was observed (0.335 ±0.093) in the month of December and minimum (0.170 ±0.04) in the month of May. The maximum gross primary productivity was observed (.796 ±0.123) in the month of January and minimum (.569 ±0.0379) in the month of May. The maximum net community respiration was observed (.479 ±0.0575) in the month of January and minimum (.399 ±0.0102) in the month of April. The higher productivity in the present studied was concomitant with temperature range from 14°C to 18°C. Singh and Swaroop (1980) observed positive correlation with productivity and water temperature. A positive correlation existed between gross primary productively and calcium in Cavery (Lakshminarayan, 2001). Vashney *et al.* (1983) present study a positive correlation was recorded between gross primary productivity and dissolved oxygen while the negative correlation between gross primary productivity and temperature and free carbon dioxide.

Table 9: Preliminary Study of Biotic Communities in Sahastradhara Stream, Dehradun

Family/Phylum	*Genus/Species*
Flora:	
A) Chorophyceae	*Ulothrix, Volvox, Cladophora, Chlorella, Vaucheria, Zygnema, Pediasterum*
B) Bacillariophyceae	Diatoms
C) Rhodophyceae	*Batrachospermun*
D) Cyanophyceae	*Rivularia, Nostoc*
Fauna:	
A) Protozoans	*Vorticalla, Amoeba, Paramoecium, Chrysamocha, Volvox*
B) Coelentrata	*Hydra, Ceratella*
C) Annelida	Pheretima
D) Arthropods	Mayfly nymph
E) Macroinvertibrate	Snails, Leeches, Flatworms, Beetles

Net production efficiency shows the positive correlation with dissolved oxygen, while the negative correlation between net production efficiency and carbon dioxide. The maximum mean value of net production efficiency was observed (43.79%) in the month of January and minimum (29.88%) in the month of April. Similar trend was observed by Yeragi and Shaikh (2003) on the primary productivity of Tansa River. Singh *et al.*(1980) and Kar *et al.* (1978) however, recorded low and high productivity in summer and winter respectively.

Sahastradhara stream has a wide biodiversity of small invertebrates, including some benthos, nekton, phytoplankton, zooplankton, which maintain the water quality of aquatic ecosystem. Planktonic genus and other fauna available in the water of Sahastradhara hill-stream at Dehradun depicted in Table 9.

The endemic fish species about 18 in number occurs in the natural aquatic system of Sahastradhara (Table 10). Among these, four to six species may be undertake as sport fishery to enhance or attract the fish anglers on the tourist sites. The limnological and biological status of Sahastradhara stream have shown optimum suitable environment to accelerate the growth and population of endemic fish diversity. There has taken place to increasing use of aquatic resources to cater the needs of tourism. As the present conditions are in sites development of these water bodies has to be taken up for the protection of natural habitats and rehabilitate as fish sanctuaries. The transplantation of healthy stocks of desirable sport fishes have to be done on scientific lines on the basis of optimum biological productivity of the stream. The conservation and management of aquatic ecosystem of hill-streams should involve the management of aquatic life including fishes and multiplicity of uses of a whole ecosystem as amenity, ecotourism etc.

Table 10: Fish Diversity in Sahastradhara Hill-stream at Dehradun

Scientific Name (Genus/Species)	*Local Name*
Schizothorax richardsonii (*Gray*)	Asella
Schizothorax plagiostomus	Dhibrua
Schizothorax sinatus	Maseen
Puntius chola (*Ham.*)	–
Puntius hexasticus	Khront
Barilius barila (*Ham.*)	
Barilius bendelisis (*Ham.*)	Chal
Barilius vagra (*Ham.*)	Chal
Noemacheilus savona (*Ham.*)	–
Glyptothorax pectinopterus (*McClell.*)	–
Mastacembelus armatus (*Lac.*)	–
Garra lamta (*Ham.*)	–
Garra gotyla gotyla (*gray*)	Gunthala
Danio devario (*Ham.*)	Patukari
Chagunia chagunio (*Ham.*)	Gelhari
Botia durlo (*Ham.*)	Baghaua
Chipisoma garua (*Ham.*)	Raikari
Colisa fasciatus (*Block and Schn.*)	Khosti

Conclusion

Sahastradhara hill-stream ecosystem has suitable conditions for the habitation and survival of different biotic communities including plankton, nekton and benthos. In the Sahastradhara hill-stream Calcium and Magnesium level is high especially in the summer season. All the parameters studied had minor differences at different sites during the observation. Water quality of Sahastradhara stream has widely affected by tourists activities hence industrial pollution is no more here. Primary productivity is high in winter season whereas production efficiency was influenced by various physico-chemical parameters at different sampling sites.

The water quality is quite rich in natural nutrients which play an important implication for use the drinking purpose after making sure the bacterial and other hygienic condition after clean technology. The conservation measures must be directed towards understanding of the intricate relationship between all biotic organisms either plants or animals along with surrounding environment.

References

Ahamed, S. and Hasnain, S.I. 2001. Snow and stream water chemistry of the Ganga headwater basin, Garhwal Himalaya, India, *Hydrological Sciences Journal* 46(1): 103-111.

Allen, W.E. 1920. A quantitative and statistical study of the plankton of the San Joaquin River and its tributaries in a near Stockton California in 1913. *Univ. Calif. Publ. Zool.* 22(1): 1-24.

APHA 1995. Ecological methods for the examination of water. *American Public Health Association,* 1015 fifteen street NW, Washington, 19: 1-1134.

Badola, S.P. and Singh, H.R. 1981. Hydrobiology of the river Alaknanda of Garhwal Himalaya *Indian J. Ecol.,* 8(2): 269-276.

Chopra, A.K., Patrick, Nirmal, J. 1994. Effect of domestic sewage on self-purification of Ganga water at Rishikesh. *A. Bio.science,* 13(11): 75-82.

Das, S.M. and Pathani, S.S. 1978. A study on the effect of lake ecology on production of Mahaseer (*Tor tor and T. putitora*) in Kumaon lake. *Indian Matsya.* 4: 25-31.

Das, S.M. and Srivastava, V.K. 1956. Studies of freshwater plankton II correlation between plankton and hydro-biological factors *Proc. Nat. Acad. Sci. India,* (13) 26: 243-253.

Dobriyal, A.K. 1985. Ecology of limnofauna in the small streams and their importance to the village life in Garhwal Himalya. *Uttar Pradesh J. Zool.* 5 (2): 139-144.

Eddy, S. 1934: A study of freshwater plankton communities. *Illinois Biol. Monogr.* 12 (4): 1-93.

Hutchinson, G.C. 1957. A treatise on limnology, geography, physical and chemical, Vol.-I, New York: *John Wiley and Sons, Inc.,* pp: 1-1015.

Hynes, H.B.N. 1970. The ecology of running waters. *Liverpool University Press, Liverpool, 4th impression*: 1-555.

Juttner I., Heike Rothfritz and Steve J. Ormerod 1995. *University of Wales, Cardiff, CFI 3TL UK*- 'Diatom Communities in Himalayan hill-streams, pp: 589-597.

Joshi, B.D., Bisht, R.C.S. and Semval, V.P. 1995. Primary productivity in western Ganga Canal at Hardwar. *Indian J.Ecol.* 22(2): 123-126.

Kar, O.K., P.C. Mishra, M.C. Das and R.C. Das 1978. Pollution studies in river Ib. III Plankton, pollution and primary productivity, 175.

Khan, A.A. and Siddiqui, A. 1971. *Hydrobiologia*, 37:447.

Khanna, D.R., Badola, S.P., Sing, H.R. and Dobriyal, K., Anoop 1992. Observations on seasonal trends in diatomic diversity in the river Ganga at Sapt-sarover, Hardwar. In: Recent research in cold water: Fisheries, Ed. by K.L. Sehgal, *Today and Tomarrow printers and publishers, New Delhi*: 99-107.

Khanna, D.R. 1993. Ecology and pollution of Ganga River, *Ashish Publishing House*, New Delhi. pp: 1-241.

Khanna, D.R., Malik, D.S. and Rana, D.S. 1998. Phytoplanktonic communities in relation to certain physico-chemical parameters of Ganga canal at Hardwar. *Him. J. Env. Zool.*, Vol-12: 193-197.

Khanna, D.R and Singh. R.K. 2000. Seasonal fluctuations in the plankton of Suswa River at Raiwala Dehradun. *Env. Conservations J.* 1(2 and 3): 89-92.

Khanna, D.R., Bhutiani, R. and Chandra, K. S. 2005. Modeling to assess effect of light on phytoplanktonic growth dynamics: a review, *Env. Conservations J.*, 6(3): 103-107.

Lakshminarayana and R.K. Someshekar. 2001. Ecology of polluted water by Arvind Kumar Vol-1, chapter II, pp. 51-60, *APH Pub. Corp.* New Delhi-110002.

Nautiyal, P. 1982. Some aspects of bio ecology of Tarputitora in relation to hydrobiology of some Garhwal hill-stream. *D.Phill. Thesis;* Garhwal University.

Pande, R.K. and Asha Mishra 2000. Water quality study of freshwaters of Dehradun (Sahastradhara stream and Mussoorie lake). *Aquacult.* Vol- (1): 57-62.

Quadri, M.Y. and Shah, G.M. 1984. Hydro-biological feature of Hoassar. A typical wetland of Kashmir-I, Biotope. *Indian J. Ecol.*, 2(2): 203-206.

Santhanam, R.; Velayntham, P. and Jegatheesan, G. 1989. A manual of freshwater ecology. *Daya publishing house Delhi*-110006: 3-17, 53-92.

Sarin, M.M., Krishnaswamy, S.K., Trivedi, J.R. and Sharma, K.K. 1992. Major ion chemistry of the Ganga source waters: weathering in high altitude Himalaya. In: *Proc, Indian acad. Sci.* (*Earth Planet Sci.*) 1, 89-98.

Schwoerbel, J. 1991. Handbook of Limnology, *Ellis Horwood Limited, Chichester, England:* pp- 95-114.

Shrama, R.C. 1986. Effect of physico-chemical factors on benthic fauna of Bhargirathi River Garhwal Himalaya. *Indian. J. Ecol.* 13(1): 133-137.

Singh, S.N.; Gupta, M.L.; and Prakash, P. 1980. Hydro-biological studies of some eutrophic ponds of Rohtash, Bihar. *Environment and Ecology.* 16 (2): 457-462.

Subramanian, V. 1989. Chemical and suspended sediment characteristics of river of India. *J. Hydrol*, 44: 37-55.

Trivedi, R.K. and Goel, P.K. 1984. Chemical and biological methods for water pollution studies Karad: *Environmental publication*, pp.1-251.

Valdiya, K.S. 1975. Emergence of the Himalayas, Science today, 9: 14-18.

Vashney, P.K.; R. Vijayalakshmi, Nair and S.H.H. Abidi.1983. Primary productivity in near shore water of Thai Maharashtra coast, India. *J.Mar. Sci.* 12:27-30.

Yeragi, S.G. and Nisar Shaikh. 2003. Studies on primary productivity of Tansa River. *J. Natcon* 15 (1): 125-130.

Chapter 4
Nutrients and Ions

Contents

3.1 General

Water is a universal solvent. Water may be found in nature as vapour and humidity in the atmosphere; as a liquid in rain; as surface water in rivers, streams, ponds, lakes, watersheds and interior seas; or forming part of sea and oceans. Water is also found as Groundwater, in vadose or unsaturated zones, occluded as interstitial water in the free spaces of soil and sediments, in springs and aquifers, or forming part of minerals as hydrates. Water exists as a solid in glaciers, icebergs, hail, snow and ice. Natural water may contain varying amount of a myriad of chemical compounds that come from natural or anthropogenic sources, or both.

The composition of water in each site depends on its geological environment, as well as on the dissolution and chemical reactions of this solvent with solids, liquids and gases during the water cycle. Many nutrients may dissolve into the water through various geochemical processes. Many interdependent parameters are thus involved and no generalizations or correlations can be easily established for the composition of natural water. Several individual or combined processes contribute to the presence of different species that affect the composition and properties of natural waters.

Chiefly, the water composition depends on the geochemical nature of bedrock, the weathering regimes, the environmental climatic conditions, biogeochemical processes taking place in the zone, Chemistry of components of the bedrock and Environmental inputs from anthropogenic activities. Water quality is affected by various ways and different physico-chemical parameters of water itself and also some external factors. Many internal and external factors are responsible to govern the water quality on a significant level.

Pollution of surface and subsurface water resources by nutrients is of growing concern worldwide as high nutrient concentrations can have harmful effects on both ecosystem and human health. Understanding river-aquifer connectivity is an important aspect of nutrient management. In addition to natural sources such as soil and organic matter, agricultural and urban activities are also contributing nutrient contamination to surface water and subsurface water systems. Nutrients of greatest concern are nitrogen (N) and phosphorus (P).

Both nutrients occur in numerous chemical and physical forms and originate from a variety of diffuse and point sources. Although eutrophication is a natural process in the aging of water bodies and some estuaries, human activities such as agricultural runoff, urban runoff, leaking septic systems, sewage discharges and eroded stream banks can increase the flow of nutrients and organic substances into aquatic systems.

The relative importance of different sources of nitrogen and phosphorus varies between catchments. In general, phosphorus tends to be bound to sediment whereas nitrogen is predominantly found in the dissolved state. The dominant sources of phosphorus are hill slope erosion, gully and bank erosion, as dissolved form in runoff as well as in urban point discharges. Dissolved nitrogen in runoff comprises a greater proportion of the total load than dissolved phosphorus. Total nitrogen loads are mainly derived from hill slope erosion and dissolved nitrogen in runoff. In landscapes where subsurface water and surface waters interact, the occurrence of high levels of dissolved nutrients can have implications for water quality. For example, the discharge of groundwater high in nitrogen into lakes, wetlands, streams and marine environments can cause eutrophication of the receiving surface water body and cause algal blooms to develop. Modeling of nutrient budgets has traditionally focused on the major pathways for nutrients transported through surface water systems. However, a missing link in these budgets is the contribution of dissolved nutrients from a subsurface water source, in the case of a gaining river system, or losses, in the case of a stream that loses water to the subsurface.

3.2 Parameters

The main nutrients parameters in hill-stream ecology are:

- ✰ Phosphate (PO_4)
- ✰ Nitrate (NO_3)
- ✰ Sulfate (SO_4)

Sahastradhara is famous for sulfur water springs, so some concentration of sulfate can be found easily in the stream ecosystem.

Phosphate and nitrate are the major nutrient parameters of a water body. The status and concentration of both nutrients described the age and status of water body, *i.e.* atrophic or eutrophic. Besides these ions, few other nutrients can also be studied for the further and deep study of an aquatic ecosystem.

Cations and anions play an important role in the chemistry of aquatic ecosystem. A list of main cations and anions is also given here for systematic study of any aquatic ecosystem:

Table 4.2.1: A List of Cations and Anions in Aquatic Ecosystem

Sl.No.	*Cation*	*Anion*
1	Ca	
2	Mg	Cl
3	Mn	PO_4
4	Sr	HCO_3
5	Fe	pH
6	Na	NO_3
7	K	SO_4

Following nutrients parameters of Sahastradhara water were selected for the assessment of water quality:

- ☆ Calcium (Ca^{++})
- ☆ Magnesium (Mg^{++})
- ☆ Potassium (K^{+})
- ☆ Sodium (Na^{+})
- ☆ Chloride (Cl^{-})

3.3 Historical Resume

According to *Hippocrates* (460 B.C. – 345 B.C.), the father of medicine, "water contributes much to health" and averted the rain water should be used after boiling and filtering, otherwise it would smell bed and cause harshness (Borchart and Wotton, 1971). Today we are going fast toward the way of success. Although man in touching the high of perfection yet on the other side he is the prime amuse for the explosion of the planet and its water resource. The very fast criteria, standard criteria for drinking water was reported in the literature in 1921 when United States published USPH standard for drinking water, But it specified only bacteriological parameters.

This review includes some of the important contribution made from various parts of world. Various workers discussed the various aspects of water quality time to time from India and abroad nationally or internationally.

Clark (1924) analyzed the composition of river and lake water of United States. Galtsoff (1924) and Reinnard (1931) studied the limnology of upper Mississippi. Ghosuddin (1934) studied the algal flora of the river Moori. Ganpati (1940) studied the ecology of the temple tank containing a permanent bloom of *Microcystis aeruginousa*. Ganpati and Alikunni (1950) observed that water of river Ganga was heavily polluted which dangerous to the human health. Motiawant *et al.* (1956), Ganpati and Chacko (1957) and Daivid (1957-59) observed about the pollution of Ganga water.

Verma (1964) carried out hydro-biological survey of Dalsagar tank. Baloni and Sarkar (1965) observed the pollution of Yamuna River at Okhla water intake out at Delhi. Saxena *et al.* (1966) observed pollution of the Ganga near Kanpur. Reynold and Johnson (1972), melt water demonstrates that chemical weathering takes place beneath the glacier.

Stround and Martin (1973) said reservoir releases might be made from either the surface or the bottom of the impoundment, with resultant opportunity to control downstream water temperature. Kand and Kachroo (1973 and 1974) studied the limnology of Kashmir lakes. Edgington and Rolfe (1974) reporting on sampling. Agarwal *et al.* (1976) analyzed the hydrobiology of river Ganga at Varanasi. Kaul (1977) studied in Kashmir. Major lowland rivers have been studied, for example, in the Kathmandu valley.

Goldberg *et al.* (1978), D' Elia *et al.* (1986), Officer *et al.* (1984) observed that nutrient pollution has been linked to eutrophication in the Chesa Peak Bay estuary for at least the several decades. Plummer and Back (1980); Christophersen and Wright (1981); Elder (1985) and Badola and Singh (1981) studied hydrobiology of Alaknanda. Gopal *et al.* (1981) studied the limnology of a freshwater reservoir of Jaipur. Meyback (1981), Stallard and Edmond (1983), (1987) concluded in tropical regions, erosion of silicates is more enhanced in response to both an increase in silica degradation rate with higher temperature and abundant rainfall and vegetation.

In Nepal, Upadhyaya and Roy (1982), Tiwari and Ali (1987); in the Kumoun Region, Uttaranchal, (Paul and Verma, 1990; Bhatt and Pathak, 1992) in the Andhra Pradesh region, India. Naidu *et al.* 1989), Mayewski *et al.* (1986), Nijampurkar *et al.* (1993) studied of snow chemistry form high altitude Himalayan glaciers have been reported concentration of No_3 and So_4 of magnitudes comparable to those experienced in areas of North-West Europe.

Hu *et al.* (1982), Sarin and Krishnaswami (1984), Sarin *et al.* (1989), Zhang *et al.* (1990 a) reported the chemistry of some large Asian rivers such as the Ganges/ Brahmaputra, Changjiang and Huanghe etc. have been of scientific interest for the last decade. Ferro (1982); Lohmunn *et al.* (1988), Jones *et al.* (1989) attention to the chemical quality of lakes and impoundments in the Himalayas has focused on the problems of eutrophication and salinity, in Nepal. Whitfield (1983) and Hall *et al.* (1991) have previously used E.C data in describing water quality within the Fraser basin. Raina *et al.* (1984) made pollution studied of river Jhelum. Chattopadhyay *et al.* (1984) made a study on the pollution status of river Ganga at Kanpur.

Officer *et al.* (1984), D' Elia *et al.* (1986) observed that nutrient pollution has been linked to eutrofication in the Chesa Peak Bay estuary for at least the several decades.

Telang (1985) observed form the Machenzie River, which drains into the Beauford Sea in the arctic, where the occurrence of carbonates in the drainage eosin accounts for the dominance of Ca^{+2} any Mg^{+2} in the river.

Renss and Johnson (1986) said that in early spring, the increased sulphate and nitrate concentrations in the early melt water fraction input into a stream can drop the pH of the stream to a Harmful level for the aquatic life. Berner and Berner (1987) demonstrated the weathering of rock forming minerals with minor contribution from cyclic sea salt and pollution, is the major source of ions in river water.

Cooper *et al.* (1987) reported runoff decrease of the concentration of most ions to a minimum in melt water. Latimer *et al.* (1988), Yuretich and Batchelder (1988) observed that the chemical mass balance approach has been used extensively during recent years to study in stream reactions and sediment dynamics. Larson *et al.* (1988) studied the assessment of attainable surface water quality. Galloway (1989) observed the deposition of acidic oxide is likely to increase in the future in the developing areas of Asia. Sarin *et al.* (1989) indicate that the water chemistry of highland tributaries is dominated by carbonate weathering in the Ganges/Brahmaputra system. Paul and Verma (1990); Zhang *et al.* (1990a) studied the atmospheric input accounts for less than 5-10% of total river in dissolved fluxes for most of the major species. Zhang *et al.* (1990 c) analyzed heavy minerals account for 5-10%, of which magnetite, hematite, pyroxene, hornblende, limonite, garnet, appetite and zircon are quite common.

Weinberg (1990) Coffey *et al.* (1992); Robillard *et al.* (1992) suggested that the importance of controlling water pollution at the agricultural watershed level is increasing day by day. Walcott *et al.* (1990) observed that in rural areas, nutrients and pesticides are released in surface and groundwater and may degrade the quality of water and cause various health problems to human. Tranter *et al.* (1992), found a sharp increase in the concentration of Cl^- is probably the result of selective Cl^- removal by rainwater over snow and ice. Bales (1992) also described sulphate and nitrate loaded meltwater pulses in North America and Europe. Jain (1992), Jain *et al.* (1997) reported the chemical characterizations of Kali River with special reference to disposal of municipal and industrial wastes.

Chauhan and Hasnain (1993) reported the negative correlation between solute concentration and discharge near the source area. The TDS and EC values for the Samples of the lower Alaknanda are high during high flow in June. Tyler and Ormerod (1993), Wilkinson *et al.*(1995), Ormerod and Juttner (1996), Juttner *et al.* (in press) studies in 5-15 sub- catchments of the Likhu Khola and Kathmandu valley.

Kosi at Purnia. Ormerod *et al.* (1994) observed that stream communities vary in composition and function with altitudes.

Callow and Petts, (1994), Norris *et al.* (1995) recognized that rivers integrate processes in whole catchments and their biota is regularly monitored to detect change on this scale. Correll *et al.* (1994) suggested that factors such as lithology and topography, affect the flux of nutrient to nearby rivers. Helgesen *et al.* (1994) and McMahon *et al.* (1994) observed that nitrate and phosphate concentration were more related to irrigated cropland and to urban areas than to range land or forest sites in the south plain river basin. Ormerod *et al.* (1994), Brewin and Ormerod (1994), Brewin *et al.* (1995) carried the survey of 20 tributaries in the Lang tang and Trishuli systems.

Collins, R. (1995) studied the stream water acidification in response to anthropogenic pollution inputs at forested and cultivated catchments in the middle

Hills, Nepal. Jenkins, A. (1995) studied the stream chemistry in the middle hills and high mountains of the Himalayas, Nepal.

Kumar, (1995) studied on pollution is river Mayurakshi in south Bihar. Shivsubramani and Mahadevan, (1995) evaluated the water quality of river Suruliyar in Tamilnadu and western Ganga cannel at Hardwar. Jenkins, A. (1995) analyzed the hydro-chemical characteristics of headwater streams in the middle Hills and high mountains of the Himalayas, Nepal. J. Zhang *et al.* (1995) described the major element chemistry of the Huanghe (Yellow River), China-Weathering processes and chemical fluxes. Brenner and Mandok (1995) observed N and P pollution in the glacial tills of the Shenango River.

Jain (1996), Jain *et al.* (1998) used indirect monitoring to study the contribution of point and non-point source of pollution to the river Kali. Puckett (1996) studies the natural source of nutrients pollution in Potomac River. Ormerod *et al.* (1996), Jenkins *et al.* (1996) carried out a regional survey of 76 sites in the Simihot, Dunai and Makalu regions. Collins and Jenkins (1996) observed increased levels of nitrate, sulphate, chloride and base cations in streams near agricultural terraces in Nepal.

Rasmussen (1996) measured higher levels of nitrate downstream of manure row crops than chemically fertilized row crops. Cameron (1996) studied the hydro-geochemistry and seasonal variation in major and minor components of the Fraser River, British Columbia. Jain (1996), Dolan and Elshearawi (1989), Berndtsson (1990) utilized the approach to determine the metallic load to the rivers.

Miller *et al.* (1997) analyzed nutrients in stream during base flow in selected environmental settings of the Potomac River basin. Stolllemyer (1997) analyzed the stream water chemistry in water shads receiving different atmospheric inputs of H^+, NH_4^+, No^-_3 and So_4^{--}.

Bond (1997), Caine and Thurman (1990) demonstrated the annual stream hydrograph, two factors account for most seasonal variations in stream water chemistry: the annual hydrologic cycle, and the degree to which snowmelt is partitioned between overland and sub-surface flow. Singh and Hasnain (1998) studied the major ion chemistry and weathering control in a high altitude basin of Alaknanda River, Garhwal Himalaya India.

Jain (2000) described application of chemical mass balance approach to determine nutrient loading in the river Kali.

Ahamad and Hasnain (2001) described the snow and stream water chemistry of the Ganga headwater basin, Garhwal Himalayas, India. Kumar *et al.* (2003) studied on water quality of the river Ambarampalayam, Coimbatore District, Tamilnadu.

Graening and Brown (2003) observed ecosystem dynamics and pollution effects in an Ozark cave stream. Bharti (2004) described the limnological aspects and physico-chemical characteristics of Sahastradhara hill-stream in Doon velly. Iqbal *et al.* (2004) highlighted the Seasonal Variations of Physico-Chemical Characteristics of River Soan Water at Dhoak Pathan Bridge (Chakwal), in Pakistan. Malik and Bharti (2005b) also described the nutrient dynamics in the water of stream Sahastradhara at Dehradun.

CPCB (2006) reported the water quality status of Yamuna river (1999-2005). Sikoki and Zabbey (2006) described the environment gradients and benthic community of the middle reaches of Imo River, South Eastern Nigeria. Sunderay *et al.* (2006) analysed the multivariate statistical techniques for the evaluation of spatial and temporal variation in water quality of Mahanadi riverestuarine system (India) in a case study. Panda *et al.* (2006) described the application of Factor and cluster analysis for characterization of river and estuarine water systems in a case study of Mahanadi River (India).

Prasad and Patil (2008) made a study of physico-chemical parameters of Krishna river water particularly in western Maharashtra. Saksena *et al.* (2008) evaluated the water quality and pollution status of Chambal river in National Chambal sanctuary, Madhya Pradesh. Karbassi *et al.* (2008) made a study on metal pollution assessment of sediment and water in the Shur river.

Dragun *et al.* (2009) described the preliminary assessment of total dissolved trace metal concentrations in Sara river water. Altin *et al.* (2009) made an assessment of seasonal variations of surface water quality charecteristics for Porsuk stream. Hartig *et al.* (2009) evaluated a long term ecosystem monitoring and assessment of the Detroit river and western Lake Erie. Ahmed *et al.* (2009) made a study on heavy metals in some environmental samples. Trivedi *et al.* (2009) made a study on the evaluation of Water Quality: Physico-Chemical Characteristics of Ganga River at Kanpur by using Correlation Study. Agbaire and Obi (2009) evaluated the seasonal Variations of Some Physico-Chemical Properties of River Ethiope Water in Abraka, Nigeria. Amantray *et al.* (2009) analysed an assessment of Water Quality Index in Mahanadi and Atharabanki Rivers and Taldanda Canal in Paradip Area, India. Fulazzaky (2009) highlighted the water quality evaluation system to assess the Brantes river water.

Wang *et al.* (2010) studied on the assessment of heavy metals in sediments from a typical catchment of the Yangtze river, China. Varunprasath and Daniel (2010) analysed the physico-Chemical Parameters of River Bhavani in Three Stations, Tamilnadu, India. Fulazzaky *et al.* (2010) made an assessment of Water Quality Status for the Selangor River in Malaysia. Solai *et al.* (2010) highlighted the implications of physical parameters and trace elements in surface water off Pondicherry, Bay of Bengal, South East Coast of India.

Rani *et al.* (2011) made an assessment of temporal variations in water quality of some important rivers in middle Gangtic plains, India. Jindal and Sharma (2011) studied on water quality of Sutlej river around Ludhiana with reference to physic-chemical parameters. Kannel *et al.* (2011) pointed out the chemometrics in assessment of seasonal variation of water quality in freshwater systems. Wang *et al.* (2011) highlighted the analysis and evaluation of the sources of heavy metals in the water of the river Changjiang.

Kapsikar *et al.* (2011) evaluated the physico-chemical features of Kali river, Karwar,west coast of India. Kumar *et al.* (2011) analysed the aquachemistry, Zooplankton and bacterial diversity in three ponds of Karwar district, Karnataka.

3.4 Methodology

Calcium

Calcium is one of the most abundant substances of the natural water. Being present in high quantities in the rocks, it is leached from there to contaminate the water. The quantities in natural waters generally very from 10 to 100 mg/l depending upon the types of the rocks.

Reagents

(A) EDTA solution 0.01 N: Dissolved 3.723 gm of disodium salt of EDTA in distilled water to prepare 1 liter of solution store in polythene or pyrex bottle.

(B) Sodium hydroxide (1N): Dissolved 40 gm of NaOH in distilled water and dilute to 1 liter.

(C) Murexide indicator: Mix 0.2gm of ammonium perpurate with 100 gm of NaCl and grind it.

Procedure

Take 50 ml sample in conical flask. If the sample is having high alkalinity use smaller volume diluted to 50 ml. Add 2 ml of NaOH solution in the sample Add 100-200 mg of murexide indicator a pink colour develops titrate against EDTA solution until the pink colour change to purple.

Calculation

$$\text{Calcium (mg/l)} = \frac{\text{Volume of EDTA} \times 400.8}{\text{ml of sample}}$$

Magnesium

Calcium and magnesium form a complex of wine red colour with Eriochrome black-T at pH 10.0. The EDTA has got a stronger affinity for Ca^{++} and Mg^{++}, the former complex is broken down and a new complex of blue colour is formed. The value of Mg^{++} can be obtained by subtracting the value of calcium from the total of Ca^{++} + Mg^{++}.

Reagents

(A) EDTA solution,.01M: Dissolve 3.723 g of disodium salt of EDTA in distilled water to prepare 1 liter of solution store in polythene or pyrex bottle.

(B) Buffer solution:

  (*a*) Dissolve 16.9 g. Ammonium chloride in 143 ml of concentrated ammonium hydroxide (NH_4OH).

  (*b*) Dissolve 1.179g of Disodium EDTA and 0.780 g of $MgSO_4 \cdot 7H_2O$ in 50 ml distilled water. Mix both (a) and (b) solution and dilute to 250 with distilled water.

(C) Eriochrome Black-T indicator: Mixed 0.40g of Eriochrome Black T with 100g NaCl (A.R.) and grind.

Procedure

1. Find out the volume of EDTA used in calcium determination.
2. Also find out the volume of EDTA used in hardness (Ca^{++} + Mg^{++}) determination with same, volume of the sample as taken in the calcium determination.

Calculation

$$\text{Magnesium (mg/l)} = \frac{y - x \times 400.8}{\text{ml of sample} \times 1.645}$$

where,

y: EDTA used in hardness determination

x: EDTA used in calcium determination for the same volume of the sample.

$$Mg^{++}, \text{mg/l} = \text{Total hardness (as mg/l } CaCo_3) - \text{Calcium hardness (as mg/l } CaCo_3) \times 0.244$$

where,

$$\text{Calcium hardness (as mg/l. } CaCo_3) = Ca, \text{mg/l} \times 2.497$$

Sodium

A characteristic light is produced due to excitation of electron when the sample with sodium is sprayed into a flame. The intensity of this characteristic radiation is proportional to the conc. of sodium and can be read at 589 nm by using suitable filter devices

Reagent and Apparatus

(A) Flame photometer

(B) Stock sodium solution (1000mg/l Na): Dissolved 2.542gm NaCl dried at 140°C in distilled water to make 1 liter of solution.

(C) Intermediate sodium solution (100mg/l Na): Dilute the stock sodium solution 10 times.

(D) Standard sodium solution (10mg/l Na): Dilute the intermediate solution further 10 times.

(E) Nitric acid conc.

(F) Hydrochloric acid conc.

(G) Hydrogen peroxide, 30%.

(H) NH_4OH conc.

Procedure

Filter the sample through a filter paper to remove any suspended matter which other wise may clog the capillary of the instruments. Find out the concentration of sodium using flame photometer follow the instructions provided by the manufacture for use, because of the differences in the makes and models of different instruments.

All the instruments require preparation of a calibration curve in the ranges of 0 to 1, 0 to 10, 0 to 100 mg/l of sodium by using the various standard solution of sodium use any of these curve for determination of Na for accurate results, it is better to use smaller ranges and if sample is having more Na, it can diluted to come in the range of determination.

Calculation

Sodium (mg/l) = (mg/l Na in diluted aliquot) × Dilution factor.

Potassium

Like sodium, potassium can also be determined accurately by flame photometer. The characteristic radiation for potassium is 768 nm, the intensity of which can be read on a scale by using a filter for this wavelength.

Apparatus and Reagents

(A) Flame Photometer

(B) Stock potassium solution (1000mg/l K): Dissolved 1.907 gm of KCl, dried at 110°C, in distilled water to prepare 1 liter of solution.

(C) Intermediate potassium solution (100mg/l K): Dilute the stock solution 10 times.

(D) Standard potassium solution (10mg/l K): Dilute the intermediate solution further 10 times.

Procedure

Follow the same procedure as described for determination of sodium except that to use filter for potassium at 768 nm wavelengths instead of sodium filter.

Calculation

K (mg/l) = (mg/l K in diluted aliquot) × Diluted factor).

Chloride

Chloride gain access in many way *viz.* solvent power of water dissolve salts from top soil, spray form Ocean, Seas invading freshwaters during tides, underground formation and sewage, human excreta etc.

Reagents

(A) Potassium chromate indicator: Dissolved 50 gm of potassium chromate in a small quantity of distilled water. Add $AgNo_3$ solution to produce a light red precipitate allows standing night and filter makes up 1.0 liter.

(B) Silver Nitrate solution: (N/35.5)- Dissolved 4.78 gm of silver nitrate in 1.0 liter of distilled water standard with standard sodium chloride solution.

Procedure

Take 100 ml of sample in a conical flask Add 1-2 drops of potassium chromate solution. Titrate the contents against 0.02 N $AgNO_3$ until a persistent red tinge appears. Note the amount of titrant used.

Calculation

$$\text{Chloride (mg/l)} = \frac{\text{N} \times \text{ml of AgNO}_3 \text{ used} \times 1000 \times 35.5}{\text{ml of sample}}$$

3.5 Role of Nutrients

Pollution of surface and subsurface water resources by nutrients is of growing concern worldwide as high nutrient concentrations can have harmful effects on both ecosystem and human health. Understanding river-aquifer connectivity is an important aspect of nutrient management. In addition to natural sources such as soil and organic matter, agricultural and urban activities are also contributing nutrient contamination to surface water and subsurface water systems. Nutrients of greatest concern are nitrogen (N) and phosphorus (P).

Eutrophication is a condition found in aquatic ecosystems whereby high nutrient concentrations, especially nitrogen (N) and phosphorus (P), stimulate excessive production of aquatic plants, including algae and periphyton. Both nutrients occur in numerous chemical and physical forms and originate from a variety of diffuse and point sources. Although eutrophication is a natural process in the aging of lakes and some estuaries, human activities such as agricultural runoff, urban runoff, leaking septic systems, sewage discharges and eroded stream banks can increase the flow of nutrients and organic substances into aquatic systems. Algal blooms on the surface of the water prevent the penetration of sunlight essential for underwater plant life while decay of algae depletes dissolved oxygen levels in the water, essential to most aquatic organisms. This disrupts the health and diversity of fish, plant and animal populations in the aquatic environment. Blue-green algae blooms can also contain compounds toxic to humans and stock.

Human health can also be affected by ingesting waters high in nitrate (NO_3^-). Bacteria in the digestive tract convert (reduce) nitrate to nitrite which can be absorbed into the bloodstream and oxidize the haemoglobin. The methaemoglobin that forms is unable to function in the transport of oxygen to the tissues and in high enough concentrations can lead to the disease Methaemoglobinaemia. Infants under the age of 3 months are particularly vulnerable, and the disease can be fatal in this age group.

The relative importance of different sources of nitrogen and phosphorus varies between catchments. In general, phosphorus tends to be bound to sediment whereas nitrogen is predominantly found in the dissolved state. According to the Australian Agriculture Assessment 2001, the dominant sources of phosphorus are hill slope erosion, gully and bank erosion, as dissolved form in runoff as well as in urban point discharges. Dissolved nitrogen in runoff comprises a greater proportion of the total load than dissolved phosphorus. Total nitrogen loads are mainly derived from hill slope erosion and dissolved nitrogen in runoff. Approximately 19,000 tonnes of total phosphorus and 141,000 tonnes of total nitrogen per year are exported down rivers to the coast from areas of intensive agriculture (www.audit.ea.gov.au).

In landscapes where groundwater and surface waters interact, the occurrence of high levels of dissolved nutrients can have implications for water quality. For example, the discharge of groundwater high in nitrogen into lakes, wetlands, streams and marine environments can cause eutrophication of the receiving surface water body and cause algal blooms to develop. In Australia, groundwater has been found to be a significant source of nitrogen to freshwater (Lamontagne 2002), estuarine (Linderfelt and Turner 2001) and coastal environments (Smith *et al.* 2003).

Modelling of nutrient budgets has traditionally focused on the major pathways for nutrients transported through surface water systems. However, a missing link in these budgets is the contribution of dissolved nutrients from a subsurface water source, in the case of a gaining river system, or losses, in the case of a stream that loses water to the subsurface. For catchments where groundwater is a significance source of nutrients to surface waters, there is likely to be an underestimation of nutrient inputs, which due to lag times may not be realised for many years (Lamontagne et al, 2003).

3.6 A Case Study (Malik and Bharti, 2005a)*

Abstract

Sahastradhara hill-stream is a major tributary of river Song, 15 Km. far from Dehradun. It has a great importance as a picnic tourist spot of the region, whereas there is no more industrial and agricultural pollution. Hill-streams of the area are the cradle of nutrients especially calcium and magnesium in the form of ions. Anthropogenic factors mainly tourists activities and catchments runoff may influence the index of nutrients in stream water. Nutrients play a vital role into niche restoration maintenance, self-regulation and water quality. Location variation in nutrients concentration of the stream was studied with special reference to correlation with physico-chemical parameters of the stream water. Calcium and Magnesium were observed in higher range in Sahastradhara stream as comparison to other hill-streams. Calcium and Magnesium were found maximum 104.21 mg/l and 68 mg/l respectively in summer season.

Keywords: Nutrient dynamics, Sahastradhara stream, Rithron zone, Water quality.

Introduction

The Himalayas are the cradle of a large number of streams and mighty rivers. Lesser Himalaya consists of a huge part of Uttaranchal. Dehradun, Hardwar and Rishikesh are the main religious and beautiful cities, which are situated in the foothills of Garhwal Himalaya. A hill-stream Sahastradhara, 15 Km. far from Dehradun city is the study site for the accounting of nutrients in natural water and fluctuations at the different locations along with the stream. Adequate understanding of the Himalayan proglacial streams is extremely important for the development of a realistic program for utilizing the potential of water that exist in the form of snow and ice in the area.

---

* (***Reference***: *Malik, D. S. and Bharti, P.K. (2005a): Nutrient dynamics in Rithron zone of Shivalik Himalayan stream Sahastradhara, Dehradun (Uttaranchal), Env. Cons. J. 6 (2): 63-68.*)

The present study reveals to characteristics the water nutrient chemistry, influenced by tourist's activity and quarrying of the geologically sedimental environments and to determine the nature and degree of anthropogenic impacts on qualitative and quantitative variations occurred in nutrients in relation to physico-chemical parameters of stream.

Materials and Methods

The water samples were collected monthly from sampling site "Sahastradhara stream" from different sampling stations, Site-I, Site-II, Site-III, Site-IV, and Site-V during December, 2003 to May, 2004 in morning period 9:00 A. M. to 10:00 A. M.

The samples for nutrients and physico-chemical parameters were collected and analyzed by using rinsed borosil glassware, with the help of the procedure described by APHA (1995), Trivedi and Goel (1984), Santhanam *et al.* (1989).

Results and Discussion

Sahastradhara stream is flowing throughout a valley of Dehradun mountain chain in foothills of Shivalik Himalaya, enriched with limestone and lignite rocks, which affect the water quality of stream according to the locations. Nutrients concentration and related physico-chemical parameters from selected five sites are depicted in tables.

Sahastradhara stream has the spatio-temporal variations of water temperature, which plays a vital role in all physico-biochemical reactions and self-purification power of aquatic system (Badola and Singh, 1981). Higher value of temperature was found 18 °C in summer and minimum 12 °C in winter season. A direct relationship was established between the water temperature and free carbon dioxide (Hynes, 1970). Turbidity is striking characteristic of the physical status of the water bodies. Although in Sahastradhara stream water is clear because there is no more pollution, siltation was the main source of turbidity in tributaries. Detritus and other non-organic material being added to water mass due to rainfall and tourist activities (Camron, 1996). Maximum turbidity was recorded 7.0 JTU during rainy days and minimum 1.0 JTU in December. The maximum depth of photic zone provides the better biological production for all aquatic organisms.

Total solids were found in the range of 955 mg/l to 1535 mg/l towards summer season, due to the gradual increases in velocity of river which favoured effective sedimentation (Subramanian, 1979). Chemical oxygen demand represents chemically oxidizable organic matter load in water, while biochemical oxygen demand is only biodegradable materials. In the present study high values observed during summer months may be attributed maximum biological activities and high temperature, stimulate the growth of microorganisms (William *et al.*, 1993).

The pH of natural water was controlled in a great extent by the interaction of hydroxyl ions arising from the hydrolysis of bicarbonate (Sharma, 1986). The pH of Sahastradhara stream was recorded slightly alkaline (7.2–8.1). Hardness is mainly due to percentage of calcium and magnesium salts of bicarbonates, carbonates, sulphates and chlorides, while the value of alkalinity occured due to presence of

Table 1: Nutrients Parameters (Mean values) of Sahastradhara Stream

Parameters (mg/l)	Site–I	Site–II	Site–III	Site–IV	Site–V
Chloride	12.78±1.73	13.73±1.93	15.26±2.1	13.49±3.25	11.6±3.06
(Range)	(11.36–15.62)	(11.36–16.58)	(12.78–18.46)	(9.94–18.46)	(8.52–16.58)
Calcium	84.67±3.58	85.67±4.28	91.68±10.13	89.18±8.26	88.43±6.19
(Range)	(80.160–88.176)	(80.160–92.184)	(77.154–104.208)	(79.158–99.198)	(80.16–96.192)
Magnesium	48.66±3.09	57.33±3.29	64.66±2.36	55.33±2.49	51.0±5.29
(Range)	(45–53)	(55–62)	(63.0–68.0)	(52.0–28.0)	(45.0–55.0)
Sodium	7.375±0.96	7.725±0.506	8.75±0.75	8.87±1.14	9.25±1.35
(Range)	(6–8.5)	(7.0–8.2)	(8.0–9.5)	(7.0–10.0)	(7.5–11.0)
Potassium	15.13±0.74	15.75±0.901	16.62±0.65	16.5±0.79	17.0±1.35
(Range)	(14–16)	(14.5–17.0)	(16.0–17.5)	(15.5–17.5)	(16.0–18.0)

bicarbonates. The highest concentration of hardness was analyzed 250 mg/l during warm months. A positive relationship between hardness and alkalinity was recorded in river Ganga at Rishikesh (Chopra and Patric, 1994).

Table 2: Physico-chemical Parameters (Mean values) of Sahastradhara Stream

Parameters	*Site–I*	*Site–II*	*Site–III*	*Site–IV*	*Site–V*
Temperature (°C)	15.75±1.14	15.37±1.63	15.0±1.41	15.75±1.6	15.75±2.277
(Range)	(14–18)	(13–17.5)	(13–17)	(13.5–18)	(12–18)
Velocity (m/s)	0.3±0.14	0.9±0.1	0.35±0.05	0.8±0.02	0.65±0.05
(Range)	(0.3–0.4)	(0.28–0.32)	(0.8–1.0)	(0.78–0.82)	(0.6–0.7)
Turbidity (JTU)	2.75±1.47	3.25±1.30	4.5±1.15	3.75±1.48	4.75±1.48
(Range)	(1.0–5.0)	(2.0–5.0)	(3.0–6.0)	(2.0–6.0)	(3.0–7.0)
Total solids (mg/l)	1218±183.2	1234.2±89.8	1277.25±122.6	1305.7±166.1	1290.75±146.1
(Range)	(955–1427)	(1090–1332)	(1115–1443)	(1135–1520)	(1148–1535)
TDS (mg/l)	1093.25±175	1094.25±120.5	1140.5±134.6	1189±158.01	1134.25±176.1
(Range)	(840–1278)	(895–1217)	(1010–1322)	(1039–1380)	(965–1420)
TSS (mg/l)	124.75±14.39	140.0±28.16	136.75±40.95	116.75±13.8	156.5±41.69
(Range)	(113–149)	(119–195)	(105–207)	(105–140)	(115–211)
pH	7.625±0.43	7.6±0.28	7.75±0.15	7.75±1.66	7.6±0.339
(Range)	(7.2–8.1)	(7.3–8.1)	(7.5–7.9)	(7.6–8.0)	(7.2–8.1)
Free CO_2 (mg/l)	1.6525±0.39	1.75±0.017	1.825±0.25	1.74±0.09	1.87±0.21
(Range)	(1.40–1.69)	(1.62–1.92)	(1.62–2.20)	(1.65–1.85)	(1.62–2.20)
DO (mg/l)	8.41±1.62	8.46±1.18	8.65±0.95	7.55±0.87	7.49±1.36
(Range)	(7.04–11.08)	(6.84–10.07)	(7.04–9.47)	(6.04–9.06)	(6.04–9.47)
BOD (mg/l)	1.875±0.162	1.98±0.23	2.25±0.18	2.0±0.14	2.05±0.15
(Range)	(1.60–2.0)	(1.7–2.2)	(2.0–2.5)	(1.8–2.2)	(1.9–2.3)
COD (mg/l)	2.55±0.32	2.6±0.25	2.9±0.22	2.68±0.22	2.7±0.18
(Range)	(2.1–3.0)	(2.2–2.9)	(2.6–3.2)	(2.4–3.0)	(2.4–2.9)
Hardness (mg/l)	196.25±8.2	200.0±15.41	222.5±19.2	200.0±18.71	198.75±21.02
(Range)	(190–210)	(185–220)	(200–250)	(180–230)	(185–235)
Alkalinity (mg/l)	250.0±134.7	262.5±140.8	305±172.1	292.5±168.8	317.5±175.2
(Range)	(150–480)	(140–500)	(170–600)	(130–570)	(120–540)

Maximum chloride concentration was recorded (17.14 mg/l) in the month of May and minimum in December (11.36 mg/l). Chloride and hardness showed a positive relationship to one another (Chopra and Patric, 1994). Chloride was found in the form of chloride ion, and one of the major inorganic anion present in natural water.

Calcium and magnesium the dominant cations, and these represent the main weathering products, but significant hydro-chemical differences between the five sampling sites associated with the bedrock geology exist (Jenkins *et al.*, 1995) Calcium is one of the essential nutrients, which plays an important role in biological system. Maximum calcium concentration was recorded (104.21 mg/l) in the month of May and minimum in January (77.154 mg/l). Calcium concentrations were found maximum about 7.5% of the total solids present in the stream water. Positive relationship between, calcium and temperature was also reported by Khanna and Singh (2000) in river Suswa, Dehradun. Magnesium is also an essential element but it is toxic at higher concentration. The amount of magnesium in Sahastradhara was found maximum (68.0 mg/l) in the month of April and minimum (45.0 mg/l) in December.

During the summer season nutrients concentration in hill-streams became more. Miller et al.(1997) described the nutrients availability in selected environmental settings of the Potomac River and Cameron, E. M. (1996) showed the similar type of fluctuation in Fraser river of British Columbia. Sodium is one of the most common cation have no adverse effect on human health at lower concentration. Bond, H W. (1979) described similar nutrients concentration pattern in a stream draining a mountain ecosystem in Utah. Maximum sodium concentration in Sahastradhara was recorded (11.0 mg/l) in the month of May and minimum in January (6.0 mg/l).

Table 3: Correlation (=CORREL) between Nutrients (Mean values) and Physico-chemical Parameters (Mean values) of Sahastradhara Stream

Parameters	*Chloride*	*Calcium*	*Magnesium*	*Sodium*	*Potassium*
Temperature (°C)	–0.86097	–0.51833	–0.92056	–0.01186	–0.14275
Velocity (m/s)	–0.17595	–0.12077	0.007842	0.179873	0.225839
Turbidity (JTU)	0.012697	0.818834	0.400371	0.92284	.0.959357
Total solids (mg/l)	–0.00448	0.788427	0.273292	0.949891	0.906666
TDS (mg/l)	0.133154	0.71132	0.25802	0.764443	0.682478
TSS (mg/l)	–0.35586	0.096981	0.004271	0.35689	0.46296
pH (pH unit)	0.681329	0.761113	0.623067	0.395679	0.345766
Free CO_2 (mg/l)	–0.03224	0.686443	0.396104	0.833271	0.90927
DO (mg/l)	0.679888	–0.12231	0.471533	–0.65112	–0.55633
BOD (mg/l)	0.607899	0.912138	0.845587	0.615583	0.694262
COD (mg/l)	0.595229	0.954861	0.801927	0.654354	0.704159
Hardness (mg/l)	0.814816	0.795954	0.897315	0.312648	0.386789
Alkalinity (mg/l)	–0.04111	0.829565	0.331085	0.97707	0.985243

Potassium is naturally occurring element, released by the clay minerals, weathering and leaching from growing vegetation and decomposition of organic matter (Berndtsson, 1990). Maximum potassium concentration was recorded (18.0 mg/l) in the month of April and minimum in December (14.0 mg/l). Pande and Mishra (2000) also observed similar results on Sahastradhara hill-stream Dehradun. Relationship between nutrients and other physico-chemical parameters are given in the Table 3 and percentages of nutrients among the total solids are given in Table 4, during the study period. These high concentrations confirm the location of the calcareous formation associated with the Central Himalaya thrust. Similarly, samples from stream draining the slope of Doon valley, exhibit high concentrations of Mg relative to K and Na. Again this can presumably be attributed to local geological features. In general, the stream at site III with high Ca concentrations also exhibit relatively low K concentrations compared to the other sites.

Table 4: Percentage of Different Nutrients among the Total Solids at Different Location of Sahastradhara Stream at Dehradun

Nutrients	*Site–I*	*Site–II*	*Site–III*	*Site–IV*	*Site–V*
Total solids	100%	100%	100%	100%	100%
Chloride	1.0492%	1.1125%	1.1948%	1.0331%	0.8987%
Calcium	6.951%	6.941%	7.178%	6.830%	6.851%
Magnesium	3.995%	4.645%	5.062%	4.238%	3.951%
Sodium	0.6055%	0.6263%	0.6852%	0.6793%	0.7166%
Potassium	1.242%	1.276%	1.301%	1.264%	1.317%

The present results conclude that significant differences in stream water nutrient concentrations exist among different environmental settings within the five subunits. The environmental setting with the highest potential by more soluble nutrients, fluctuations in nutrient concentrations were the land use and carbonate bedrock that was predominated in the Doon valley especially, at main tourist spot and sulphur springs site III.. Ca and Mg are the dominant cations in this alkaline tributary of river Song. Rock weathering is the most important mechanism controlling the water chemistry. The high concentrations of alkali earth metals, high alkalinity and the high (Ca+Mg)/(Na+K) ratio indicate that the water chemistry of the stream is controlled largely by carbonate weathering and partially by run-off process and tourists activities. The spatial variations in TDS are attributed to climatic and lithological control over the ionic concentrations.

References

APHA (1995): Standard methods for examination of water and waste water. *American Public Health Association, 19th edition. Inc, New York.* pp:1970.

Alan Jenkins; Jeremy Wilkinson and Robert Collins (1995): Hydro-chemical characteristics of headwater stream in the middle hills and high mountains of the Himalayas, Nepal. *Atmospheric Hydrologic and Ecological interaction- Part C. International conference on ecohydrology of high mountain areas. pp: 255-263.*

Badola, S.P. and Singh, H.R. (1981) Hydrobiology of the river Alaknanda of Garhwal Himalaya. *Indian J. Ecol.*, 8(2): 269-276.

Berndtsson, R. (1990): Transport and sedimentation of pollutants in a river reach: A chemical mass balance approach. *Wat. Resour. Res.* 26(7): 1549-1558.

Bond, H. B. (1979): Nutrient concentrations patterns in a stream draining a montane ecosystem in Utah. *Ecology*. 60(6): 1184-1196.

Cameron, E. M. (1996): Hydrogeo-chemistry of the Fraser River British Columbia: Seasonal variation in major and minor components. *J. Hydrol.* 182(1-4): 209-255.

Chopra, A. K. and Patrick, N. J. (1994): Effect of domestic sewage on self-purification of Ganga water at Rishikesh. *A. Bio. Science.* 13(11): 75-82.

Hussain, S. I.; Subramanian, V. and Dhanpal, K. (1989): Chemical characteristics of meltwaters from a Himalaya glacier, India. *J. Hydrol.* 106: 98-106.

Hynes, H.B.N. (1970). The ecology of running waters. *Liverpool University Press, Liverpool, 4th impression*: 1-555.

Jenkins, A., Sloan W.T. and Cosby, B.J. (1995) Stream chemistry is the middle hills and high mountain of the Himalaya, Nepal. *Journal of Hydrology.* Vol-166, No-1-4: 61-79.

Khanna, D.R and Singh. R.K. (2000). Seasonal fluctuations in the plankton of Suswa River at Raiwala Dehradun. *Env. Conservations J.* 1(2 and 3): 89-92.

Miller, C. V.; Denis, J. M.; Ator, S. W. and Brakebill, J. W. (1997): Nutrients in stream during baseflow in selected environmental settings of the Potomac river basin. *J. American Wat. Resources Association.* 33(6): 1155-1171.

Odum, E. P. (1971): Fundamentals of Ecology. New York. W. B. *Saunders and Co.* pp: 1-344.

Pande, R. K. and Asha Mishra (2000): Water quality study of freshwaters of Dehradun (Sahastradhara stream and Mussoorie Lake). *Aquacult.* 1: 57-62.

Santhanam, R.; Velaynatham, P. and Jegatheesan, G. (1989): A manual for freshwater ecology. *Daya Publishing House, Delhi- 110006*:1-92.

Shrama, R.C. (1986). Effect of physico-chemical factors on benthic fauna of Bhagirathi River Garhwal Himalaya. *Indian. J.Ecol.* 13(1): 133-137.

Subramanian, V. (1979) Chemical and suspended sediment characteristics of river of India. *J. Hydrol,* 44: 37-55.

Trivedi, R. K. and Goel, P. K. (1984): Chemical and biological methods for water pollution studies. Karad. Environmental publication. pp: 1-25.

William, M.W., Brown, A. and Melack, J.M. (1993). Geochemical and hydrologic controls on the composition of surface water in the high elevation basin, *Sierra Navada. Limnol. Oceanogr,* 38: 775-797.

Chapter 5
Planktonic Diversity

Contents

5.1 General

The biotic community in the streams and rivers is quite different from that in the ponds and lakes. The differences in the community are largely due to fluctuations in the physical, and chemical conditions of their environment.

The ecological conditions of a river or stream have a direct bearing upon the different producer to consumer level in aquatic life and physico-chemical parameters impart a major role in determination of the quality of any water body and can influence the structure and function of aquatic ecosystem. The planktonic diversity is largely interrelated with the temperature, turbidity, velocity, suspended solids, free carbon dioxide, dissolved oxygen, biochemical oxygen demand and some other physico-chemical parameters, which influenced the planktonic diversity adversely as well as positively.

Plankton are the heterogeneous assemblage of minute organisms present in the natural water. The plankton has greatest importance for ecological point of view. All natural water contains a variety of plankton as the natural flora and fauna. The phytoplankton community is a heterogeneous group of tiny plants adapted to suspension in the sea and freshwater. The quantitative fluctuation of the planktonic diversity has a great effect on the ecology of river.

5.2 Parameters

- ☆ Total plankton
- ☆ Phytoplankton
- ☆ Zooplankton
- ☆ Diatoms
- ☆ Green algae
- ☆ Blue green algae

5.3 Historical Resume

Today we are going fast toward the way of success. Although man in touching the high of perfection yet on the other side he is the prime amuse for the explosion of the planet and its water resource. However, it is difficult to give the name of scientists, limnologists and hydro-biologists, who worked on the various aspects of water quality and aquatic ecology. This review includes some of the important contribution made from various parts of world. Various workers discussed the various aspects of water quality time to time from India and abroad nationally or internationally.

Clark (1924) analyzed the composition of river and lake water of United States. Galtsoff (1924) and Reinnard (1931) studied the limnology of upper Mississippi. Ghosuddin (1934) studied the algal flora of the river Moori. Ganpati (1940) studied the ecology of the temple tank containing a permanent bloom of *Microcystis aeruginousa*. Chakraborty (1959) survey of the plankton and physico-chemical conditions of the Jamuna River at Allahabad.

Singh (1960) studied the chlorophyceae of Kumaon, Needham and Needham (1962), Macan (1974) and Petta (1984) indicated hydrologic conditions such as floods or low flows create habitats that may represent limiting conditions for flora and fauna, both vertebrates and invertebrates. Venkateswarlu (1969) investigated the role of algal in relation to pollution of river Moori of Hyderabad. Rai (1970) studied the ecology of algal community of river Ganga at Varanasi.

Kand and Kachroo (1973 and 1974) studied the limnology of Kashmir lakes. Kant and Anand (1978) investigated the interrelationship of phytoplankton and physical parameters in Mansar lake of Jammu. Stalnakar (1979) attention in management of fish habitat is targeted on the floral composition of the stream.

Gopal *et al.* (1981) studied the limnology of a freshwater reservoir of Jaipur. Bhatt *et al.* (1985) explained the ecology and phytoplankton population in relation to physico-chemical factors of river Ganga at Patna. Larson *et al.* (1988) studied the assessment of attainable surface water quality. Nautiyal (1990) explained the ecology of the Ganga River system in the upland of Garhwal Himalayan environment. Round (1991) indicates diatoms are the most common and diverse primary producers in rivers.

Pathak (1991) studied some aspects of ecology of the river Sarju and Gomati of the Kumoan Himalaya. Karr, (1993) examined the river biota regarded as indicators of ecosystem healthy degradation and integrity.

Joshi *et al.* (1993) evaluated the physico-chemical characteristics of river Bhagirthi in the uplands of Garhwal Himalaya. Khanna *et al.* (1993) studied about the plankton ecology of river Ganga at Chandi Ghat, Hardwar. Ormerod *et al.* (1994) observed that stream communities vary in composition and function with altitudes.

Leland (1995), Lobo *et al.* (1995) said diatoms are being recognized as bio-indicators of environmental change and pollution.

Shivsubramani and Mahadevan, (1995) evaluated the water quality of river Suruliyar in Tamilnadu and western Ganga cannel at Hardwar.

Shyam sunder (1996) studied the biotic communities of a Kumoan Himalayan river. Srivastava *et al.* (1996) evaluated the phytoplankton productively and physico-chemical properties of Rapti river. Juttner *et al.* (1997) studied the diatom communities in Himalaya Hill-stream

Joshi and Singh (1997) estimated the phytoplanktonic population in relation to certain physico-chemical characteristic of river Ganga at RishikeshSingh and Sharma (1998) studied the community structure of plankton in fishponds mannered with three organic manures. Joshi and Kathiat (1998) studied the limnological characteristics of three tributaries of river Ganga between Devprayag and Rishikesh.

Khanna *et al.* (1998) studied phytoplanktonic communities in relation to certain physico-chemical parameters of Ganga canal at Hardwar. Khanna and Singh (2000) evaluated seasonal fluctuations in the plankton of Suswa River at Raiwala, Dehradoon. Pande and Mishra (2000) studied water quality of freshwaters of Sahastradhara Lake and Mossoorie Lake, Dehradoon.

Fokmare and Musaddiq (2002) studied on physico-chemical characteristics of Kapsi Lake and Purna river waters in Akola District of Maharastra. Jhajhria (2002) made a report on limn biotic studies of Shekhawat pond at Jodhpur with special reference to plankton. Kumar *et al.* (2003) studied on water quality of the river Ambarampalayam, Coimbatore District, Tamilnadu.

Khanna and Bhutiani (2003) studied the limnological characteristics of the river Ganga at Haridwar. Khanna and Bhutiani (2003) also evaluated the limnological status of Satikund pond at Hardwar. Graening and Brown (2003) observed ecosystem dynamics and pollution effects in an Ozark cave stream. Bharti (2004) described the limnological aspects and physico-chemical characteristics of Sahastradhara hill-stream in Doon velly.

Malik and Bharti (2005a) also described the planktonic population in the water of stream Sahastradhara at Dehradun.

CPCB (2006) reported the water quality status of Yamuna river (1999-2005). Ghavzan *et al.* (2006) highlighted the limnological evaluation of an urban freshwater river with special reference to phytoplankton. Sridhar *et al.* (2006) evaluated the water quality and phytoplankton characteristics in the Palk Bay, southeast coast of India. Negi *et al.* (2006) evaluated the impact of river flow regulation on the planktonic population in Ganga river at Rishikesh (Uttaranchal). Malik and Bharti (2007) described the ecology of Sahastradhara Hill-stream at Dehradun (Uttaranchal).

Zabbey *et al.* (2008) find out the plankton assemblages and environmental gradients in the middle reaches of the Imo River, Niger Delta, Nigeria. Bharti *et al.* (2008) studied on the influence of Heavy Metals on Abundance of Cyanophyceae Members in Three Spring-fed Lake in Kempty, Dehradun.

Bernatowicz *et al.* (2009) made a study on linking biological and physic-chemical water quality. Trivedi *et al.* (2009) made a study on the evaluation of Water Quality: Physico – Chemical Characteristics of Ganga River at Kanpur by using Correlation Study. Agbaire and Obi (2009) evaluated the seasonal Variations of Some Physico-Chemical Properties of River Ethiope Water in Abraka, Nigeria. Fulazzaky (2009) highlighted the water quality evaluation system to assess the Brantes river water.

Madhu *et al.* (2010) analyzed short term variability of water quality and implication on phytoplanktons production in a tropical estuary (Cochin backwaters-India). Resende *et al.* (2010) pointed out the use of biological indicators to assess water quality of the Ul river (Portugal). Ogbonna (2010) evaluated the seasonal dynamics of microbial population and physicochemical characteristics of a water body receiving industrial pollutants in Port Harcourt, Nigeria. Tessitore (2010) evaluated the effects of Eutrophication on benthic life within the littoral zone of freshwater lakes.

Juahir *et al.* (2011) analysed the spatial water quality assessment of Langat River Basin (Malaysia) using environmetric techniques.

Kapsikar *et al.* (2011) evaluated the physico-chemical features of Kali river, Karwar,west coast of India. Kumar *et al.* (2011) analysed the aquachemistry, Zooplankton and bacterial diversity in three ponds of Karwar district, Karnataka. Vasanthkumar and Vijaykumar (2011) calculated the diurnal variation of physico-chemical properties and primary productivity of phytoplankton in Bheema river. Kamble *et al.* (2011) analysed the seasonal variations in algal population of Ajanta water–fall.

5.4 Methodology

Collection of Phytoplankton

Phytoplankton collection in the open water of a water body consists of surface and/or deep grab sampling. A Van Dorn bottle is the most common tool for collecting the deep samples. For phytoplankton samples, Plankton nets are not recommended for quantitative samples. They are size selective and very non-quantitative. They can be used however for identification of the species present as the higher density assists in the taxonomic work, particularly of rarer species.

For collecting surface phytoplankton samples, first of all, anchor the boat at the designated sample site, obtain a labeled, 1 litre sample bottle and remove the lid without touching the inner surface of either the bottle or lid. Reach out an arm length from the boat to take the sample. Ensure that the person in the stern is providing counterbalance (working over the opposite side of the boat). Plunge the bottle under the surface and move it slowly towards the current (the direction the boat is facing) until the bottle is entirely full. Standard sampling depths for "surface" water samples are 0.1 m and 0.5 m.

Preserve the sample with 1-3 mL of Lugol's solution (1-3 mL per 1 litre of sample). Different water chemistry and density of algal material require different concentration of preservative. A general guideline is that there be sufficient Lugol's to turn the sample the colour of weak tea.

Collection of Zooplankton

The zooplankton collection involves primarily the filtration of water by net, collecting the water in bottles/water samplers or by pumps. The sampling success will largely depend on the selection of a suitable gear; mesh size of netting material, time of collection, water depth of the study area and sampling strategy. The gear should be used keeping in view the objectives of the investigation. There are three main methods of zooplankton collection, which are as follows:

Bottles/Water Samplers

This method is used mainly for collecting smaller forms or microzooplankton. The water is collected at the sampling site in bottles or water samplers of 5 to 20 litre capacity. The sterile bottles should be preferred. Surface water can be collected by scooping water into the bottle of suitable size. While collecting the water samples, there should be minimum disturbance of water to prevent avoidance reaction by plankton. The Von Dorn bottles or water samplers with closing mechanisms are commonly used for obtaining samples from the desired depths.

The microzooplankton are then concentrated by allowing them to settle, centrifuging or fine filtration. The advantage of this method is that it is easy to operate and sampling depths are accurately known. The disadvantage is that the amount of water filtered is less. The bigger or macrozooplankton and rare forms are usually not collected by this method and so it is unsuitable for qualitative and quantitative estimations.

Pumps

The gear is normally used on board the vessel/boat. The sampling can also be carried out from a pier. In this method, the inlet pipe is lowered into the water and the outlet pipe is connected to a net of suitable meshsize. The net is particularly submerged in a tank of a known volume. This prevents damage to the organisms. The zooplankton is filtered through the net. A meter scale on the pump records the volume of water filtered. This method is used for quantitative estimation and to study the small scale distribution of plankton. The frictional resistance of the sampled water in the hose can cause turbulence; damaging the larger plankton especially the gelatinous forms *viz.* medusae, ctenophores and siphonophores etc. The advantage of the method is that the volume of the water pumped is known. Again the continuous sampling is possible. However, the sampling depth is limited to a fewmeters and it is difficult to obtain samples from deeper layers.

Nets

The most common method of zooplankton collection is by a net. The amount of water filtered is more and the gear is suitable both for qualitative and quantitative studies. The plankton nets used are of various sizes and types. The different nets can broadly be put into two categories, the open type used mainly for horizontal and oblique hauls and the closed nets with messengers for collecting vertical samples from desired depths. Despite minor variations, the plankton net is conical in shape and consists of ring, the filtering cone and the collecting bucket for collection of organisms.

The collecting bucket should be strong and easy to remove from the net. The netting of the filtering cone is made of bolting silk, nylon or other synthetic material. The material should be durable with accurate and fixed pore size. The mesh should be square and aperture uniform. The mesh size of the netting material will influence the type of zocplankton collected by a net. The nets with finer mesh will capture smaller organisms, larval stages and eggs of planktonic forms and fish eggs while those with coarse netting material are used for collecting bigger plankton and fish larvae. Sometimes combinations of nets with mesh of different pore sizes are used. There is a great variety of mesh available from the finest to the coarse pore sizes. The mesh size of 0.2 mm of monofilament nylon is usually used for collecting zooplankton for taxonomic and productivity studies. In addition to the mesh size, the type, length

Figure 5.4.1: Collection of Plankton in Sahastradhara Hill-stream

and mouth area of the net, towing speed, time of collection and type of haul will determine the quality and quantity of zooplankton collected.

The zooplankton collections can be made by horizontal, oblique and vertical hauls. In the horizontal sampling the net is towed at a slow speed usually for 5 to 10 minutes. The towing speed of the net should be such that the maximum amount of water enters through the mouth of the net for better filtration and gear used can withstand the strain. The towing speed of the net recommended for horizontal samples is 1.5 to 2.0 knots. When the towing speed is more, a static cone of water develops thus diverting water outside the net and consequently reducing the effective filteration. The net may also be damaged. Most of the zooplankters migrate vertically in response to light conditions. Their occurrence is poor in upper layers during daytime. For better quantitative and qualitative zooplankton collections, the suitable time for horizontal zooplankton sampling would be before dawn, after dusk or night. The net should be submerged in water. When the currents are strong the depressors are used to keep the nets in desired position.

The horizontal collections are mostly carried out for the surface and subsurface layers. In oblique hauls, the net is usually towed above the bottom. The disadvantage of this method is that the sampling depth may not be accurately known. The net may be damaged if it touches the substratum. The vertical haul is made to sample the water column. The net is lowered to the desired depth and hauled slowly upwards. The zooplankton sample collected is from the water column transversed by the net. Closing mechanisms are used to sample a specific body of water. The samples taken with closing nets are analysed to study zooplankton abundance at different depths.

For quantitative plankton sampling it is imperative to know the actual amount of water passed through the net. For this purpose, an instrument called flow meter is used. It should not be mistaken for current meter. The flow meter has a multi bladed propeller, which is rotated by the flow of water. There is a counter, which records the number of revolutions. The flow meter should be positioned in such a way so that it records the actual flow of water passing through the net. The volume of the water filtered is normally expressed in cubic meters.

It is calculated as follows.

$$V = A \times R/K$$

where,

K: Calibration constant

A: Mouth area of the net

R: Flow meter reading and

V: Volume of water filtered.

When the net traverses through a water column, the volume is

$$V = A \times d$$

where,

A: Mouth area of the net and

d: Depth of haul.

When a circular net is used, the volume of water filtered can be calculated by the formula given below:

$$V = ð\, r^2\, d$$

where,

V: Volume of water filtered

r: The radius of the mouth of the net

d: Length of the water column traversed by the net.

In case of a square net, calculation is as follows

$$V = S^2\, d$$

where,

S: Length of the side of the frame.

d: Depth of haul.

The collection of zooplankton samples particularly from the deeper waters is expensive as it involves proper gear, considerable time and expertise. Records of the sampling procedures, prevailing environmental conditions and other information should be maintained in the field log sheet. Observation on live plankton could be made in the field for their colouration, abundance and composition prior to fixation and subsequently analysis in the laboratory. The samples should be transported with care otherwise their durability and usefulness would be seriously jeopardized.

Periphyton

Periphyton are defined as attached species of microflora (algae) and are primarily found on hard, immobile surfaces such as rocks, large stones (cobbles, boulders) and on aquatic plants. Analysis of periphyton communities, particularly for the purpose of biomass calculations, involves collecting the algae from a known surface area. To do so, the water bottles, tooth brush, preservative and a piece of equipment to outline are required.

Fixation of Samples

After the sampling, the fixation of samples should be carried out, as early as possible, at least within 5 minutes after the collection to avoid damage to animal tissue by bacterial action and autolysis. The necessity of proper fixation and preservation of zooplankton needs no emphasis. The whitish precipate and ruptured exoskeletons can be seen in the improper fixed samples. The zooplankton deteriorates rapidly in tropics. An ideal fixative should be cheap and which kills the animals quickly. Again it should be non-corrosive or toxic in nature. The most common fixing and preserving reagent is (4-5%) formaldehyde (formalin). It is the cheapest fixative and the zooplankton samples can be stored for number of years. The other fixatives occasionally used are ethanol, picric acid, acetic acid etc. Analytical grade formalin should be used for fixation as the commercial formalin is often contaminated with iron compounds which produce a brow precipitate of iron hydroxide which renders the zooplankton identification difficult.

Dilution of Formalin

The concentrated formalin should be diluted with freshwater, seawater or preferably with water from the sampling area to avoid undesirable osmotic effects. The dilution is in the ratio of 1 part formalin and 9 parts of freshwater or seawater. The pH of the fixative should be around 8.0. It is advisable to use buffered formalin. The commonly used buffers are borax (sodium tetraborate) or hexamethyene teteramine. The buffers are added in an amount of 200 g to one litre of concentrated formalin. The fixative usually renders the zooplankton body tissues hard and brittle. The additives *viz.* propylene phenoxetal and propylene glycerol (2 to 5 %) are added to fixatives for flexibility of specimens, resistance to bacteria and moulds.

Preservation

Allow 10 days as the minimum fixation periods. After fixation, the zooplankton are transferred and stored in airtight containers with sufficient quantity of preservative. While transfering, due care should be taken so that no part of the zooplankton sample is lost. Various types of preservatives are available. The buffered formalin (4 to 5%) is mostly used both as fixative and as the preservative. The other preservative used is 70% ethanol or 40% isopropanol. The ethanol is used for preserving museum specimens but it is costly and volatile. Glycerin is often added to formalin to prevent shrinkage of specimens, drying of the material and to facilitate retaining colours of zooplankters.

For better shelf life of the zooplankton samples, the preservative should be changed within the first 6 months. It would be better to store the preserved zooplankton samples in well ventilated room at temperature less than 25°C. The samples should be kept in the wide mouth glass jars. A good quality preprinted labels, on which the collector's name, fixative and preservative used and other field information are written should be put into the jars for ready reference at the time of sample analysis.

Analysis of the Samples

The basic analysis consists of measurements of biomass (standing stock), enumeration of common taxa and species.

The sample is usually splitted into 4 subsamples. One of the subsamples is used for estimation of dry weight, the second for counting the specimens of common taxa, the third for relative abundance of species and the fourth fraction is kept as reference collection. Plastic or glass pipettes are also used to take the subsample for counting. The stempel pipette is used to obtain a certain volume (0.1 to 10 ml). The zooplankton sample in a glass container is diluted to a known volume and is stirred gently. The stampel pipette is then used to remove the subsample or aliquot for counting.

Counting

After splitting, the next step in the analysis is to sort and count the specimens. There is a primary and secondary sorting. In the former type the sample is separated into 30 to 40 taxonomic groups. Whereas in the secondary stage the important groups of organisms or specimens are further separated or sorted into their respective families and genera. The zooplankton groups diversity is higher in the marine environment. In the fresh or limnetic waters the number of groups is less. The common taxa observed there are protozoans, cladocerans, copepods (adults and lifehistory stages), decapods larvae, mysids etc. The counting should be done under the microscope and when the specimen of a particular group is seen, a tally mark is made on the sheet. When different groups are to be counted simultaneously the multiple counter is used.

All the specimens present in the subsample are counted with proper records on the data sheet. The total number of specimens are later calculated for the whole sample depending on the percentage of subsamples examined. Image analysis systems are being tried for rapid counting of common taxa and their species. The illustrations of common groups occuring in fresh and marine waters are usually given in the introductory books on Limnology and Marine Biology. For sorting, the help of illustrations could be taken.

Species Identification

Species is defined as a group of individuals capable of interbreeding. Correct species identification is prerequisite for understanding distributional pattern, seasonal variability and community structure of zooplankton in an aquatic ecosystem. It is a specialized work and requires patience, experience and sufficient published literature. The initial identification of common species could be done with the help of illustrated checklists. The taxonomic experts should later confirm the identification. The identified and labelled specimens should be kept properly for further reference. For identification of species a stereoscopic dissecting microscope, good quality glass slides, coverslips, stainless steel fine forceps, dissecting needles, pipettes and chemical reagents are required. It involves various steps such as cleaning of specimens, staining, dissection and slide preparation. For identification of very common and abundant forms from a particular area, the live specimens are put in a drop of distilled water and examined under the microscope.

5.5 Classification

This section covers the minimum requirements to ensure quality and consistency of the field aspects of biological data collection. The essential tasks in biological sampling are to collect representative samples that meet the requirements of the program, and to prevent deterioration and contamination of the samples before analysis. Following the protocols outlined in this chapter will aid field staff in collecting reliable, representative samples.

The protocols presented here are the most acceptable ones used at present. It should be emphasized that in unusual circumstances or with development of new methods, experienced professional judgment is a necessary component of method choice and application. It is intended that this document will be updated as the need arises to incorporate new knowledge. For specialized sampling needs, a considerable literature exists that can be consulted. This is particularly the case with benthic stream invertebrates.

Preparation for Site Visit

Preparation for each sampling trip is critical since oversights are not usually noticed until staffs reach the first station. The most effective way to prepare for a sampling trip is with a checklist that is designed to meet the requirements of each project.

Other than considering site-specific instructions, the checklist should identify the needful items.

Locating the Site in the Field

It is the responsibility of the field staff to locate all sampling stations accurately. Only if the same location is sampled consistently can temporal changes in the quality of water be interpreted with confidence. Therefore, actual station location descriptions that identify key landmarks must be prepared on the first visit to every sampling site. Fair photographic documentation is the best way of ensuring that each site is easily recognized. A map that labels the sample sites should accompany the site identification logbook. The logbook can be in the form of a 3-ring binder with a 1:50 000 maps. The basic site location data *viz.* latitudes, longitudes, map sheet number, site identification number, etc. should be incorporated into the database.

Field Notes/Observations

Appropriate sampling practice always involves the use of detailed field notes. Specific information about seemingly unimportant facts such as the time of day or weather conditions is often important when interpreting data. A field logbook for each project is mandatory. All field measurements like DO, temperature, conductivity, etc. should be entered by date directly into this field logbook. All information recorded in the logbook should be initialled by the data recorder and entered into the database as soon as possible upon return from the field. The field note book is a very important document and it should be stored as an archival document for future reference.

Zooplankton

Zooplankton means planktonic animals are microscopic free floating and suspended in open or pelagic waters. Zooplankton are generally collected with a conical net that has a specific mesh size (ranging from as small as 64 µm to as large as 256 µm). Small mesh openings will clog more readily than larger ones, but small organisms will pass readily through larger openings. The mesh size required for a particular water body will depend on the productivity of the water body and the purpose of the study. The size of the mesh and the diameter of the net opening used for each Ministry of Water, Land and Air Protection project will be clearly outlined in the project design. The preferred net mesh, when appropriate, is 64 µm with a net mouth diameter of 20 cm.

The net is lowered to a particular depth and pulled directly up through the water column (known as a vertical tow). Alternatives to the vertical tow are the horizontal and oblique tows in which various strata of the water body are sampled individually (a horizontal tow) or as a composite (oblique tow). These are elaborate techniques that require specialized equipment rigged to the boat and a tow net that has remote open and close capabilities. Unless there is specific need for data from horizontal and oblique tows they are not used. Therefore, the vertical tow is the only protocol that will be mentioned here.

Zooplankton (Greek: Zoon, animal; planktos, wandering) are myriads of diverse floating and drifting animals with limited power of locomotion. Majority of them are microscopic, unicellular or multicellular forms with size ranging from a few microns to a millimeter or more. In addition to size variations, there are differences in morphological features and taxonomic position.

The zooplankton play an important role to study the faunal bio-diversity of aquatic ecosystems. They include representatives of almost every taxon of the animal kingdom and occur in the pelagic environment either as adults (holoplankton) or eggs and larvae (meroplankton). By sheer abundance of both types and their presence at varying depths, the zooplankton are utilized to assess energy transfer at secondary trophic level. They feed on phytoplankton and facilitate the conversion of plant material into animal tissue and in turn constitute the basic food for higher animals including fishes, particularly their larvae. The zooplankton occurrence and distribution influence pelagic fishery potentials. The fishes mostly breed in areas where the planktonic organisms are plenty so that their young ones could get sufficient food for survival and growth. Certain planktonic organisms are capable of concentrating radioisotopes and can act as indicator of certain pollutants, the study of which is important to marine environmental science.

Table 5.5.1: Major Taxonomy of Zooplankton

Sl.No.	*Zooplankton*
1.	Protozoan
	(*a*) *Arcella*
	(*b*) *Paramecium*
	(*c*) *Bursaria*
	(*d*) *Vorticella*
2.	Rotifera
	(*a*) *Brachionas*
	(*b*) *Trichoceraca*
3.	Cladocera
	(*a*) *Daphnia*
	(*b*) *Bosmina*
4.	Copepoda
	(*a*) *Cyclops*
5.	Decapoda
6.	Ostracoda

The planktonic forms with calcareous or siliceous shells or tests contribute to the bottom sediments. The zooplankton are more varied as compared to phytoplankton, their variability in any aquatic ecosystem is influenced mainly by patchiness, diurnal vertical migration and seasons. Evaluation of zooplankton production in any particular area will largely depend on use of correct zooplankton methodology that involves collection of samples, fixation, preservation, analysis and computation of data.

Phytoplankton

Few examples of phytoplankton are given below:

Cyclotella, Nitzchia, Navicula, Scenedesmes,Tetradron, Pediastrum, Kirchneriella, Crucigenia, Selenastrum, Actinastrum, hatzschia, Spirulina, Laxissima, Chrococcus, Oscillotoria, etc.

Phytoplankton can be classified taxonomically in these groups:

Cryptophyta, Bassillariophyta, Chrysophyta, Chlorophyta, Zygnemaphyta, Cyanophyta, Dinophyta, Euglenophyta, Xanthophyta, Rhodophyta, Mixophyta.

Table 5.5.2: Major Taxonomy of Phytoplankton

Sl.No.	*Phytoplankton*
1.	Chlorophyceae
	(*a*) *Hydrodictyon* sp.
	(*b*) *Ulothrix* sp.
	(*c*) *Spirogyra* sp.
	(*d*) *Microspora* sp.
	(*e*) *Cladophora* sp.
2.	Basillariophyceae
	(*a*) *Melosira* sp.
	(*b*) *Diatoma* sp.
	(*c*) *Frastalia* sp.
	(*d*) *Navicula* sp.
3.	Cynophyceae
	(*a*) *Microcystis* sp.
	(*b*) *Nostoc* sp.
	(*c*) *Oscillatoria* sp.

5.6 Identification

Fundamentals of an aquatic food chain are producers (Phytoplankton) and primary consumers (Zooplankton) at primary and secondary trophic level. Planton can be identified with the help of standard books like APHA, Edmondson, etc. Few species are given here to identify their name:

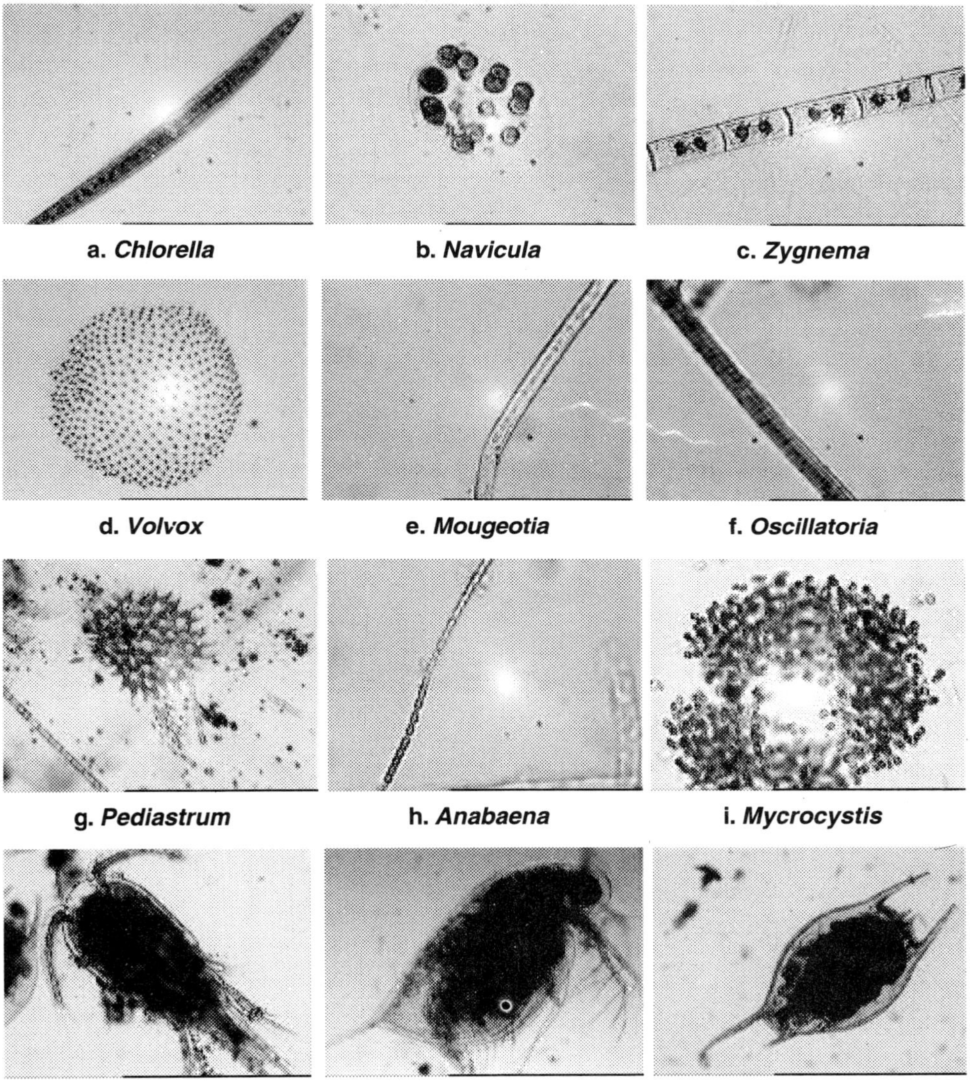

a. *Chlorella* b. *Navicula* c. *Zygnema*

d. *Volvox* e. *Mougeotia* f. *Oscillatoria*

g. *Pediastrum* h. *Anabaena* i. *Mycrocystis*

j. *Cyclops* k. *Dephnia* l. *Kerratella*

Figure 5.6.1a-i: Some Species of Meroplanktonic Population in Sahastradhara Hill-stream Aquatic Ecosystem (General species occurred in some places of Sahastradhra, where water is quite stagnant)

5.7 Significance

The plankton has greatest importance for ecological point of view. All natural water contains a variety of plankton as the natural flora and fauna. Plankton are the heterogeneous assemblage of minute organisms present in the natural water. The quantitative fluctuation of the planktonic diversity has a great effect on the ecology of river. The phytoplankton community is a heterogeneous group of tiny plants adapted to suspension in the sea and freshwater.

The ecological conditions of a stream or river have a direct bearing upon the different producer to consumer level in aquatic life and physico-chemical variables impart a major role in determination of the quality of any water body and can influence the structure and function of aquatic ecosystem. The planktonic diversity is largely interrelated with the temperature, turbidity, velocity, suspended solids, free carbon dioxide, dissolved oxygen, biochemical oxygen demand and some other physico-chemical parameters, which influenced the planktonic diversity adversely as well as positively.

Plankton are the base of an ecosystem especially, phytoplankton are the primary producer for aquatic ecosystem. They trap the solar energy by photosynthesis reaction in sunlight and make the food for higher trophic levels. All the consumers are dependent on plankton directly or indirectly. Few planktonic species are the favorite food for few small fishes.

5.8 A Case Study (Malik and Bharti, 2005a)*

Abstract

Plankton play an important role in every aquatic ecosystem, espicially at primary trophic lavels of food chain existing in aquatic habitat. Phytoplankton, an abundant autotrophic biota contributing in planktonic population, serve as producers, which tap energy directly from the sun by photosynthesis reaction. Variation in physico-chemical caracterstics of the ecosystem influences the number and distribution of planktonic population in the aquatic system. Plankton also act as the indicator of water quality and degree of pollution. Water quality of Sahastradhara hill-stream has deteriorated considerably due to increased human interferences and anthropogenic activities in several ways *viz.* Bathing, Dumping of domestic waste, Sewage discharge etc.

An investigated was conducted on planktonic diversity and water quality of Sahastradhra hill-stream during 2004. The distribution pattern of plankton was found in the stream as Total plankton > Phytoplankton > Zooplankton and abundance of phytoplankton was found as Bacillariophyceae > Chlorophyceae > Cynophyceae.

Keywords: *Plankton, Aquatic biota, Autotrophs, Anthropogenic factors, Producers.*

Introduction

Water is one of the important natural resource and a regular supply of clean water is essential for the survival of all living organisms. Water covers about 73% of the earth's surface, of the total volume of water available as 97% in vast ocean, 2% stored in the form of ice sheets and less than 1% is available as freshwater (Pande and

---

(***Reference***: *Malik, D. S. and Bharti, P.K. (2005b): Fluctuation in planktonic population of Sahastradhara hill-stream at Dehradun (Uttaranchal), Aquacult. 6 (2): 191-198.*)

Mishra, 2000). Water quality includes all physical, chemical and biological factors that influance the beneficial use of water. lotic habitats are those existing in relatively fast running streams, springs, rivers and brooks. Lentic habitats are represented by the lakes, ponds, wetlands, marshes and swamps. A hill-stream consists of two zones, rithron and potamon. Aquatic biodiversity is abundantly occured in potamon zone due to the slow velocity of running water. In streams the community consists of the population of following groups:

Neuston, Plankton, Necton, Benthos, Periphyton and Aquatic Macrophytes.

The biotic community in the streams and rivers is quite different from that in the ponds and lakes. The differences in the comunity are largely due to fluctuations in the physical, and chemical conditions of their environment (Singh, 2001). From the point of view of ecohydrology, for the main elements of an ecosystem including inorganic and organic compound, producers and consumers both the quantity and quality, the chemistry of water have a decisive impact on its biomass and biotic composition. Information obtained form current hydro-chemical analyses of water specimens is very important but it is sometimes difficult to Ganga the overall situation especially the occurrence of plankton, which may be very important to an ecosystem. The plankton have greatest importance for ecological point of view. All natural water contains a variety of plankton as the natural flora and fauna. The phytoplankton community is a heterogeneous group of tiny plants adapted to suspension in the sea and freshwater. The quantitative fluctuation of the planktonic diversity has a great effect on the ecology of river.

The impact on water quality of anthropogenic pollution from industrial, agricultural, sources, quarrying and tourists activity has concerned environmentalists and scientists for the past two decades. Plankton is the primary producer of any aquatic ecosystem, which can be as an indicator of water quality. Dissolved oxygen is decreases or increases in an aquatic ecosystem due to the plankton. Plankton takes sunlight directly and makes food for the total ecosystem through the photosynthesis process. Plankton may vary at place-to-place and season-to-season.

Lesser Himalaya consists of a huge part of Uttaranchal, and Dehradun, Haridwar and Rishikesh are the main religious and beautiful cities, which are situated in the foothills of Himalaya. A hill-stream *Sahastradhara,* 15km far from Dehradun and situated in Doon valley, is the study site for investigation of planktonic population and their correlation with physico-chemical parameters of the same.

Materials and methods

The water samples were collected monthly from sampling site "Sahastradhara stream" from different sampling stations, Site-I, Site-II, Site-III, Site-IV, and Site-V during December, 2003 to May, 2004 in morning period 9:00 hrs. to 10:00 hrs. The samples for plankton and physico-chemical parameters were collected and analyzed by using rinsed borosil glassware, with the help of the procedure described by APHA (1995), Trivedi and Goel (1984), Santhanam *et al.* (1989). Plankton net,Culture tube, Sedgwick rafter counting cell, Microscope and Formalein 4% are the materials used during the experiments.

The volume of water filtered is calculated as follows.

$$V = r^2 \times D$$

where,

r: Radius of the nets orifice in m. and

D: The depth of net has been sent in water m.

Preserve it by formalein and count with Sedgwick-Rafter counting cell with the help of microscope.

No. of Plankton/ml = No. of organisms counted/No. of replicates taken

N (Plankton/l) = (A × 1000) C/L

where,

N: No. of plankton/liter

A: Average no. of plankton in a small chamber

C: ml. of plankton concentrations,

L: Volume of original water filtered in liter

Results and Discussion

Sahastradhara stream is flowing throughout a valley of Dehradun mountain chain in foothills of Shivalik Himalaya, enriched with limestone and lignite rocks, which affect the water quality and plankton diversity of stream according to the location. Plankton population and related physico-chemical parameters from selected 5 sites are depicted in Tables 1 to 5.

Table 1: Planktonic Population (Mean values) of Sahastradhara Stream

Parameters	*Site–I*	*Site–II*	*Site–III*	*Site–IV*	*Site–V*
Total plankton (n/l)	1130.25±316.8	1133±316	1101.5±323.9	1063.75±346.9	1163.25±339.4
(Range)	(700–1540)	(725–1525)	(693–1480)	(700–1490)	(730–1583)
Phytoplankton (n/l)	1018.25±286.1	1023.75±291.5	992.5±296.3	951.25±318.2	1037.5±259.5
(Range)	(625–1380)	(635–1380)	(615–1345)	(635–1340)	(640–1410)
Zooplankton (n/l)	112±31.61	109.25±27.09	109±28.6	112.5±31.72	125.75±36.66
(Range)	(75–160)	(77–145)	(78–140)	(65–150)	(90–173)
Total diatoms (n/l)	764.75±206.6	784.5±218.5	772.25±247.3	732.5±236.5	807±250.5
(Range)	(492–1022)	(645–1015)	(480–1064)	(495–1035)	(495–1108)
Green algae (n/l)	190.5±59.86	179.5±64.96	161±40.72	164.5±57.21	157.5±50.13
(Range)	(105–275)	(98–278)	(102–205)	(105–228)	(102–220)
Blue green algae (n/l)	63±24.53	57.25±21.57	59.25±17.72	54.25±25.86	58±32.04
(Range)	(21–83)	(27–87)	(33–76)	(27–83)	(23–97)

Table 2: Distribution Pattern and Contribution of Various Family in Phytoplanktonic Population

Planktonic Groups	Site-I	Site-II	Site-III	Site-IV	Site-V
Phytoplankton	100%	100%	100%	100%	100%
Basillariophyceae	75.1%	76.6%	77.8%	77.0%	77.8%
Chlorophyceae	18.7%	17.5%	16.2%	17.3%	15.2%
Cynophyceae	6.19%	5.61%	5.97%	5.70%	5.59%

The seasonal fluctuation of pH depends chiefly on amount of free carbon- dioxide, which is ultimately related to the rate of photosynthesis and also the decomposition of organic matter. The pH of natural water was controlled in a greater extent by the interaction of hydroxyl ions, resulting form the dissociation of carbonic acid, and form hydroxyl ion arising from the hydrolysis of bicarbonate.

Table 3: Preliminary Study of Biotic Communities in Sahastradhara Stream, Dehradun

Family/Phylum	Genus/Species
Flora:	
A) Chorophyceae	*Ulothrix, Volvox, Cladophora, Chlorella, Vaucheria, Zygnema, Pediasterum*
B) Bacillariophyceae	Diatoms
C) Rhodophyceae	*Batrachospermun*
D) Cyanophyceae	*Rivularia, Nostoc*
Fauna:	
A) Protozoans	*Vorticalla, Amoeba, Paramoecium, Chrysamocha, Volvox*
B) Coelentrata	*Hydra, Ceratella*
C) Annelida	Pheretima
D) Arthropods	Mayfly nymph
E) Macroinvertibrate	Snails, Leeches, Flatworms, Beetles

Free carbon dioxide and dissolved oxygen showed a negative relationship to one another. Free carbon dioxide released during the decomposition of certain substances and respiration of living organism since higher temperature accelerate the decomposition of organic substances as well as the respiratory activity of the biota a direct relationship was established between the water temperature and free Carbon dioxide Hynes (1970).

An inverse relationship between dissolved oxygen and free carbon- dioxide by Khan and Siddiqui (1971). The highest rate of photosynthesis decreases free carbon-dioxide content due to the production of oxygen dissolved in water of that aquatic ecosystem and higher rate of decomposition of organic matter and dead parts of living organisms, increases free carbon dioxide in to related water body. The dissolved oxygen showed an inverse relationship with temperature as reposted by Das and

Srivastava (1956) and Dobriyal (1985) that warm water have a tendency to bear less dissolved oxygen in comparison to water has a low temperature. The dissolved oxygen in water is often attributed to the fact that the oxygen is dissolved more during the period of active photosynthesis.

Table 4: Physico-chemical Parameters (Mean values) of Sahastradhara Stream

Parameters	*Site–I*	*Site–II*	*Site–III*	*Site–IV*	*Site–V*
Temperature (°C) (Range)	15.75±1.14 (14–18)	15.37±1.63 (13–17.5)	15.0±1.41 (13–17)	15.75±1.6 (13.5–18)	15.75±2.277 (12–18)
Velocity (m/s) (Range)	0.3±0.14 (0.3–0.4)	0.9±0.1 (0.28–0.32)	0.35±0.05 (0.8–1.0)	0.8±0.02 (0.78–0.82)	0.65±0.05 (0.6–0.7)
Turbidity (JTU) (Range)	2.75±1.47 (1.0–5.0)	3.25±1.30 (2.0–5.0)	4.5±1.15 (3.0- 6.0)	3.75±1.48 (2.0–6.0)	4.75±1.48 (3.0- 7.0)
Total solids (mg/l) (Range)	1218±183.2 (955–1427)	1234.2±89.8 (1090–1332)	1277.25±122.6 (1115–1443)	1305.7±166.1 (1135–1520)	1290.75±146.1 (1148–1535)
TDS (mg/l) (Range)	1093.25±175 (840–1278)	1094.25±120.5 (895–1217)	1140.5±134.6 (1010–1322)	1189±158.01 (1039–1380)	1134.25±176.1 (965–1420)
TSS (mg/l) (Range)	124.75±14.39 (113–149)	140.0±28.16 (119–195)	136.75±40.95 (105–207)	116.75±13.8 (105–140)	156.5±41.69 (115–211)
pH (Range)	7.625±0.43 (7.2–8.1)	7.6±0.28 (7.3–8.1)	7.75±0.15 (7.5–7.9)	7.75±1.66 (7.6–8.0)	7.6±0.339 (7.2–8.1)
Free CO_2 (mg/l) (Range)	1.6525±0.39 (1.40–1.69)	1.75±0.017 (1.62–1.92)	1.825±0.25 (1.62–2.20)	1.74±0.09 (1.65–1.85)	1.87±0.21 (1.62–2.20)
DO (mg/l) (Range)	8.41±1.62 (7.04–11.08)	8.46±1.18 (6.84–10.07)	8.65±0.95 (7.04–9.47)	7.55±0.87 (6.04–9.06)	7.49±1.36 (6.04–9.47)
BOD (mg/l) (Range)	1.875±0.162 (1.60–2.0)	1.98±0.23 (1.7–2.2)	2.25±0.18 (2.0–2.5)	2.0±0.14 (1.8–2.2)	2.05±0.15 (1.9–2.3)
COD (mg/l) (Range)	2.55±0.32 (2.1–3.0)	2.6±0.25 (2.2–2.9)	2.9±0.22 (2.6–3.2)	2.68±0.22 (2.4–3.0)	2.7±0.18 (2.4–2.9)
Hardness (mg/l) (Range)	196.25±8.2 (190–210)	200.0±15.41 (185–220)	222.5±19.2 (200–250)	200.0±18.71 (180–230)	198.75±21.02 (185–235)
Alkalinity (mg/l) (Range)	250.0±134.7 (150–480)	262.5±140.8 (140–500)	305±172.1 (170–600)	292.5±168.8 (130–570)	317.5±175.2 (120–540)

Hutchinson (1957) reported that when the water has low temperature has greater capacity for holding dissolved gases, increasing of temparature may cause low efficiency for holding them. Khanna *et al.* (1992) and Joshi (1996) stated that the higher value during winter months can be attributed to increased solubility of oxygen at lower water temperature and high photosynthetic rate due to increasing number of phytoplankton in abundance form than the other groups of organisms. Eddy (1993) pointed out that plankton production is mainly influenced by temperature. Badola and Singh (1981) reported high values of plankton during January to March due to the favourable conditions for the growth of planktonic diversity and effective rate of photosynthesis.

Table 5: Correlation Between Plankton and Physico-chemical Parameters of Sahastradhara Stream

Parameters	Total Plankton	Phytoplankton	Zooplankton	Total Diatom	Green Algae	Blue Green Algae
Temperature °C	0.140144	0.040568	0.561048	–0.12814	0.203944	–0.06004
Velocity (m/s)	–0.09075	–0.11978	0.096464	–0.00984	–0.18658	–0.81972
Turbidity (JTU)	0.103772	0.005161	0.537763	0.394692	–0.95776	–0.35417
Total solids (mg/l)	–0.40534	–0.52983	0.405479	–0.18218	–0.91516	–0.73149
TDS (mg/l)	–0.70298	–0.80425	0.139674	–0.54607	–0.71164	–0.72652
TSS (mg/l)	0.823334	0.77943	0.635537	0.966082	–0.40829	0.080955
pH	–0.88664	–0.89145	–0.42828	–0.71618	–0.42595	–0.36483
Free CO_2 (mg/l)	0.27888	0.196314	0.548124	0.578174	–0.89315	–0.36232
DO (mg/l)	0.028383	0.184226	–0.75181	0.04589	0.505435	0.574037
BOD (mg/l)	–0.18081	–0.18513	–0.07095	0.161374	–0.74373	–0.20002
COD (mg/l)	–0.27454	–0.29116	–0.05821	0.047125	–0.75928	–0.19054
Hardness (mg/l)	–0.2978	–0.25029	–0.38539	–0.01229	–0.45865	0.023773
Alkalinity (mg/l)	–0.00781	–0.12433	0.568959	0.262619	–0.98348	–0.44697

According to Das and Pathani (1978) increase in turbidity reduces the plankton production and their number because turbidity especially in monsoon season reduces the light penetration in the water bodies and also reduces the euphotic zone of that water body, which is essential for photosynthesis and production of oxygen whereas transparency of water helps in photosynthesis activity as well as for increasing the euphotic zone. Here, study shows the negative correlation between planktonic diversity and total solids because solids enhance the turbidity and turbidity reduce the light penetration and photosynthesis rate in aquatic medium.

According to Khanna (1993) the plankton were maximum in the month of winter probably due to low temperature, high content of dissolved oxygen, low velocity and transparency of water and other suitable conditions, which are nessesory for the growth of planktonic diversity. Allen (1920) stated that water currant is the chief factor influencing the plankton of stream. He has shown that the water current above the moderate speed is directly inhibitory to plankton development. Juttner *et al.* (1995) also reported the similar trend of diatom communities in Himalayan Hill-streams. Joshi and Singh (1997) observed the relation of phytoplanktonic population to certain physico-chemical characteristics of River Ganga at Rishikesh. Similar observations have been reported by Khanna *et al.* (1998) in relation to phytoplanktonic communities of Ganga canal at Haridwar. Khanna *et al.* (2000) described the phytoplanktonic population of a pond at Haridwar. Similar observations were also reported; by Nautiyal (1982) in Alaknanda River and Khanna (1993) in river Ganga at Hardwar.

The distribution pattern of plankton was found in the stream as Total plankton > Phytoplankton > Zooplankton and abundance of phytoplankton was found as Bacillariophyceae (Total diatoms) about 77% > Chlorophyceae (Green algae) about 17% > Cynophyceae (Blue green algae) about 6%. Khanna *et al.* (2000) observed the similar distributional pattern and abundance of phytoplanktonic diversity in a family wise manner. Khanna *et al.* (2000) also supported the percentage of distribution and abundance of various families among the phytoplankton. Among the total plakton, Bacillariophyceae dominated over Chlorophyceae, Cyanophyceae and zooplankton. Same trend of domination was reported by Khanna (1993) and Joshi *et al.* (1996).

Plankton are the heterogeneous assemblage of minute organisms present in the natural water, maximum population of total plankton in the headwater of Sahastradhara stream was recorded 1583 n/l in the month of January and minimum 693 n/l during May. Khanna and Singh (2000) reported the similar trend of planktonic diversity in Suswa River, Raiwala; Dehradun. They observed the highest value of phytoplankton in winter and minimum in summer season due to some favourable conditions developed by their physico-chemical environments in aquatic ecosystem.

The ecological conditions of a river or stream have a direct bearing upon the different producer to consumer level in aquatic life and physico-chemical parameters impart a major role in determination of the quality of any water body and can influence the structure and function of aquatic ecosystem. The planktonic population is largely interrelated with the temperature, turbidity, velocity, suspended solids, free carbon dioxide, dissolved oxygen, biochemical oxygen demand and some other physico-chemical parameters, which influenced the planktonic diversity adversely as well as positively.

References

Allen, W. E. (1920): A quantitative and statistical study of the plankton of the San Joaquin river and its tributaries near stockton California, 1913. *Univ. Calif. Publ. Zool.*, 22(1):1-24.

APHA (1995): Standard methods for examination of water and waste water. *American Public Health Association, 19th edition. Inc, New York.* pp:1970.

Badola, S.P. and Singh, H.R. (1981) Hydrobiology of the river Alaknanda of Garhwal Himalaya *Indian J. Ecol.*, 8(2): 269-276.

Berndtsson, R. (1990): Transport and sedimentation of pollutants in a river reach: A chemical mass balance approach. *Wat. Resour. Res.* 26(7): 1549-1558.

Bond, H. B. (1979): Nutrient concentrations patterns in a stream draining a montane ecosystem in Utah. *Ecology.* 60(6): 1184-1196.

Cameron, E. M. (1996): Hydrogeo-chemistry of the Fraser river British Columbia: Seasonal variation in major and minor components. *J. Hydrol.* 182(1-4): 209-255.

Chopra, A. K. and Patrick, N. J. (1994): Effect of domestic sewage on self-purification of Ganga water at Rishikesh. *A. Bio. Science.* 13(11): 75-82.

Das, S.M. and Srivastava, V.K. (1956) Studies of freshwater plankton II correlation between plankton and hydro-biological factors *Proc. Nat. Acad. Sci. India,* (13) 26: 243-253.

Das, S.M. and Pathani, S.S. (1978) A study on the effect of lake ecology on production of Mahaseer (*Tor tor and T. putitora*) in Kumaon lake. *Indian Matsya.* 4: 25-31.

Dobriyal, A.K. (1985). Ecology of limnofauna in the small streams and their importance to the village life in Garhwal Himalya. *Uttar Pradesh J. Zool.* 5 (2): 139-144.

Eddy, S. (1993). A study of freshwater plankton communities. *Illinois Biol. Monogr.* 12 (4): 1-93.

Hussain, S. I.; Subramanian, V. and Dhanpal, K. (1989): Chemical characterstics of meltwaters from a Himalaya glaciar, India. *J. Hydrol.* 106: 98-106.

Hutchinson, G.C. (1957). A treatise on limnology, geography, physical and chemical, Vol.-I, New York: *John Wiley and Sons, Inc.*, pp: 1-1015.

Hynes, H.B.N. (1970). The ecology of running waters. *Liverpool University Press, Liverpool, 4th impression*: 1-555.

Joshi, B. D., Bisht, R. C. and Joshi, Namita (1996):Planktonic population in relation to certain physico-chemical factors of Ganga canal at Jwalapur (Hardwar). *Him. J. Env. Zool.*,10:75-77.

Joshi, B.D. and Rajendra Singh (1997) 'Phytoplanktonic population in relation to certain physiochemical characteristics of river Ganga at Rishikesh. *Him. J. Env. Zool.*, Vol-11: 61-64.

Juttner,Ingrid; Heike Rothfritz and Steve J. Ormerod (1995) *University of Wales, Cardiff, CFI 3TL UK*- 'Diatom Communities in Himalayan hill-streams. pp-589-597.

Khan, A.A. and Siddiqui, A. (1971). *Hydrobiologia,* 37:447.

Khanna, D.R., Badola, S.P., Sing, H.R. and Dobriyal, K., Anoop (1992). Observations on seasonal trends in diatomic diversity in the river Ganga at Sapt-sarover, Hardwar. Recent research in cold water: Fisheries, ed. by K.L. Sehgal, Today and Tomarrow printers and publishers, New Delhi: 99-107.

Khanna, D.R; (1993) Ecology and pollution of Ganga River. *Ashish Publishing House,* New Delhi. pp: 1-241.

Khanna, D.R., Malik, D.S. and Rana, D.S. (1998). Phytoplanktonic communities in relation to certain physico-chemical parameters of Ganga canal at Hardwar. *Him. J. Env. Zool.,* Vol-12: 193-197.

Khanna, D. R. and Singh, R. K. (2000): Seasonal fluctuations in the plankton of Suswa river at Raiwala, Dehradun. *Env. Conserv. J.* 1(1-2): 89-92.

Khanna, D. R., Ashutosh Gautam, Tarun Chugh and Praveen Sarkar (2000): Impact of abiotic factors on the phytoplanktonic population of a pond. *Env. Conserv. J.* 1(1): 41-46.

Miller, C. V.; Denis, J. M.; Ator, S. W. and Brakebill, J. W. (1997): Nutrients in stream during baseflow in selected environmental settings of the Potomac river basin. *J.American Wat. Resources Association.* 33(6): 1155-1171.

Nautiyal, P. (1982) Some aspects of bio ecology of Tarputitora in relation to hydrobiology of some Garhwal hill-stream. *D.Phill. Thesis;* Garhwal University.

Odum, E. P. (1971): Fundamentals of Ecology. New York. W. B. *Saunders and Co.* pp:1-344.

Pande, R. K. and Asha Mishra (2000): Water quality study of freshwaters of Dehradun (Sahastradhara stream and Mussoorie Lake). *Aquacult.* 1: 57-62.

Quadri, M.Y. and Shah, G.M. (1984) Hydro-biological feature of Hoassar. A typical wetland of Kashmir-I, Biotope. *Indian J. Ecol.,* 2(2): 203-206.

Santhanam, R.; Velaynatham, P. and Jegatheesan, G. (1989): A manual for freshwater ecology. *Daya Publishing House, Delhi- 110006*:1-92.

Sing, H.R- (2001)- 'Introduction to animal ecology and environmental Biology'. *S. Nagin and Co., Jalandhar.* pp: 150-165, 348-357.

Trivedi, R. K. and Goel, P. K. (1984): Chemical and biological methods for water pollution studies. Karad. Environmental Publication. pp: 1-25.

Chapter 6
Primary Productivity

Contents

6.1 General

The amount of plant tissue built up by process of photosynthesis over time is primary production of any ecosystem. The majority of primary production is accomplished by small, dispersed pelagic phytoplankton rather than marine plants (plants only account for 5-10% of total marine productivity. The total amount of organic material produced in the sea by photosynthesis represents the gross primary productivity.

As a portion of the organic material produced by photosynthesis is utilized in cellular respiration, any excess production is referred to as net primary production.; represents amount of organic material available to support consumers, non-photosynthetic protists, and decomposers.

The standing stock refers to the number of organisms per unit area or per unit volume of water at the moment of sampling; can count numbers of phytoplankton from filtered seawater samples.

In recent days, instead of using the total amount of phytoplankton, chlorophyll *a* concentration is used because it is more accurate; chlorophyll *a* can be measured by taking advantage of its ability to fluoresce when excited by an appropriate wavelength of light or by directly extracting it

Biomass is defined as the total weight (total numbers × average weight) of all organisms in a given area or volume; this measure is used in preference to standing stock because phytoplankton vary in size and total numbers of all organisms as not as ecologically meaningful as estimates of their biomass.

Production rates are usually reported in units of grams of organic carbon fixed by photosynthesis under a square meter of sea surface per day or per year.

Its typically measured in the past with light (transparent) and dark (opaque) containers. Phytoplankton samples and their surrounding water are collected in these bottles and replaced at the depth from which they were collected; after a few hours, the paired samples are retrieved and the oxygen content of the water in each bottle is measured.

Decreases in dissolved oxygen are used to estimate cellular respiration in the absence of light. These decreases are subtracted from the oxygen content in the light bottles to provide a measure of net photosynthesis (*i.e.*, excess of phytoplankton production after respiration).

Nowadays, the primary productivity is measured using radioactive carbon (^{14}C); paired light and dark bottles are injected with a known quantity of bicarbonate containing labeled ^{14}C. The amount of assimilated radioactive carbon is measured and net primary productivity is then computed using a conversion factor; is much more accurate than the oxygen measurements, particularly when the productivity is very low.

6.2 Parameters

- ☆ Net Primary Productivity
- ☆ Gross Primary Productivity
- ☆ Community Respiration
- ☆ Net Production Efficiency

6.3 Historical Resume

The importance of water reveals from the beginning of civilization always took place near the water sources. According to *Hippocrates* (460 B.C. – 345 B.C.), the father of medicine, "water contributes much to health" and averted the rain water should be used after boiling and filtering, otherwise it would smell bed and cause harshness (Borchart and Wotton, 1971). Life can't exist without water it is an universal truths. However, it is difficult to give the name of scientists, limnologists and hydro-biologists, who worked on the various aspects of water quality and aquatic ecology. This review includes some of the important contribution made from various parts of world. Various workers discussed the various aspects of water quality time to time from India and abroad nationally or internationally.

Galtsoff (1924) and Reinnard (1931) studied the limnology of upper Mississippi. Clark (1924) analyzed the composition of river and lake water of United States. Ghosuddin (1934) studied the algal flora of the river Moori. Ganpati (1940) studied the ecology of the temple tank containing a permanent bloom of *Microcystis aeruginousa*. Ganpati and Alikunni (1950) observed that water of river Ganga was heavily polluted which dangerous to the human health. Motiawant *et al.* (1956), Ganpati and Chacko (1957) and David (1957-59) observed about the pollution of Ganga water.

Rao and Govind (1964) carried out the hydrobiology of Tungbhadra reservoir. Verma (1964) carried out hydro-biological survey of Dalsagar tank. Venkateswarlu (1969) investigated the role of algal in relation to pollution of river Moori of Hyderabad. Rai (1970) studied the ecology of algal community of river Ganga at Varanasi. Kand and Kachroo (1973 and 1974) studied the limnology of Kashmir lakes.

Stalnakar (1979) attention in management of fish habitat is targeted on the floral composition of the stream. Gopal *et al.* (1981) studied the limnology of a freshwater reservoir of Jaipur. Bhatt *et al.* (1985) explained the ecology and phytoplankton population in relation to physico-chemical factors of river Ganga at Patna.

Nautiyal (1990) explained the ecology of the Ganga River system in the upland of Garhwal Himalayan environment. Round (1991) indicates diatoms are the most common and diverse primary producers in rivers. Pathak (1991) studied some aspects of ecology of the river Sarju and Gomati of the Kumoan Himalaya. Karr, (1993) examined the river biota regarded as indicators of ecosystem healthy degradation and integrity.

Shivsubramani and Mahadevan, (1995) evaluated the water quality of river Suruliyar in Tamilnadu and western Ganga cannel at Hardwar. Shyam sunder (1996) studied the biotic communities of a Kumoan Himalayan river. Srivastava *et al.* (1996) evaluated the phytoplankton productivity and physico-chemical properties of Rapti river.

Joshi and Kathiat (1998) studied the limnological characteristics of three tributaries of river Ganga between Devprayag and Rishikesh. Khanna *et al.* (1998) studied phytoplanktonic communities in relation to certain physico-chemical parameters of Ganga canal at Hardwar. Pande and Mishra (2000) studied water quality of freshwaters of Sahastradhara Lake and Mossoorie Lake, Dehradoon.

Jhajhria (2002) made a report on limnobiotic studies of Shekhawat pond at Jodhpur with special reference to plankton. Yeragi and Shaikh (2003) analyzed the primary productivity of Tansa River. Khanna and Bhutiani (2003) studied the limnological characteristics of the river Ganga at Haridwar. Bharti (2004) described the limnological aspects and physico-chemical characteristics of Sahastradhara hill-stream in Doon velly.

Malik and Bharti (2005c) also described the primary productivity in the water of stream Sahastradhara at Dehradun. Malik and Bharti (2007) described the ecology of Sahastradhara Hill-stream at Dehradun (Uttaranchal).

Zabbey *et al.* (2008) find out the plankton assemblages and environmental gradients in the middle reaches of the Imo River, Niger Delta, Nigeria. Prasad and Patil (2008) made a study of physico-chemical parameters of Krishna river water particularly in western Maharashtra. Bernatowicz *et al.* (2009) made a study on linking biological and physic-chemical water quality. Fulazzaky (2009) highlighted the water quality evaluation system to assess the Brantes river water.

Madhu *et al.* (2010) analysed short term variability of water quality and implication on phytoplanktons production in a tropical estuary (Cochin backwaters-India). Resende *et al.* (2010) pointed out the use of biological indicators to assess water quality of the Ul river (Portugal). Varunprasath and Daniel (2010) analysed the physico-Chemical Parameters of River Bhavani in Three Stations, Tamilnadu, India. Ogbonna (2010) evaluated the seasonal dynamics of microbial population and physicochemical characteristics of a water body receiving industrial pollutants in Port Harcourt, Nigeria.

Rani *et al.* (2011) made an assessment of temporal variations in water quality of some important rivers in middle Gangtic plains, India. Jindal and Sharma (2011) studied on water quality of Sutlej river around Ludhiana with reference to physic-chemical parameters. Kumar *et al.* (2011) analysed the aquachemistry, Zooplankton and bacterial diversity in three ponds of Karwar district, Karnataka. Vasanthkumar and Vijaykumar (2011) calculated the diurnal variation of physico-chemical properties and primary productivity of phytoplankton in Bheema river.

6.4 Methodology

Primary productivity is the rate at which the sun's radiation energy is stored by photosynthetic activity of producer organisms. There are four successive steps of production process:

A) Gross Primary Productivity (GPP)

It is the rate of photosynthesis and includes the organic matter used up in the respiration during the measurement period.

B) Net Primary Productivity (NPP)

It is the rate of storage of organic matter in plant tissues in excess of the respiratory utilization by the producer during the period of measurement.

C) Net Community Productivity (NCP)

It is the rate of organic matter not used by heterotrophs during the period under consideration.

(D) Secondary Productivity

It is the rate of energy storage at consumer level.

The respiration rate of primary producers is referred as R and that of heterotrophs as RH. The whole situation can be understood by these equations.

$$GPP = NPP + R$$

$$NPP = GPP - R$$

$$NCP = NPP - RH$$

Figure 6.4.1: Assembly for Measurement of Primary Productivity

Measurement of Primary Productivity

The basic equation of photosynthesis is:

$$6\,Co_2 + 6\,H_2O \xrightarrow[\text{Chlorophyll}]{\text{Light}} C_6\,H_{12}O_6 + 6O_2 + \text{Energy}$$

There are two methods of measurement of primary productivity:

1. Biomass method
2. Light and Dark bottles method

We generally choose the *light and dark bottle method* of Gaarder and Gran for estimation of primary productivity.

Apparatus and Reagents

A) BOD bottles, 300 ml (*Few darkened*)

B) Reagents and Glassware for measuring dissolved oxygen

C) Sacchi disc

D) Water sampler

Procedure

Determine depth of the euphotic zone by using sacchi disc. Fix depth intervals for suspension of bottles. For extremely shallow water, select only surface and bottom. Collect water by using a water sampler; transfer it gently to a bucket or trough. Fill avoiding agitation, 3 sets of bottles, initial, light and dark. Suspend light and dark bottles at desired depths and determine oxygen in the initial bottle immediately. Incubate for selected number of hours. After the expiry of incubation period, carefully remove the bottles and determine oxygen in them immediately.

Calculation

$$\text{Net Primary Productivity } (O_2 \text{ mg/l/hr}) = \frac{D_L - D_I}{h}$$

$$\text{Gross Primary Productivity } (O_2 \text{ mg/l/hr}) = \frac{D_L - D_D}{h}$$

$$\text{Community Respiration } (O_2 \text{ mg/l/hr}) = \frac{D_I - D_D}{h}$$

where,

D_I: D.O. in *initial* bottle in mg/l
D_L: D.O. in *Light* bottle in mg/l
D_D: D.O. in *Dark* bottle in mg/l
h: Duration of exposure in *hours*.

Net Production Efficiency

$$\text{Net Production efficiency } (\%) = \frac{NPP \times 100}{GPP}$$

where,

NPP: Net primary productivity
GPP: Gross primary productivity

6.5 Factor affecting

6.5.1 Light

Photosynthesis is only possible when light reaching the algal cell is above a certain intensity; light is influenced by a number of meteorological features such as clouds, dust, etc., reducing the amount of available light; it is also influenced by the water itself due to reflection, scattering by suspended water particles, and absorption of various wavelengths (reds and violets are absorbed within first few meters; greens and blues are absorbed less rapidly and may penetrate farther).

The amount of photosynthesis increases with light intensity up to a maximum value known as P_{max}, which is specific for each species; beyond this value, the rate of photosynthesis declines due to photoinhibition–light intensity at which productivity exactly equals respiration is the compensation intensity; the depth at which this occurs is the compensation depth.

6.5.2 Nutrients

Major inorganic nutrients that are required by phytoplankton are nitrogen and phosphorus (diatoms and dinoflagellates required silica also); all of these nutrients occur in small amounts and are thus limiting factors for Primary productivity; each species of phytoplankton has a particular response to different concentrations of limiting nutrients and each has a maximum growth rate.

6.5.3 Hydrographic Conditions

Factors that move water masses around in the oceans (currents, upwellings, and diffusion); upwelling occurs when the surface water moves away from shore and is replaced by nutrient-rich deep water brought to the surface; divergence of currents also brings up deeper nutrient-rich water; vertical mixing brings up nutrients and pushes down phytoplankton (as long as it doesn't push it down beyond the photic zone, the phytoplankton will be able to continue photosynthesizing).

Amount of wind mixing (which brings nutrients up to the surface) increases from the tropics to the Polar Regions, thus the abundance of light and nutrients forms an inverse relationship which determines the pattern of phytoplankton production in different latitudes.

6.6 Significance

The rate of production of organic matter per unit time is termed as productivity with the two levels; primary and secondary in producers and consumers respectively. The amount of new organic matter as plant tissue built up by photosynthesis is termed as primary production. Primary productivity is the rate at which the sun's radiation energy is stored by photosynthetic activity of producer organisms. The animal and plant communities inhabiting water bodies are considered as the direct manifestation of the productivity. It is well established that the primary productivity is controlled by several physico-chemical and biotic interactions.

There are few successive steps of production process; Gross Primary Productivity (GPP) rate of photosynthesis and includes the organic matter used up in the respiration; Net primary productivity (NPP) the rate of storage of organic matter in plant tissues in excess of the respiratory utilization by the producer; Net community productivity (NCP) or community respiration (CR) the rate of organic matter not used by heterotrophs. Production efficiency depends upon net primary productivity. If NPP is relatively high, than production efficiency will be automatically high in the particular ecosystem.

6.7 Aquatic Macrophytes

Aquatic plants are collected for one of three purposes: first, biomass studies for the determination of how much plant material is present on an area or lake basis; second, tissue analyses for the detection of pesticides, metals and plant products; or third, taxonomic analyses as part of ecological or impact studies (permanent records of community structure over time) and to serve as reference specimens for the above two analyses. These reference specimens are a valuable scientific record and their subsequent handling collection should be done with care so that much of the time and expense that has gone into their collection is not wasted. Reference specimens are stored in herbaria that provide permanent records of what was found and allow identifications to be re-verified, if necessary.

Even when the major thrust of the work is for biomass studies or tissue analyses, representative specimens must still be collected and saved as vouchers of the species that were analyzed. With respect to sampling for taxonomic purposes, Warrington (1994) documents techniques regarding the processing of individual taxa within each of the three groups of aquatic plants (submerging, floating, and emergent). This methodology gives a general overview of the protocols for collecting aquatic plants for taxonomic purposes.

6.8 A Case Study (Malik and Bharti, 2005c)*

Abstract

An investigation was conducted on primary productivity and water quality of Sahastradhra hill-stream for evaluation of aqatic ecosystem status in different environmental settings along with the stream. The factors such as temperature, pH, carbon dioxide and plankton on which primary productivity depends were studied. It was pointed out that the Gross primary productivity showed a negative relationship with temperature, pH and carbon dioxide.

The present paper deals with the production efficiency of Sahastradhara hill-stream, dehradun and maximum production efficiency of Sahastradhara stream was found 66.66% at sampling site- III in the month of December 2003, while minimum production efficiency was recorded 20.79% at site- IV during May 2004.

Keywords: *Production efficiency, Primary productivity, Photosynthesis.*

Introduction

Sahastradhara stream originated basically from the hills of Mussoorie. Upstream of Sahastradhara is connected with river Badli near village Karligarh. River Badli is dividing in to two branches JhanduNala and Dhadola at 840-1310 msl. Geologically, Sahastradhara hills are enriched with limestone. It is also famous for limestone quarrying, which is prohibited by Government after the appeals of M.C. Mehta (1985, *R.L.E case Dehradun Vs state of U.P*). Geographically, Sahastradhara is situated in the globe on Latitude 29.57°–31.20° E and Longitude 77.35°–79.20° N. The water of Sahastradhara is very beneficial for skin disease due to sulphur. Skin disease can be cure after bathing regularly in this water. The downstream of Sahastradhara meets with Kali Rao, which is mostly dry during study period and quarrying is running regularly in its basin. This stream meets with Song River, which is a tributary of River Ganga.

The rate of production of organic matter per unit time is termed as productivity with the two levels; primary and secondary in producers and consumers respectively.

---

* (***Reference***: *Malik, D. S. and Bharti, P.K. (2005c): Primary production efficiency of Sahstradhara hill-stream, Dehradun, Env. Cons. J. 6 (3): 117-121.*)

the amount of new organic matter as plant tissue built up by photosynthesis is termed as primary production. Primary productivity is the rate at which the sun's radiation energy is stored by photosynthetic activity of producer organisms. The animal and plant communities inhabiting water bodies are considered as the direct manifestation of the productivity. It is well established that the primary productivity is controlled by several physico-chemical and biotic interactions.

There are few successive steps of production process; Gross Primary Productivity (GPP) rate of photosynthesis and includes the organic matter used up in the respiration; Net primary productivity (NPP) the rate of storage of organic matter in plant tissues in excess of the respiratory utilization by the producer; Net community productivity (NCP) or community respiration (CR) the rate of organic matter not used by heterotrophs. Production efficiency depends upon net primary productivity. If NPP is relatively high, than production efficiency will be automatically high in the particular ecosystem.

Material and Methods

Five sampling site were selected for the measurement of primary production and efficiency in Sahastradhara river. We choose the *light and dark bottle method* of Gaarder and Gran for estimation of primary productivity. The water samples were collected monthly from five sampling stations of 'Sahastradhara stream' during December 2003 to May 2004 in morning period 9:00 hrs. to 10:00 hrs. The samples for plankton and physico-chemical parameters were collected and analyzed by using rinsed borosil glassware, with the help of the procedure described by APHA (1995), Trivedi and Goel (1984), Santhanam *et al.* (1989).

$$\text{NPP} (O_2\ \text{mg/l/hr}) = D_L - D_I/h$$
$$\text{GPP} (O_2\ \text{mg/l/hr}) = D_L - D_D/h$$
$$\text{CR} (O_2\ \text{mg/l/hr}) = D_I - D_D/h$$

where,

D_I: D.O. in *initial* bottle in mg/l,
D_L: D.O. in *Light* bottle in mg/l,
D_D: D.O. in *Dark* bottle in mg/l,
h: Duration of exposure in *hours.*

Net Production efficiency (%) = NPP × 100/GPP

where,

NPP: Net primary productivity
GPP: Gross primary productivity

Result and Discussion

It is well established that the primary productivity is controlled by several physico-chemical and biotic interactions. The biotic communities inhabiting water bodies are considered as the direct manifestation of the productivity. The maximum gross primary productivity of Sahastradhara stream was observed during winter season. Kar *et al.* (1978) recorded high productivity also in winter season.

Table 1: Primary Productivity (Mean values in mg/l) of Sahastradhara Stream

Parameters	*Site–I*	*Site–II*	*Site–III*	*Site–IV*	*Site–V*
NPP	(0.200–0.355)	(0.200–0.255)	(0.140–0.500)	(0.105–0.320)	(0.200–0.330)
Mean	0.271±0.069	0.220±0.0215	0.336±0.108	0.231±0.086	0.265±0.0522
GPP	(0.605–0.805)	(0.600–0.705)	(0.550–1.01)	(0.505–0.900)	(0.580–0.810)
Mean	0.6925±0.074	0.640±0.0776	0.716±0.1344	0.729±0.0975	0.676±0.0826
CR	(0.405–0.450)	(0.400–0.450)	(0.390–0.480)	(0.400–0.580)	(0.380–0.480)
Mean	0.420±0.0184	0.420±0.0635	0.421±0.0394	0.498±0.156	0.411±0.0375
NP Effic. (%)	(33.05–44.09)	(33.33–36.17)	(25.45–66.66)	(20.79–37.03)	(34.48–42.55)
Mean	38.77±4.7	34.29±1.101	44.15±15.56	30.485±6.445	38.87±3.069

Table 2: Planktonic Diversity (Mean values) of Sahastradhara Stream

Plank. Population	*Site–I*	*Site–II*	*Site–III*	*Site–IV*	*Site–V*
Total plankton	(700–1540)	(725–1525)	(693–1480)	(700–1490)	(730–1583)
Mean	1130.25±316.8	1133±316	1101.5±323.9	1063.75±346.9	1163.25±339.4
Phytoplankton	(625–1380)	(635–1380)	(615–1345)	(635–1340)	(640–1410)
Mean	1018.25±286.1	1023.75±291.5	992.5±296.3	951.25±318.2	1037.5±259.5
Zooplankton	(75–160)	(77–145)	(78–140)	(65–150)	(90–173)
Mean	112±31.61	109.25±27.09	109±28.6	112.5±31.72	125.75±36.66

Temperature plays a vital role in all physico-biochemical reactions and self-purification power of aquatic system. Temperature fluctuation measurement is useful to determine the trends of biochemical and biological activities. The Sahastradhara stream have a difference in the fluctuation of water temperature was recorded maximum (17.7°C ± 0.4) in the month of May and minimum (13.1°C±0.66) in January. The temperature of water decreases form September and increases from January onward. Badola and Singh (1981) observed similar trend in the river Alaknanda in the Garhwal region. Joshi and Kathait (1998) also reported similar trend in three Tributaries of river Ganga. The higher productivity in the present studied was concomitant with water temperature range from 14°C to 18°C. Singh and Swaroop (1980) observed positive correlation with productivity and water temperature. A positive correlation existed between gross primary productively and calcium in Cavery (Lakshminarayan, 2001). Vashney *et al.* (1983) recorded a positive correlation was between gross primary productivity and dissolved oxygen while the negative correlation between gross primary productivity and temperature and free carbon dioxide. Sumithra (1971) reported a distinct correlation between productivity and alkalinity, we have also the similar on individual values but there may be a standard error in correlations due to the mean value of parameters during the different months.

Table-3: Physico-chemical parameters (mean values) of Sahastradhara stream.

Parameters	*Site–I*	*Site–II*	*Site–III*	*Site–IV*	*Site–V*
Temperature °C	(14–18)	(13–17.5)	(13–17)	(13.5–18)	(12–18)
Mean	15.75±1.14	15.37±1.63	15.0±1.41	15.75±1.6	15.75±2.277
Velocity (m/s)	(0.3–0.4)	(0.28–0.32)	(0.8–1.0)	(0.78–0.82)	(0.6–0.7)
Mean	0.3±0.14	0.9±0.1	0.35±0.05	0.8±0.02	0.65±0.05
Turbidity (JTU)	(1–5)	(2.0–5.0)	(3–6)	(2–6)	(3–7)
Mean	2.75±1.47	3.25±1.30	4.5±1.15	3.75±1.48	4.75±1.48
Total solids (mg/l)	(955–1427)	(1090–1332)	(1115–1443)	(1135–1520)	(1148–1535)
Mean	1218±183.24	1234.2±89.8	1277.25±122.6	1305.7±166.1	1290.75±146.1
TDS (mg/l)	(840–1278)	(895–1217)	(1010–1322)	(1039–1380)	(965–1420)
Mean	1093.25±174.9	1094.25±120.5	1140.5±134.6	1189±158.01	1134.25±176.1
TSS (mg/l)	(113–149)	(119–195)	(105–207)	(105–140)	(115–211)
Mean	124.75±14.39	140.0±28.16	136.75±40.95	116.75±13.8	156.5±41.69
pH	(7.2–8.1)	(7.3–8.1)	(7.5–7.9)	(7.6–8.0)	(7.2–8.1)
Mean	7.625±0.43	7.6±0.28	7.75±0.15	7.75±1.66	7.6±0.339
Free CO_2 (mg/l)	(1.40–1.69)	(1.62–1.92)	(1.62–2.20)	(1.65–1.85)	(1.62–2.20)
Mean	1.6525±0.39	1.75±0.017	1.825±0.25	1.74±0.09	1.87±0.21
DO (mg/l)	(7.04–11.08)	(6.84–10.07)	(7.04–9.47)	(6.04–9.06)	(6.04–9.47)
Mean	8.41±1.62	8.46±1.18	8.65±0.95	7.55±0.87	7.49±1.36
BOD (mg/l)	(1.60–2.0)	(1.7–2.2)	(2.0–2.5)	(1.8–2.2)	(1.9–2.3)
Mean	1.875±0.162	1.98±0.23	2.25±0.18	2.0±0.14	2.05±0.15
COD (mg/l)	(2.1–3.0)	(2.2–2.9)	(2.6–3.2)	(2.4–3.0)	(2.4–2.9)
Mean	2.55±0.32	2.6±0.25	2.9±0.22	2.68±0.22	2.7±0.18
Hardness (mg/l)	(190–210)	(185–220)	(200–250)	(180–230)	(185–235)
Mean	196.25±8.2	200.0±15.41	222.5±19.2	200.0±18.71	198.75±21.02
Alkalinity (mg/l)	(150–480)	(140–500)	(170–600)	(130–570)	(120–540)
Mean	250.0±134.7	262.5±140.8	305±172.1	292.5±168.8	317.5±175.2

In this study it was recorded that the pH was always slightly alkaline. The pH of natural water was controlled in a greater extent by the interaction of hydroxyl ions, resulting form the dissociation of carbonic acid, and form hydroxyl ion arising from the hydrolysis of bicarbonate, was recorded highest (8.02 ± 0.1166) in December and lowest (7.4 ± 0.1414) in the month of April. The higher rate of photosynthesis decreases free carbon dioxide content and increases dissolved oxygen (Denham, 1938) while higher rate of decomposition increases free carbon dioxide. Similar observations were found in Sahastradhara stream during investigating period. Vashney *et al.* (1983) observed negative correlation between productivity and turbidity, total dissolved solids and suspended solids because these factors deceases the light penetration and further affects the rate of photosynthesis in aquatic ecosystem (Khanna, 1993), while negative correlation between GPP and pH, temperature and free carbon dioxide.

The maximum value of free carbon dioxide was observed (2.2 mg/l ±0.155) in May and minimum value in January (1.70 mg/l ±0.066) free carbon dioxide and dissolved oxygen showed a negative relationship to one another. Free carbon dioxide released during the decomposition of certain substances and respiration of living organism since higher temperature accelerate the decomposition of organic substances as well as the respiratory activity of the biota a direct relationship was established between the water temperature and free Carbon dioxide. The highest rate of photosynthesis decreases free carbon-dioxide content and higher rate of decomposition increases free carbon dioxide.

Table 4: Correlation Between Primary Productivity and Physico-chemical Parameters of Sahastradhara Stream

Parameters	*NPP*	*GPP*	*CR*	*NP Efficiency*
Temperature °C	–0.59945	0.006189	0.311429	–0.57232
Velocity (m/s)	–0.82147	–0.40554	0.387568	–0.78591
Turbidity (JTU)	0.459379	0.237629	–0.09751	0.389256
Total solids (mg/l)	0.086601	0.565255	0.544701	–0.16675
TDS (mg/l)	0.01787	0.761621	0.801179	–0.33031
TSS (mg/l)	0.165469	–0.58282	–0.73453	0.444083
pH	0.409892	0.87509	0.647625	0.023325
Free CO_2 (mg/l)	0.335796	–0.03623	–0.24934	0.360837
D O (mg/l)	0.43596	–0.20694	–0.47748	0.522691
BOD (mg/l)	0.715985	0.330189	–0.11921	0.583037
COD (mg/l)	0.757185	0.484589	–0.01968	0.572202
Hardness (mg/l)	0.811178	0.38677	–0.13668	0.659382
Alkalinity (mg/l)	0.380434	0.349649	0.067672	0.259953

The maximum net primary productivity was observed (0.335 ±0.093) in the month of December and minimum (0.170 ±0.04) in the month of May. The maximum gross primary productivity was observed (0.796 ±0.123) in the month of January and minimum (0.569 ±0.0379) in the month of May. The maximum net community respiration was observed (0.479 ±0.0575) in the month of January and minimum (0.399 ±0.0102) in the month of April. Net production efficiency shows the positive correlation with dissolved oxygen, while the negative correlation between net production efficiency and carbon dioxide. The maximum net production efficiency was observed (43.79%) in the month of December and minimum (29.88%) in the month of May. Similar trend was observed by Yeragi and Shaikh (2003) on the primary productivity of Tansa River. Singh *et al.* (1980) and Kar *et al.* (1978) however, recorded low and high productivity in summer and winter respectively.

References

APHA (1995): Standard methods for examination of water and waste water. *American Public Health Association, 19th edition. Inc, New York.* pp: 1970.

Badola, S.P. and Singh, H.R. (1981): Hydrobiology of the river Alaknanda of Garhwal Himalaya *Indian J. Ecol.*, 8(2): 269-276.

Denham, S.C. (1938): A limnological investigation of the West Fork and common branch of White river, Invest. *Indian lakes and streams,* 1: 17-71.

Joshi, B.D. and Kathait, R.S. (1998): Limnlogical characteristics of three tributaries of river Ganga between Devprayag and Rishikesh. *Him. J. Env. Zool.* Vol-12: 225-243.

Kar, O.K., P.C. Mishra, M.C. Das and R.C. Das (1978): Pollution studies in river Ib. III Plankton, pollution and primary productivity, 175.

Kathri, T.C. (1984): Seasonal variation in ecosystem of Lakhotia lake in Rajasthan. *Indian J. Fish.,* 31: 122-129

Khanna, D.R. (1993): Ecology and pollution of Ganga River. *Ashish Publishing House,* N.Delhi.: 1-241.

Lakshminarayana and R.K. Someshekar (2001): Ecology of polluted water by Arvind Kumar Vol. I, Chapter II, pp. 51-60. *APH Pub. Corp. New Delhi-* 110002.

Pande, R. K. and Asha Mishra (2000): Water quality study of freshwaters of Dehradun (Sahastradhara stream and Mussoorie Lake). *Aquacult.* 1: 57-62.

Santhanam, R.; Velaynatham, P. and Jegatheesan, G. (1989): A mannual for freshwater ecology. *Daya Publishing House, Delhi- 110006*: 1-92.

Singh, S.R. and K. Swaroop (1980): Studies on primary production of phytoplankton in Surha lake (Ballia India). Int. Revue. Ges. *Hydrobiol.* 65(5): 706-717.

Sumitra, V. (1973): Seasonal variation in primary production in three tropical ponds. *Hydrobiologia.* 48: 117-123.

Trivedi, R. K. and Goel, P. K. (1984): Chemical and biological methods for water pollution studies. Karad. *Environmental publication.* pp: 1-251.

Vashney, P.K.; R. Vijayalakshmi, Nair and S.H.H. Abid (1983): Primary productivity in near shore water of Thai Maharashtra coast, India. *J. Mar. Sci.* 12: 27-30.

Yeragi, S.G. and Nisar Shaikh (2003): Studies on primary productivity of Tansa River. *J. Natcon* 15 (1): 125-130.

Chapter 7
Benthic Diversity

Contents

7.1 General

Aquatic invertebrates live in the bottom parts of our waters. They are also called benthic macroinvertebrates, or benthos, (benthic means bottom, macro means large, and invertebrate means animal without a backbone) and make very good indicators of health of water bodies, because they live in the water for all or most of their life and stay in areas suitable for their survival. Generally benthos are easy to collect and identify in a laboratory and differ in their tolerance to amount and types of pollution. These animals often live for more than one year and have limited mobility. Benthos are integrators of environmental condition.

Freshwater benthic macroinvertebrates, or more simply "benthos", are animals without backbones that are larger than ½ millimeter (the size of a pencil point). These animals live on rocks, sediment, logs, debris and aquatic plants during some period in their life. The benthos include crustaceans such as crayfish, mollusks such as clams and aquatic worms, snails and the immature forms of aquatic insects such as stonefly and mayfly nymphs.

Some benthos are found more often, and in larger number, in waters that are generally clean, or unpolluted by organic wastes. Without too much organic matter, the waters usually have lots of oxygen for the benthos. This use as an indicator of water quality has been occurring for many years. For example, stoneflies are often considered to be clean water benthos. But when thinking about worms and midges, water quality professionals often view these as indicators of dirty water, especially in streams and rivers.

Oxygen is only one factor affecting the benthos. Unfortunately, it is not always a clear decision to make. Others include toxic chemicals, nutrients, and habitat quality. Some types of stoneflies may actually be found in waters that are not so clean, and likewise some types of midges and worms can be found in clean waters. So this is important to understand that there are some more complex methods to make these types of decisions, and to determine whether waters are healthy or polluted for aquatic life. Depending upon the type of aquatic environment, such as standing waters like lakes and wetlands, the categories of clean, somewhat pollution tolerant, and pollution tolerant don't necessarily apply.

Benthic invertebrates in lakes or large slow moving rivers are generally collected in the same fashion as sediment samples. The processing of the sample once it has been collected is where the techniques differ. The type of grab sampler to be used at a particular site will depend on the site conditions and the purpose of the study. The equipment to be used will be dictated by the project design and must be outlined in the field logbook and pre-sampling checklist.

7.2 Role of Benthic Diversity

The use of benthos as an indicator of water quality has been occurring for many years. These animals are widespread in their distribution and can live on all bottom types, even on manmade objects. They can be found in hot springs, small ponds and large lakes. Some are even found in the soil beneath puddles. Many benthic species are able to move around and expand their distribution by drifting with currents to a new location during the aquatic phase of their life or by flying to a new stream during their terrestrial phase. Most species of benthos can be found throughout the year, but the largest numbers occur in the spring just before the reproductive period. In colder months, many species burrow deep within the mud or remain inactive on rock surfaces. Many aquatic insects undergo a complete metamorphosis–the transition from egg to larva to pupa and finally to adult. They remain in the water for most of their lives (typically 1 month–4 years). After becoming adults, the majority of insects live for only a brief time, usually a few hours to a few days, while they locate mates and reproduce (www.dnr.maryland.gov).

Many invertebrates feed on algae and bacteria, which are on the lower end of the food chain. Benthos is an important part of the food chain, especially for fish. Some shred and eat leaves and other organic matter that enters the water. Because of their abundance and position as middlemen in the aquatic food chain, benthos plays a critical role in the natural flow of energy and nutrients. As benthic invertebrates die, they decay, leaving behind nutrients that are reused by aquatic plants and other animals in the food chain.

Unlike fish, benthos cannot move around much so they are less able to escape the effects of sediment and other pollutants that diminish water quality. Therefore, benthos can give us reliable information on stream and lake water quality. Their long life cycles allow studies conducted by aquatic ecologists to determine any decline in environmental quality.

Many benthic macroinvertebrates are long-lived, allowing detection of past pollution events such as pesticide spills and illegal dumping. Benthos represents an extremely diverse group of aquatic animals, and the large numbers of species possess a wide range of responses to stressors such as organic pollutants, sediments, and toxicants.

Benthic communities can be used to monitor stream quality conditions over a broad area or they can be used to determine the effects of point source discharges from sources such as sewage treatment plants and factories (www.dnr.maryland.gov). Ecologists who evaluate environmental quality using the benthos often consider the following characteristics of a benthic sample to be important indicators of stream, river or lake quality:

1. Pollution tolerance: Many types of benthos are sensitive to pollutants such as metals and organic wastes. Mayflies, stoneflies, and caddis-flies are generally intolerant of pollution. If a large number of these insect types are collected in a sample, the water quality in the stream is likely to be good. If only pollution-tolerant organisms such as worms and non-biting midges are found, the water is likely to be polluted.
2. Taxa richness: A measure of the number of different types of animals; greater taxa richness generally indicates better water quality.
3. Functional groups: The presence or absences of certain feeding groups (such as scrapers and filterers) may indicate a disturbance in the food supply of the benthic animals in the stream and the possible effects of toxic chemicals.

7.3 Historic Resume

According to *Hippocrates* (460 B.C. – 345 B.C.), the father of medicine, "water contributes much to health" and averted the rain water should be used after boiling and filtering, otherwise it would smell bed and cause harshness (Borchart and Wotton, 1971).

However, it is difficult to give the name of scientists, limnologists and hydro-biologists, who worked on the various aspects of water quality and aquatic ecology. This review includes some of the important contribution made from various parts of world. Various workers discussed the various aspects of water quality time to time from India and abroad nationally or internationally.

Clark (1924) analyzed the composition of river and lake water of United States. Galtsoff (1924) and Reinnard (1931) studied the limnology of upper Mississippi. Ganpati (1940) studied the ecology of the temple tank containing a permanent bloom of *Microcystis aeruginousa*. Ganpati and Alikunni (1950) observed that water of river Ganga was heavily polluted which dangerous to the human health. Needham and Needham (1962) indicated hydrologic conditions such as floods or low flows create habitats that may represent limiting conditions for flora and fauna, both vertebrates and invertebrates. Baloni and Sarkar (1965) observed the pollution of Yamuna River at Okhla water intake out at Delhi. Saxena *et al.* (1966) observed pollution of the Ganga near Kanpur.

Gopal *et al.* (1981) studied the limnology of a freshwater reservoir of Jaipur. Sharma (1986) published a report on effect of physico-chemical factors and benthic fauna of Bhagirthi River in Garhwal Himalaya. Nautiyal (1990) explained the ecology of the Ganga River system in the upland of Garhwal Himalayan environment. Pathak (1991) studied some aspects of ecology of the river Sarju and Gomati of the Kumoan Himalaya. Karr, (1993) examined the river biota regarded as indicators of ecosystem healthy degradation and integrity. Ormerod *et al.* (1994) observed that stream communities vary in composition and function with altitudes.

Aicha Ajakane, (1995) defined ecological characteristics of the benthic macro-invertebrates of high altitude streams (Morocco). Shyam sunder (1996) studied the biotic communities of a Kumoan Himalayan river. Dutta *et al.* (1997) evaluated the variation in physico-chemical characteristics of water and micro-benthic invertebrates in river Tawi near Nagrota bypass Jammu. Joshi and Kathiat (1998) studied the limnological characteristics of three tributaries of river Ganga between Devprayag and Rishikesh.

Pande and Mishra (2000) studied water quality of freshwaters of Sahastradhara Lake and Mossoorie Lake, Dehradoon. Kumar *et al.* (2003) studied on water quality of the river Ambarampalayam, Coimbatore District, Tamilnadu. Khanna and Bhutiani (2003) also evaluated the limnological status of Satikund pond at Hardwar. Bharti (2004) described the limnological aspects and physico-chemical characteristics of Sahastradhara hill-stream in Doon velly.

Sikoki and Zabbey (2006) described the environment gradients and benthic community of the middle reaches of Imo River, South Eastern Nigeria. Sunderay *et al.* (2006) analysed the multivariate statistical techniques for the evaluation of spatial and temporal variation in water quality of Mahanadi riverestuarine system (India) in a case study. Duran and Suicmez (2007) pointed out the utilization of both benthic macroinvertebrates and physicochemical parameters for evaluating water quality of the stream Cekerek (Tokat, Turkey). Malik and Bharti (2007a) evaluated the macro-zoobanthos as pollution indicator in river Saung at Dehradun (Uttaranchal). Malik and Bharti (2007b) described the ecology of Sahastradhara Hill-stream at Dehradun (Uttaranchal). Ross *et al.* (2008) analysed the response of macroinvertibrate communities to remediation stimulating conditions in Pennsylvania streams influenced by acid mine drainage.

Resende *et al.* (2010) pointed out the use of biological indicators to assess water quality of the Ul river (Portugal). Tessitore (2010) evaluated the effects of Eutrophication on benthic life within the littoral zone of freshwater lakes. Rani *et al.* (2011) made an assessment of temporal variations in water quality of some important rivers in middle Gangtic plains, India. Jindal and Sharma (2011) studied on water quality of Sutlej river around Ludhiana with reference to physic-chemical parameters. Kannel *et al.* (2011) pointed out the chemometrics in assessment of seasonal variation of water quality in freshwater systems.

7.4 Classification

Freshwater benthic macroinvertebrates comprise chiefly three of the phyla of many animals – Arthopoda, Mollusca and Annelida. There is a fourth Phylum, Platyhelminthes that has the Class Turbellaria (flatworms) which is not described here. Almost all of the freshwater benthic macroinvertebrates you will encounter fall within the taxnomic groups below:

PHYLUM	Arthropoda (crustaceans, insects, spiders, and relatives)	**Annelida** (segmented worms)	**Mollusca** (mollusks)
CLASS	**Malacostraca** (crayfish, pill bugs, shrimp, and relatives)	**Hirudinea** (leeches)	**Gastropoda** (gastropods, slugs, and freshwater snails)
	Insecta (see Orders below)	**Oligochaeta** (aquatic earthworms)	**Bivalvia** (bivalves, mussels and clams)
ORDER	**Ephemeroptera** (mayflies)		**Basommatophora**
	Odonata (dragonflies and damselflies)		(freshwater snails)
	Plecoptera (stoneflies)		**Unionoida** (freshwater
	Hemiptera (true bugs)		mussels)
	Trichoptera (caddisflies)		**Veneroida** (asian clam)
	Lepidoptera (butterflies and moths)		
	Coleoptera (beetles)		
	Megaloptera (alderflies, dobsonflies, fishflies)		
	Neuroptera (spongillaflies)		
	Diptera (two-winged or true flies)		

Each of the orders above contains many families. Each family, especially the insects, can contain dozens of genera and each genera dozens of species, or sometimes just a few species.

General classification and few members of various groups of benthic community are given here:

Sl.No.	Benthic Organisms
1.	Oligochaeta
	(*i*) *Tubifex* sp.
	(*ii*) *Limnodrillus hoffmeisteri*
	(*iii*) *Branchivra sowerbyii*
2.	Polychaeta
	(*i*) *Namalycastis indica*
	(*ii*) *Nephthys polybranchia*
	(*iii*) *Nephthys oligobranchia*
3.	Insecta
	(*i*) *Chironomus plumosus*
	(*ii*) *Strictochironomus* sp.
	(*iii*) *Culicoides* sp.
	(*iv*) *Dragonfly nymph*
4.	Pelecypoda
	(*i*) *Parreysia favidens*
	(*ii*) *Parreysia coerutea*
	(*iii*) *Corbicula striatella* Deshayes
	(*iv*) *Noviculina gangetica*
5.	Gastropoda
	(*i*) *Bellamya crassa*
	(*ii*) *Thiara scabra*
	(*iii*) *Thiara granifera*
	(*iv*) *Thiara tuberculata*
	(*v*) *Brotia costula*

7.5 Methodology

Benthos can be sampled with mushroom shaped scooping bottom sampler which collected a sample of about 10cm x 10cm. The entire collections should brought to the laboratory for further investigation as per the method applied by Singh *et al.* (1998) and the benthos organisms are identified with the help of "*Freshwater biology*" by Edmondson (1992). After taking a sample of 200ml and passed through guarded sieves and washed with plenty of water. The organisms collected in sieve should transfer to a bottle filled with water. The benthos may first identify in living condition and than preserved in 5% formaldehyde solution.

7.6 Identification

The benthos organisms should identify with the help of "*Freshwater biology*" by Edmondson (1992). A sample of 200ml is taken out and passed through guarded sieves and washed with plenty of water. The organisms collected in sieve are transferred to a bottle filled with water. The benthos are first identified in living condition and than preserved in 5% formaldehyde solution.

There are so many different types of living organisms, that scientists long ago devised a classification system (by Linnaeus using Latin) to help keep track of how closely related they were. This system is used to name the organisms in a systematic manner. Let's use a mayfly (*Ephemerella inermis*), known to fly-fishers as the Pale Morning Dun, as an example of this taxonomic system:

TAXON	*LATIN NAME/Feature*
Kingdom	Animalia (Animal, Plant or Fungi–this is an animal)
Phylum	Arthropoda (meaning "joint-legged," are invertebrates)
Class	Insecta (insects, 6 jointed legs, head, thorax and abdomen)
Order	Ephemeroptera (mayfly, ephemeral meaning short-lived)
Family	Ephemerellidae
Genus	Ephemerella
Species	Ephemerlla inermis

7.7 Photos of Few Benthos (www.epa.gov)

Phylum Arthopoda

Class Malacostraca

Order Decapoda (Crayfish)

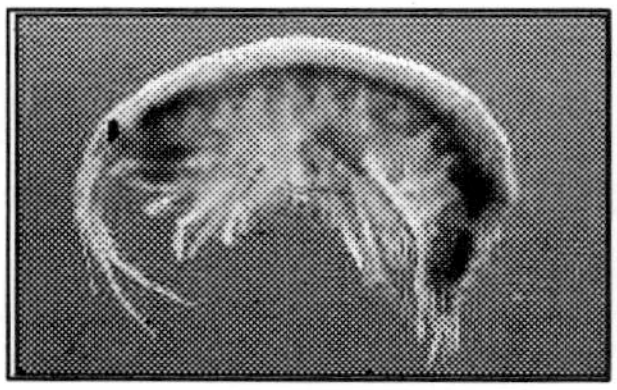

Order Amphipoda

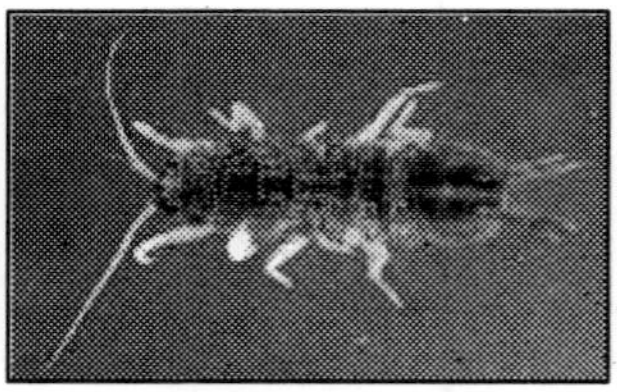

Order Isopoda

Class Insecta

Order Diptera

Family Simuliidae (Black Fly)

Order Diptera

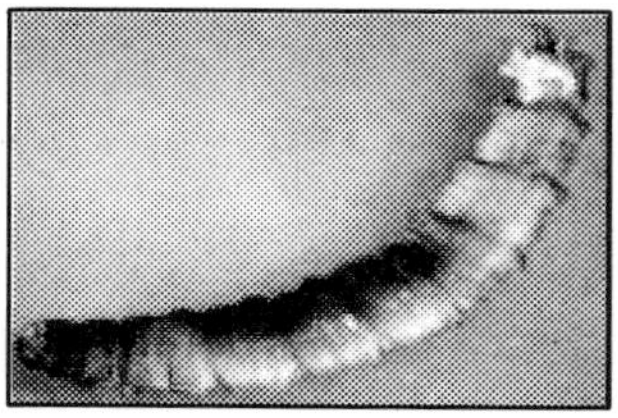

Family Tipulidae (Crane Fly)

Order Diptera

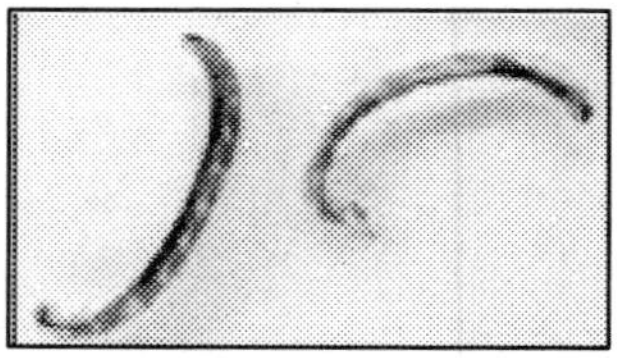

Family Chironomidae (Midge Fly)

Order Diptera

Family Athericidae (Snipe Fly)

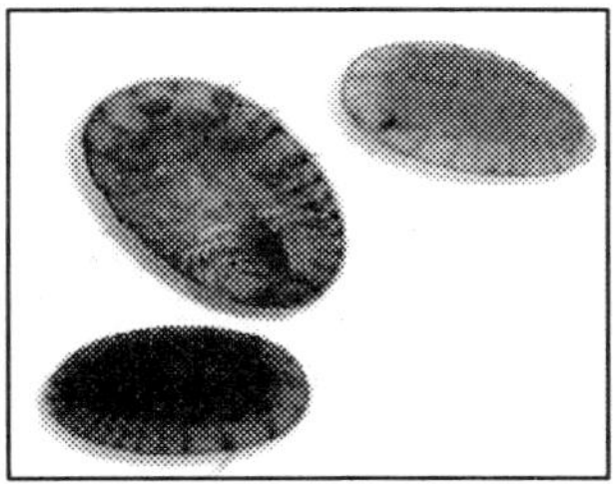

Order Coleoptera (Water Penny Beetle)

Order Coleoptera (Riffle Beetles)

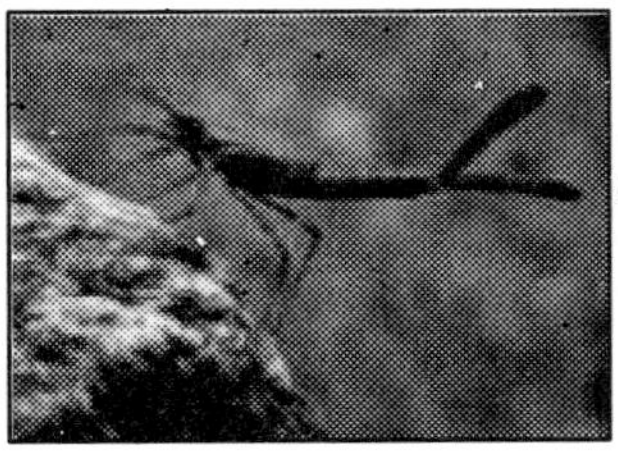

Order Odonata (Damselfly)

Order Odonata (Dragonfly)

Order Hemiptera (True Bugs)

Order Plecoptera (Stonefly)

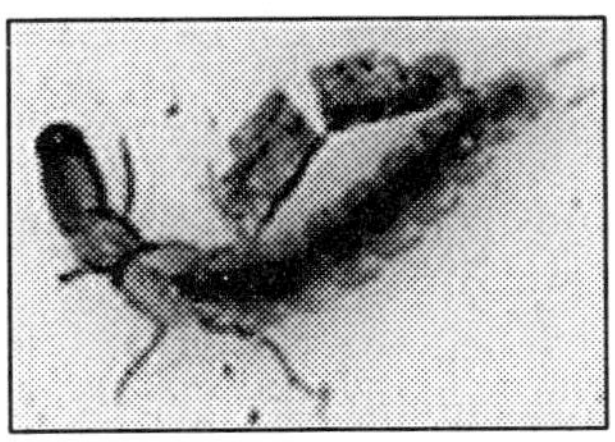

Order Trichoptera (Caddisfly)

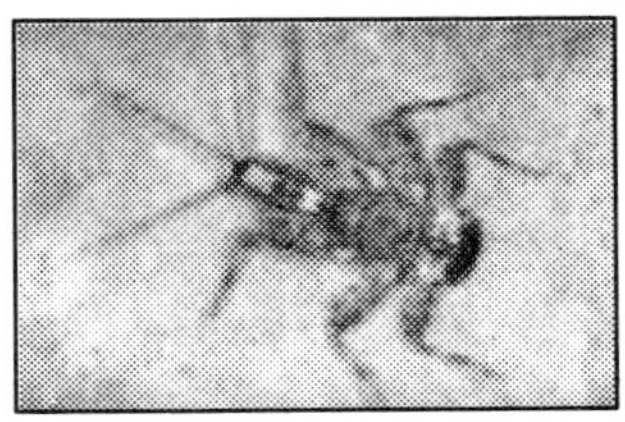

Order Ephemeroptera (Mayfly)

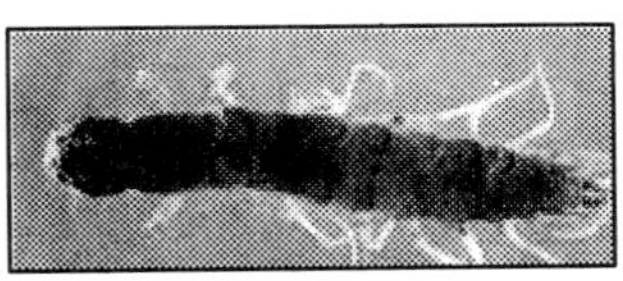

Order Megaloptera (Alderflies)

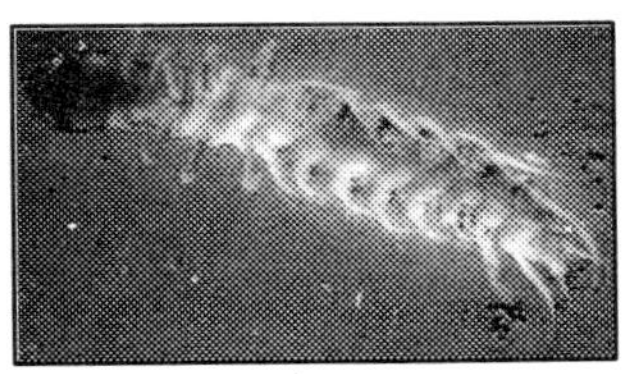

Order Megaloptera (Dobsonfly)

Phylum Annelida

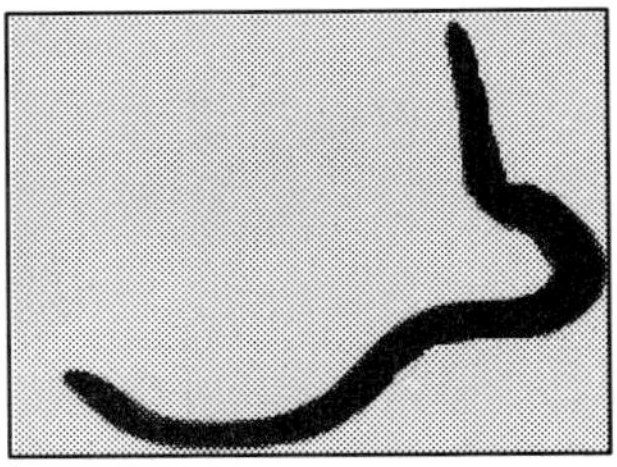

Class Oligochaeta
Worms

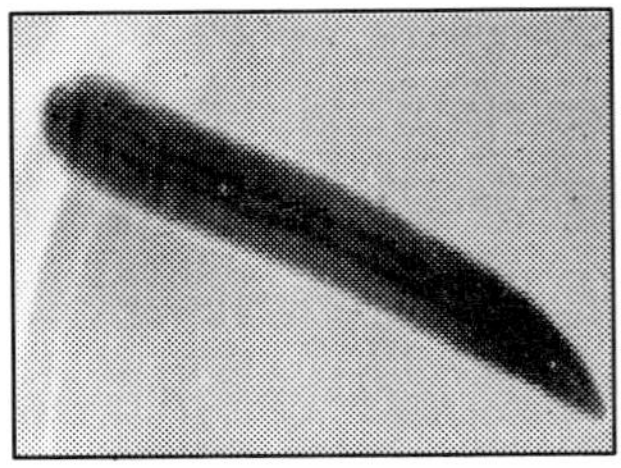

Class Hirudinea
Leeches

Phylum Mollusca

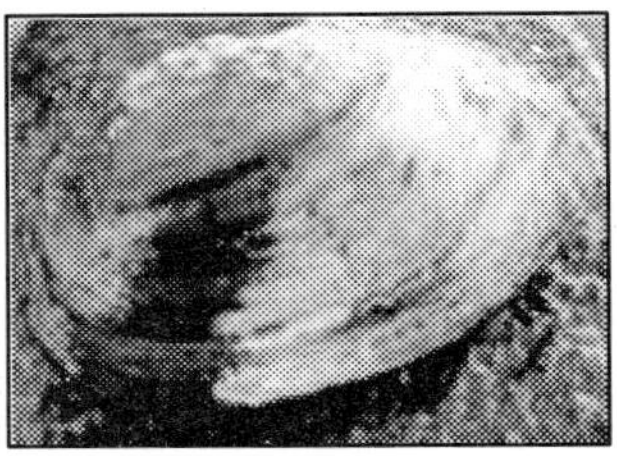

Class Bivalvia
Mussels

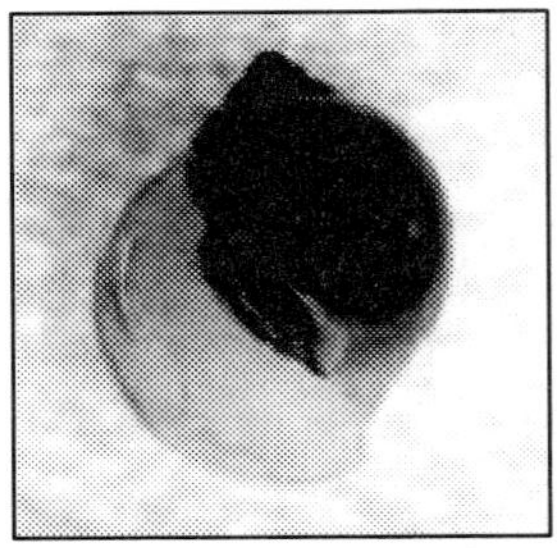

Class Gastropoda
Pouch Snail

7.8 A Case Study (Malik and Bharti, 2007b)*

Abstract

Accurate assessment of water quality, whether in relation to the requirements of intended water uses or in order to determine the impacts of an activity on the water resources, depends on the results generated by specific monitoring activities, which defines the physical, chemical and biological characteristics of the aquatic ecosystem.

It is apparent that much attention is being paid on these basic studies about the impact assessment of distillery effluents on aquatic ecology of river Saung in Shivalik Himalayan region. Present evidences supported that Gastropodes are facultative faunistic organisms along with Oligochaetes may be serve as bio-indicator of organic pollution prevailing in the Saung river due to mixing distillery effluents.

Introduction

Today very rare or no river has been spared from industrial discharge. Discharge of pollutants can degrade the quality of water and hence adverse affect the water's

---

* (***Reference***: *Malik, D.S. and Bharti, P.K. (2007b): Macro-zoobanthos as pollution indicator in river Saung at Dehradun (Uttaranchal), J. Exp. Zool. India, 10 (1): 221-222.*)

beneficial uses as well as the health of its aquatic ecosystem. Effluents from distilleries contains large amount of dissolved organic matter causes severe damage to the aquatic life in the riverine system. Though, distillery effluents do not contain any toxic substance, it create toxic conditions in the receiving stream by immediate depletion of dissolved oxygen resulting in massive fish kills, destruction of aquatic flora and fauna, production of foul odours and discolouration of stream

Pollution of a river first affects its chemical quality and then systematically destroys the community disrupting the delicate food web. Diverse uses of the river are seriously impaired due to pollution and even the polluters like industry suffer due to increased pollution of the river. River pollution has several dimensions; effective monitoring and control of river pollution require the expertise from various disciplines (Trivedy *et al.*, 1990).

An ecosystem is characterized by complex biogeochemical cycles and interrelationships among the physical and biological environment within recycling processes of materials and energy. The structure of a community in an ecosystem reacts in a dynamic equilibrium with the change in the environmental conditions. A number of groups of organisms could be used for evaluation of quality of river ecosystem e.g. Bacteria, phytoplankton, zooplankton, Macroinvertibrate and fishes (Pelmer, 1969). Benthic Macroinvertibrate community has been used extensively for the measurement of water quality and ecological status in lentic and lotic aquatic ecosystem.

Materials and Methods

Saung River is a spring-fed river originated from different small rivulets of the mountainous range of Dhanolti, crossing with Sahastradhara streams flow downwardly towards Doon valley basins. The three sampling sites have selected as site-I, site-II and site-III in the Saung River in between Dehradun and Doiwala town. The macro-benthic biota have been sampled by Eckmen's dredge and identified by Pennak (1953) and Endmondson (1959).

Results and Discussion

Macrozoobanthos are important components of the bottom biocoenosis. Invertebrate macro benthic animals mainly consisted of sessile or sedentary animals. Unlike planktonic organisms, benthic components from relatively stable community in the sediments and reflect characteristics of both sediments and the water column. The macro benthic biota principally consists of Oligochaetes, Polychaetes, Insecta, Pelecypoda and Gastropoda.

On site II, the benthic groups *i.e.* Polychaeta, Insecta and Pelecypoda were not observed and may be disappeared due to high organic pollutant nature of distillery effluents. On site III the all form of benthic biota like site I exhibited similar distributional pattern, while on site IV, Polychaeta most species of Insecta and one species of Gastropoda remained absent during the investigation. These benthic organisms can be considered as biological indicators for organic pollution emerging in to river water. Abundance of Oligochaeta, Insecta and Gastropoda were observed indicating their selective food habit and degrative nature of riverine ecosystem. In site I and site III the benthic organisms possessed a stable and uniform benthic community structure exhibited advanced mesotrophy supported dominance of the pollution to learnt species. The Oligochaetes are known to exhibit high percentage of the total benthic fauna in polluted water as reported by Howmiller and Beeton (1973) and Kulshrstha *et al.* (1991). In the present study, high density of Oligochaetes on site III and site IV clearly indicated their tolerance towards high degree of pollution. Reddy and Rao (1987) reported more *Tubifex* in the water enriched with organic matter. Brinkhurst (1966) suggested that the *Limnodrillus hoffmeristic* often dominates the benthic macrofauna community under conditions of extreme organic pollution. The occurrence of *Limnodrillus hoffmeristic* in the present study confirms to its abundance in Saung River indicated its degrative nature due to directly drains of distillery effluents.

Table 7.7.1: Comparatively Analysis for Seasonal Variation Among Macro-zoobenthic (Ind./m³) in Upstream Point at Site – I of Saung River (2001-2003)

Sl.No.		Summer	Rainy	Winter	Average
1.	Oligochaeta	57±24.42	64±27.18	78±33.77	66.33±10.69
2.	Polychaeta	98±40.27	124±45.21	132±43.58	118±17.77
3.	Insecta	138±43.56	162±50.28	184±53.32	161.3±23.0
4.	Pelecypoda	91±8.69	99±11.95	103±10.17	97.66±6.11
5.	Gastropoda	190±17.70	195±26.93	199±27.77	194.66±4.5
	Total	574±50.94	644±51.46	696±51.69	638.0±59.66

Table 7.7.2: Comparatively Analysis for Seasonal Variation Among Macro-zoobenthic (Ind./m³) in Effluent Point at Site – II of Saung River (2001-2003)

Sl.No.		Summer	Rainy	Winter	Average
1.	Oligochaeta	78±30.41	95±37.07	107±41.29	93.33±14.57
2.	Polychaeta	–	–	–	–
3.	Insecta	–	–	–	–
4.	Pelecypoda	–	–	–	–
5.	Gastropoda	34±2.48	36±5.49	40±5.09	36.66±3.05
	Total	112±28.39	131±34.74	147±39.16	130.0±17.52

Table 7.7.3: Comparatively Analysis for Seasonal Variation Among Macro-zoobenthic (Ind./m³) in Confluence Point at Site – III of Saung River (2001-2003)

Sl.No.		Summer	Rainy	Winter	Average
1.	Oligochaeta	246±107.25	262±113.22	305±129.06	271.0±30.51
2.	Polychaeta	55±18.92	56±21.95	58±23.05	56.33±1.52
3.	Insecta	93±31.94	91±29.71	91±29.02	91.66±1.15
4.	Pelecypoda	58±5.35	54±5.19	55±6.99	55.66±2.08
5.	Gastropoda	210±18.05	232±19.00	246±22.9	229.33±18.14
	Total	662±89.44	695±100.24	755±116.41	704.00±47.10

Table 7.7.4: Comparatively Analysis for Seasonal Variation Among Macro-zoobenthic (Ind./m³) in Downstream Point at Site – IV of Saung River (2001-2003)

Sl.No.		*Summer*	*Rainy*	*Winter*	*Average*
1.	Oligochaeta	625±259.57	635±265.68	605±253.52	621.66±15.27
2.	Polychaeta	–	–	–	–
3.	Insecta	9±1.00	12±4.58	16±3.00	12.33±3.51
4.	Pelecypoda	21±2.39	21±1.49	22±1.89	21.33±0.57
5.	Gastropoda	280±30.82	307±42.78	323±31.69	303.33±21.73
	Total	935±254.82	975±259.76	966±248.56	958.66±20.98

Gastropoda were found to be more tolerant of organic pollution the species, *Bellamgo crossa, Thiara scabra, Thiara granifera, Thiara culata and Brotia costula* indicates that Gastropodes have a broad tolerance range of organic enrichment. Present evidences supported that Gastropodes are facultative faunistic organisms along with Oligochaetes may be serve as bioindicator of orgnic pollution prevailing in the Saung river due to mixing distillry effluents. The resulting biocaenoses comprises benthic species that prefer a strictly limited ranges of physico-chemical conditions and others which tolerant abroad range of existing riverine conditions (Bhanot, 2004).

Thus, on the basis of present study it was concluded that river Saung that had been affected due to distillery effluent restored in same extent to physical chemical and biological characteristics up to a distance of 10-12 kilometers downstream from the confluence point by the natural process of self-regeneration.

References

Bhanot, M. (2004): effects of effluents on Doon Valley distillery on aquatic ecology of river song (Shivalk Himalaya). Ph. D. Thesis, *Gurukula Kangri University, Hardwar.* pp: 121

Brinkhurst, R.O. (1966): Tubificidae (Oligochaeta) of polluted waters. Vern. Internat. Varein, *Limnol.* 16: 854-859.

Edmondson, W.T. (1959): Freshwater Biology–Rotifera, 2nd edition, *Wiley and Sons, New York,* pp: 420-484.

Howmiller, R.P. and Beeton, A.M. (1973): Biological evaluation of environmental quality, Green Bay, Lakh Michigan. *J. Wat. Pollut. Control Fed.* 43: 123-133.

Kulshrestha, S.K.; Srivastava, M.; george, M.P.; saxena, R.; Tiwari, A. and Johri, M. (1991): Seasonal variations in Macro-zoobanthic organisms of Mansarovar reservoir, Bhopal. *Pro. Nat. Aca. Sci. India.* 61B(2): 153-162.

Pelmer, C.M. (1969): A composite rating of algae tolerating organic pollution. *J. Phyco.* 5: 78-82.

Pennak, R.W. (1953): Comparatively limnology of eighth coloorado mountains takes Univ. Colo. Studies *Ser. Biol.,* 2: 1-75.

Reddy, M.V. and Rao, B.M. (1987): Structure of benthic Macroinvertibrate populations particularly the Tubificidae and Chironamid larvae in a sewage polluted urban canal. *Poll. Res.* 6(2): 65-68.

Malik, D.S. and Bharti, P.K. (2007): Macro-zoobanthos as pollution indicator in river Saung at Dehradun (Uttaranchal), *J. Exp. Zool. India,* 10 (1): 221-222.

Trivedi, R.K.; Khatewkar, S.D; Kulkarni, A.Y. and Shrotri, A.C. (1990): Ecology and pollution of the river Krishna in Maharashtra. River Pollution in India. *Ashish Publishing House, New Delhi.* 26: 99-193.

Chapter 8
Heavy Metals

Contents

8.1 General

Metals that are naturally introduced into the water body come primarily from such sources as rock weathering, soil erosion, or the dissolution of water-soluble salts. Naturally occurring metals move through aquatic environments independently of human activities, usually without any detrimental effects. Humans consume metallic elements through both water and food. Some metals such as sodium, potassium, magnesium, calcium, and iron are found in living tissue and are essential to human life-biological anomalies arise when they are depleted or removed. Probably less well known is that currently no less than six other heavy metals including molybdenum, manganese, cobalt, copper, and zinc, have been linked to human growth, development, achievement, and reproduction (Vahrenkamp, 1979; Friberg *et al.*, 1979). Even these metals, however, can become toxic or aesthetically undesirable when their concentrations are too great. Several heavy metals, like cadmium, lead, and mercury, are highly toxic at relatively low concentrations, can accumulate in body tissues over long periods of time, and are nonessential for human health.

The toxic heavy metals entering the ecosystem may lead to geo-accumulation, bioaccumulation and biomagnifications. Heavy metals like Fe, Cu, Zn, Ni and other trace elements are important for proper functioning of biological systems and their deficiency or excess could lead to a number of disorders. Food chain contamination by heavy metals has become a burning issue in recent years because of their potential accumulation in biosystems through contaminated water, soil and air. Therefore, a better understanding of heavy metal sources, their accumulation in the soil and the effect of their presence in water and soil on plant systems seem to be particularly important issues of present-day research on risk assessments (Lokeshwari and Chandrappa, 2006).

8.2 Parameters

Following Heavy Metals were selected for the evaluation in water of Sahastradhara hill-stream:

- ☆ Cadmium
- ☆ Copper
- ☆ Iron
- ☆ Lead
- ☆ Manganese
- ☆ Nickel
- ☆ Zinc

Copper (Cu)

Copper in the natural waters also results in higher concentration due to pollution. It is used with sulphate as a pesticides and also separately as an algicide. Although, it passes as such through the body but there is evidence of accumulation of trace quantities in liver. The limits of it in the standards are not due to its toxic effects but are due to its taste producing capacity.

Preparation of 1000 Cu (µg/ml) standard: Dissolve 1 gm of Cu in 50 ml of 6N of HNO_3 and dilute to 1 L to give 1000 µg/ml Cu.

Cadmium (Cd)

Cadmium is fairy dense silver white malleable and most toxic metal, which melts at 320.9°C. Cadmium is used for dye and paint pigment production, batteries, ceramic industries, wooden industries and plastic production. The Cd found in a sample of Ca is likely in a inorganic form and may be relatively less toxic to plants and animals, while same amount of Cd when present in zinc or phosphates may be highly toxic to plants and animals, especially when there is calcium deficiency in soil or livestock rations.

Preparation of 1000 Cd (µg/ml) standard: Dissolve 1 gm of Cd Metal in 20 ml of 5N HCl containing 0.5 ml of concentrated HNO3 and dilute to 1 L to give 1000 µg/ml Cd.

Iron (Fe)

Iron is one of the most abundant elements of the rocks and soil, ranking fourth by weight. All kinds of waters including groundwater have appreciable quantities of iron. Iron has more solubility at acidic pH, therefore large quantities of iron are leached out from the soils by acidic waters. In the alkaline medium iron remain comparatively low in soluble phase.

Preparation of 1000 Fe (µg/ml) standard, dissolve 1.000 g of iron wire in 50 ml of (1+1) HNO_3 and dilute to 1 liter with de-ionized water to give 1000 µg/ml Fe.

Manganese (Mn)

Although manganese not a toxic metal, Mn imparts objectionable and tenacious stains to laundry plumbing fixtures and clothing. It occurs in domestic waste water, industrial effluents, acid mine drainage and receiving strums and therby enters water bodies. Mn is relatively non-toxic to animals, but toxic to plants at higher levels.

Preparation of 1000 Mn (µg/ml) standard: Dissolve 1 gm of Mn in 50 ml of 6N of HNO_3 and dilute to 1 L to give 1000 µg/ml Mn.

Nickel (Ni)

At high concentrations, nickel has toxic properties. Aquatic organisms have varying sensitivities to nickel salts depending on the water's pH, hardness, alkalinity and type of nickel compound under consideration. Nickel as a metal is a carcinogen.

Preparation of 1000 Ni (µg/ml) standard: Dissolve 1 gm of Ni metal in 50 ml of 6N of HNO_3 and dilute to 1 L to give 1000 µg/ml Ni.

Lead (Pb)

It is a dense soft metal and is quite resistant to corrosion. It has melting point of 327°C. Major source of lead is PbS (Galena). Lead is used for pipes, solders, electrodes, batteries, newsprint, and pigments in paints. Lead is also used in insecticides, beverages, ointments and synthetic dyes. The chemical form of lead determines its solubility in water and biological fluids, the extent of its fixation on soil and type of chemical reactions occurring in atmospheric, aquatic as well as soil environment.

Preparation of 1000 Pb (µg/ml) standard: Dissolve 1 gm of Pb metal in 20 ml of 6N of HNO_3 and dilute to 1 L to give 1000 µg/ml Pb.

Zinc (Zn)

Zinc is present in high concentrations in the wastes from pharmaceuticals, paint, galvanizing, cosmetics, dyes and pigments, etc., and their discharge increases its concentration in appreciable amounts in the waters. Zinc is very essential micronutrient in human beings and only at very high concentration it may cause some toxic effects. Zinc salts produce an undesirable taste to the water and causes water to appear milky and on boiling, a greasy surface scum may also form in the water (Mani *et al.*, 2005).

Preparation of 1000 Zn (µg/ml) standard: Dissolve 1 gm of Zn metal in 40 ml of 5N HCl and dilute to 1 L to give 1000 µg/ml Zn.

8.3 Historical Resume

According to *Hippocrates* (460 B.C. – 345 B.C.), the father of medicine, "water contributes much to health" and averted the rain water should be used after boiling and filtering, otherwise it would smell bed and cause harshness (Borchart and Wotton, 1971). The importance of water reveals from the beginning of civilization always took place near the water sources. Life can't exist without water it is a universal truths. This review includes some of the important contribution made from various parts of world. Various workers discussed the various aspects of water quality time to time from India and abroad nationally or internationally.

Clark (1924) analyzed the composition of river and lake water of United States. Galtsoff (1924) and Reinnard (1931) studied the limnology of upper Mississippi. Ganpati and Alikunni (1950) observed that water of river Ganga was heavily polluted which dangerous to the human health. Motiawant *et al.* (1956), Ganpati and Chacko (1957) and Daivid (1957-59) observed about the pollution of Ganga water. Rao and Govind (1964) carried out the hydrobiology of Tungbhadra reservoir. Verma (1964) carried out hydro-biological survey of Dalsagar tank. Baloni and Sarkar (1965) observed the pollution of Yamuna River at Okhla water intake out at Delhi. Saxena *et al.* (1966) observed pollution of the Ganga near Kanpur. Reynold and Johnson (1972) demonstrated in melt water that chemical weathering takes place beneath the glacier.

Meyback (1981), Stallard and Edmond (1983), (1987) concluded in tropical regions, erosion of silicates is more enhanced in response to both an increase in silica degradation rate with higher temperature and abundant rainfall and vegetation. In Nepal, Upadhyaya and Roy (1982), Tiwari and Ali (1987); in the Kumoun Region, Uttaranchal, (Paul and Verma, 1990; Bhatt and Pathak, 1992) in the Andhra Pradesh region, India. Naidu *et al.* 1989), Mayewski *et al.* (1986), Nijampurkar *et al.* (1993) studied of snow chemistry form high altitude Himalayan glaciers have been reported concentration of No_3 and So_4 of magnitudes comparable to those experienced in areas of North-West Europe. Hu *et al.* (1982), Sarin and Krishnaswami (1984), Sarin *et al.* (1989), Zhang *et al.* (1990 a) reported the chemistry of some large Asian rivers such as the Ganges/Brahmaputra, Changjiang and Huanghe etc. have been of scientific interest for the last decade. Ferro (1982); Lohmunn *et al.* (1988), Jones *et al.* (1989) attention to the chemical quality of lakes and impoundments in the Himalayas has focused on the problems of eutrophication and salinity, in Nepal. Raina *et al.* (1984) made pollution studied of river Jhelum. Chattopadhyay *et al.* (1984) made a study on the pollution status of river Ganga at Kanpur. Officer *et al.* (1984), D' Elia *et al.* (1986) observed that nutrient pollution has been linked to eutrophication in the Chesa Peak Bay estuary for at least the several decades.

Telang (1985) observed form the Machenzie River, which drains into the Beauford Sea in the arctic, where the occurrence of carbonates in the drainage eosin accounts for the dominance of Ca^{+2} any Mg^{+2} in the river. Berner and Berner (1987) demonstrated the weathering of rock forming minerals with minor contribution from cyclic sea salt and pollution, is the major source of ions in river water. Cooper *et al.* (1987) reported runoff decrease of the concentration of most ions to a minimum in melt water. Latimer *et al.* (1988), Yuretich and Batchelder (1988) observed that the chemical mass balance approach has been used extensively during recent years to study in stream reactions and sediment dynamics. Larson *et al.* (1988) studied the assessment of attainable surface water quality. Sarin *et al.* (1989) indicate that the water chemistry of highland tributaries is dominated by carbonate weathering in the Ganges/Brahmaputra system. Zhang *et al.* (1990 c) analyzed heavy minerals account for 5-10%, of which magnetite, hematite, pyroxene, hornblende, limonite, garnet, appetite and zircon are quite common.

Weinberg (1990) Coffey *et al.* (1992); Robillard *et al.* (1992) suggested that the importance of controlling water pollution at the agricultural watershed level is increasing day by day. Jain (1992), Jain *et al.* (1997) reported the chemical characterizations of Kali River with special reference to disposal of municipal and industrial wastes. Ormerod *et al.* (1994) observed that stream communities vary in composition and function with altitudes. Callow and Petts, (1994), Norris *et al.* (1995) recognized that rivers integrate processes in whole catchments and their biota is regularly monitored to detect change on this scale. Correll *et al.* (1994) suggested that factors such as lithology and topography, affect the flux of nutrient to nearby rivers. Jenkins (1995) studied the stream chemistry in the middle hills and high mountains of the Himalayas, Nepal. Kumar, (1995) studied on pollution is river Mayurakshi in south Bihar. Shivsubramani and Mahadevan, (1995) evaluated the water quality of river Suruliyar in Tamilnadu and western Ganga cannel at Hardwar. Jenkins, A. (1995) analyzed the hydro-chemical characteristics of headwater streams in the middle Hills and high mountains of the Himalayas, Nepal. J. Zhang *et al.* (1995) described the major element chemistry of the Huanghe (Yellow River), China-Weathering processes and chemical fluxes. Brenner and Mandok (1995) observed N and P pollution in the glacial tills of the Shenango River. Jain (1996), Jain *et al.* (1998) used indirect monitoring to study the contribution of point and non-point source of pollution to the river Kali. Collins and Jenkins (1996) observed increased levels of nitrate, sulphate, chloride and base cations in streams near agricultural terraces in Nepal. Rasmussen (1996) measured higher levels of nitrate downstream of manure row crops than chemically fertilized row crops. Cameron (1996) studied the hydro-geochemistry and seasonal variation in major and minor components of the Fraser River, British Columbia. Jain (1996), Dolan and Elshearawi (1989), Berndtsson (1990) utilized the approach to determine the metallic load to the rivers. Miller *et al.* (1997) analyzed nutrients in stream during base flow in selected environmental settings of the Potomac River basin. Stolllemyer (1997) analyzed the stream water chemistry in water shads receiving different atmospheric inputs of H^+, NH_4^+, No^-_3 and So_4^{--}. Bond (1997), Caine and Thurman (1990) demonstrated the annual stream hydrograph, two factors account for most seasonal variations in stream water chemistry: the annual hydrologic cycle, and the degree to which snowmelt is partitioned between overland and sub-surface flow. Singh and Hasnain (1998) studied the major ion chemistry and weathering control in a high altitude basin of Alaknanda River, Garhwal Himalaya India.

Jain (2000) described application of chemical mass balance approach to determine nutrient loading in the river Kali. Ahamad and Hasnain (2001) described the snow and stream water chemistry of the Ganga headwater basin, Garhwal Himalayas, India. Kumar *et al.* (2003) studied on water quality of the river Ambarampalayam, Coimbatore District, Tamilnadu. Graening and Brown (2003) observed ecosystem dynamics and pollution effects in an Ozark cave stream. Bharti (2004) described the limnological aspects and physico-chemical characteristics of Sahastradhara hill-stream in Doon velly.

Malik and Bharti (2005b) also described the nutrient dynamics in the water of stream Sahastradhara at Dehradun. Otokunefor and Obiukwu (2005) analysed the impact of refinery effluent on the physicochemical properties of a water body in the Niger Delta. CPCB (2006) reported the water quality status of Yamuna river (1999-2005). Sunderay *et al.* (2006) analysed the multivariate statistical techniques for the evaluation of spatial and temporal variation in water quality of Mahanadi riverestuarine system (India) in a case study. Panda *et al.* (2006) described the application of Factor and cluster analysis for characterization of river and estuarine water systems in a case study of Mahanadi River (India). Osibanjo and Adie (2007) identified the impact of effluent from Bodija abattoir on the physico-chemical parameters of Oshunkaye stream in Ibadan city, Nigeria. Malik and Bharti (2007) described the ecology of Sahastradhara Hill-stream at Dehradun (Uttaranchal). Saksena *et al.* (2008) evaluated the water quality and pollution status of Chambal river in National Chambal sanctuary, Madhya Pradesh. Karbassi *et al.* (2008) made a study on metal pollution assessment of sediment and water in the Shur river. Bharti *et al.* (2008) studied on the influence of Heavy Metals on Abundance of Cyanophyceae Members in Three Spring-fed Lake in Kempty, Dehradun. Dragun *et al.* (2009) described the preliminary assessment of total dissolved trace metal concentrations in Sara river water. Altin *et al.* (2009) made an assessment of seasonal variations of surface water quality charecteristics for Porsuk stream. Ahmed *et al.* (2009) made a study on heavy metals in some environmental samples.

Wang *et al.* (2010) studied on the assessment of heavy metals in sediments from a typical catchment of the Yangtze river, China. Chatterjee *et al.* (2010) monitored the waste metal pollution at Ganga estuary via the east Calcutta wetlands areas. Reza *et al.* (2010) measured the pollution level and monthly fluctuation of pollution -a study of wastewater of Chittagong city, Bangladesh. Fulazzaky *et al.* (2010) made an assessment of Water Quality Status for the Selangor River in Malaysia. Solai *et al.* (2010) highlighted the implications of physical parameters and trace elements in surface water off Pondicherry, Bay of Bengal, South East Coast of India. Rani *et al.* (2011) made an assessment of temporal variations in water quality of some important rivers in middle Gangtic plains, India. Jindal and Sharma (2011) studied on water quality of Sutlej river around Ludhiana with reference to physic-chemical parameters. Kannel *et al.* (2011) pointed out the chemometrics in assessment of seasonal variation of water quality in freshwater systems. Wang *et al.* (2011) highlighted the analysis and evaluation of the sources of heavy metals in the water of the river Changjiang.

Dai *et al.* (2011) pointed out the variation of Riverine Material Loads and Environmental Consequences on the Changjiang (Yangtze) Estuary in Recent Decades (1955-2008). Kapsikar *et al.* (2011) evaluated the physico-chemical features of Kali river, Karwar,west coast of India. Kumar *et al.* (2011) analysed the aquachemistry, Zooplankton and bacterial diversity in three ponds of Karwar district, Karnataka.

8.4 Sampling Method

Grab sampling was generally applied during the sampling. A grab sample is an ordinary sample which is taken from a particular place representing the whole water quality. This type of sample is valid only when it is certain that the water quality is not changing in a short time and effluent discharges, if any, are fairy regular. It is advisable to collect and analyze the grab samples separately at various timings, if the water quality is known to change with time. In such cases the schedule of timings shall be dependent on the frequency of discharge or change in water quality. This approach is used in studies to understand diurnal changes in pH, free CO_2, alkalinity, dissolved oxygen, etc. by collecting a 2 or 3 hour sample round the clock. In any kind of water, at least for dissolved oxygen, several grab samples spread over the whole day or even the night shall be important in limnological study.

The sampling of water from stream banks can be easily carried out using a wide mouthed polythene bottle but a sampler has to be used if the studies are to be undertaken at various strata of water. The sampling of sediments from the bottom of natural water bodies, stabilizing ponds or effluent drains is invariably carried out using special samplers. A large number of water and sediment samplers have been developed over the year with varying degree of sophistication. Most common of them and those which are readily available in India are Van Dron Water Sampler, Simple Laboratory Made Water sampler, Shallow Water sampler and Eckmen Dredge Sediment Sampler.

Stream water samples were analyzed by standard methods (APHA, 1995; Wetzel, 1975; Trivedi and Goel, 1984 and Santhanam *et al.*, 1989). The trace heavy metals were analyzed in the laboratory by Atomic absorption spectrophotometer *AAS 4129 model* (APHA, 1995; ECIL Methods Manual, 2004; ITRC Manual, 1987).

The samples were taken in BOD bottles and plastic Jeri cane for physical, chemical and heavy metals analysis.

Materials

Following materials and accessories were used in sampling process:

(1) Sampling Bottles

300ml capacity BOD bottles were used for collecting the samples. These were washed with chromic acid and then rinse well with tap water followed by rinsing with distilled water. Then these were oven dried at 160°–180° for 3 hours.

(2) Pipettes

Pipettes were washed in same manner as in above. All the pipettes used were of borosil glass certified grade pipettes used were of 1ml capacity (micro pipettes), 5ml capacity and 10ml capacity.

(3) Reagents and Glassware

Some reagents were taken for on spot analysis and sample preservation. Glassware used in study *viz.* conical flask, beaker, burettes etc. were of Borosil glass certified grade. All the glassware were washed with chromic acid and then rinsed well with tap water and then with distilled water.

(4) Jeri Canes

Jeri cane used for carrying the samples from sampling sites to laboratories. Jeri cane made of plastic and washed well with water and then rinsed well with distilled water.

(5) Chemical Bottles

Some small chemical bottles were used for transporting some necessary chemical urgently required during the sampling for immediately analysis for selected parameters.

(6) Bag

A bag of large carrying capacity was taken during the sampling for the collection of all water, soil and sediment samples.

(7) Thermometer

Mercury thermometer was used for on spot measurement of the soil and water samples.

(8) pH Meter

A handy pen pH meter was used for on spot evaluation of the pH of surface water, groundwater, soil and sediment samples.

8.5 Digestion and Dilution

Samples were collected in Borosil BOD bottles and some Jeri canes for laboratory experiments. Some parameters were determined immediately on sampling sites, for rest parameters and heavy metals; samples were stored in refrigerator at 4°C. Heavy metals may be analyzed in the 6 months period from the preservation date.

Samples were taken in Jeri canes for determination of the parameters like conductivity, total solids, pH (hydrogen ion concentration), COD, free CO_2, total alkalinity, total hardness Ca/Mg, chlorides, lead, manganese, zinc, calcium and magnesium. Caps of cans were closed tightly after filling up of cane.

For dissolved oxygen/biochemical oxygen demand, samples were collected in sterilized 300 ml capacity BOD bottles. The bottles were filled completely with sample water up to the rim and stopper was placed only avoiding any kind of air bubble inside it. DO was immediately fixed by adding 2 ml each of alkaline potassium iodide and manganese sulphate ($MnSO_4$) at sampling spot. While the sample for BOD was incubated for 5 days in BOD incubator at 20°C.

Collected, preserved, diluted water samples were prepared for the evaluation of metal concentrations with the help of AAS 4129.

Metals enter in the surface water ecosystem through the disposing of waste materials and various. For every metal a standard was required and concentration may be detected by AAS. Diluted and completely digested samples were required for metal detection by AAS 4129. Metal elements were determined with the help of Atomic absorption spectrophotometer (Model AAS 4129). Alan Walsh first developed the technique of atomic absorption spectrophotometry in 1955, and since then it has emerged as a powerful tool in quantitative analysis of more than 70 metals. The major advantages of the method are that it is free from any kind of interferences and very small concentrations are possible to be measured (De, 2002). The AAS is based on the principle that atoms of elements, which normally remain in ground state under flame condition, absorb energy when subjected to radiation of specific wavelength. The absorption of radiation is proportional to the concentration of atoms of the element. The absorption of radiation by the atoms is independent of the wavelength of absorption and temperature of the atoms. These to feature provide AAS a distinct advantage over flame spectroscopy.

8.6 About AAS

ECIL's Atomic Absorption Spectrophotometer, AAS 4129 is a PC based instrument for absorption and emission analysis. It is used for quantitative elemental analysis mainly like Copper, Iron, Zinc, Lead etc., by measuring the absorbance of a sample atomized in a flame. Some of the metals like Sodium, Potassium, Calcium, and Lithium are analyzed by emission method. PC does the data processing and partial control of the instrument.

The liquid sample is nebulised (reduce to a spray) by the support gas. The fuel gas is mixed and burnt over the burner head. A modulated light from Hollow Cathode lamp of a pre-selected element travels through the flame and enters the monochromator. The monochromator selects the appropriate resonance line of the selected element and directs it on to the PMT. The DC signal generated by the flame emission is rejected by FE compensation circuit and the original signal of the lamp is amplified, phase sensitively rectified averaged by an integrator to obtain sample signal. A computer processes the sample signal for photometric computations (% T, ABS or CONC). Instrument controls like wavelength, lamp current, gain, etc. are achieved and maintained by PC.

The cathode material of Hollow Cathode Lamp corresponds to the element of interest. ECIL's Atomic Absorption Spectrophotometer covers the complete range of Atomic Absorption applications. It incorporates State-of-the-art electronics, safety and operational convenience ensuring reliable and accurate analytical performance.

The data analysis and report making is done by the PC including selection of instrument parameters like wavelength, lamp current selection, and EHT to PMT at various wavelength. The software is user-friendly window based GUI interface using menus, function key, prompts, error messages, enabling ease of operation. Information is presented in easy read menus. In most cases recommended values are filled in.

The instrument was calibrated using regression techniques of linear and quadratic methods against standard solutions and concentration of unknown samples can be quantified. Instrument parameters and calibration parameters can be stored, as applications, which can be retrieved as and when, required. A hard copy of the results can be taken with the aid of a printer connected to one of the parallel ports of the PC.

Operating Steps of AAS

There are some main operating steps used in the operation of AAS (ECIL Instructions manual, 2004)-

1. Switch on Stabilizer (Power) and computer.
2. Double click AAS NEW software icon on desktop and click power.
3. Select the required element from list.
4. Adjust selected element lamp on top position and switch on that lamp from instrument.
5. Click HC lamp current, 1, 2, 3, or 4.
6. Click peak, A and Bb options will appear, check the lamp before, if OK then click YES.
7. A peak will appear on screen, it should be sharp and compare element wavelength with present one, and the difference should not be more than ± 1 nm.
8. If peak is not OK or difference is > ±1 then click INDEX, after index again check the peak.
9. If massage *"Signal is too high or too low for alignment"* appears, then check the lamp position, lamp and slit dial.
10. If peak is OK then align the burner with the help of line mark visiting card.
11. Switch on air compressor and open gas cylinder (pressure should be in green zone *i.e.* 5-10).
12. Open air from instant (pressure 15-20 LMP)
13. Open gas (Fuel) and adjust pressure 2-4 LMP and ignite immediately.
14. Switch On exhaust.
15. Click ANALYSIS.
16. Adjust HCL signal to green zone *i.e.* aprox. 3V with the help of EHT increase or decrease.
17. Feed blank in capillary and click zeroing.
18. Click CALIBRATION, and put the number of standard and cover of standard.
19. Feed blank in capillary and click zeroing.
20. Feed standard 1 in capillary and click READ.
21. Feed standard 2 in capillary and click READ.
22. Feed standard 3 in capillary and click READ.
23. Click CALIBRATION GRAPH and close, if graph is not OK then re-calibrate.

24. Click SAMPLE and put the number of samples and name of samples.
25. Feed blank in capillary and click zeroing.
26. Feed No. of samples one by one and click READ.
27. After taking the result of unknown click SAVE.
28. Click QUIT and close the gas cylinder tightly.
29. Switch of Air compressor and close gas from instrument.
30. Switch Off lamp 1, 2, 3 or 4.
31. Click POWER, switch of exhaust and click quit.
32. For print out results, double click AAS report, LOAD FILE, RES. OPEN, select the file and print result.
33. For print graph, load graph, print graph, res. open and print graph.
34. Now shut down PC, check the gas cylinder before closing the room and switch off printer and main power (stabilizer).

Precautions

Some precautions and highly attention is required during the handling of AAS 4129 and analyzing the heavy metals:

1. If the current wavelength is differed by ± 0.5 nanometers from the actual wavelength for any element after the peak search program, then the system needs INDEXING for correcting the ZERO error in the wavelength.
2. In-case of any emergency while the Air – Acetylene Flame / N_2O–Acetylene is On, immediately put off the fuel switch and then turn the oxidant knob to off position.
3. While igniting $N_2O - C_2H_2$ flame ensure that the N_2O burner is fixed on the burner assembly.
4. Don't try to light up the flame without switching on the air.
5. Don't try to open or remove the Nebulizer when the flame is ON. Always ensure the Nebulizer is in locked position.
6. Always ensure the drain trap is filled with water to avoid back suction and also water drains out freely from spray chamber through the drain trap to the outlet.
7. Always switch on the exhaust system when the flame is ON.
8. Always keep ready your standards, samples, distilled water and then start working on AAS.
9. Check frequently for the gas leakage at the flow points with the soap solution.
10. After completing the analysis work, always ensure that the gas cylinder, compressor outlet is in closed position. Switch Off the power supplies.

8.7 Standard and Calibration

Whenever, possible metals and metals oxides are to be preferred in the preparation of standards. This enables the analyst to dissolve them that samples and standards will contain identical elements and hence minimizes any chemical or physical interference effects.

Only concentrated standards (above 1000 µg/ml) should be held in storage. Working standards should be diluted from standards stock solutions only when needed. At low concentrations (less than 10 µg/ml) solutions have been found to deteriorate quite quickly because of the absorption on the walls of the container. Similar standard addition solutions can be prepared containing all of the required elements. This will avoid multiple splitting of the sample for individual elements and reduce the amount of time spent in preparing standards.

Before weighting, standards materials should be treated to ensure that they are in a standard state.

- ☆ Metals: Wash with acetone and ether to remove any oil layers. Remove any oxide coating by abrasion with emery cloth or by acid pickling and drying.
- ☆ Oxides: Dry at 110 °C for two hours. If necessary, heat to evaluated temperatures to remove bound water.
- ☆ Compounds: Equilibration at constant water content, or drying at 110 °C for two hours to remove any water.

Standards of known concentrations were prepared and evaluated the concentration of metal in water/soil digested sample. Every metal has some specific properties and atomic weight, so for every metal different condition of standard and calibration was applied for every metal (ECIL methods manual, 2004).

Standard Conditions for Cadmium (Cd)

Stock Standard solution

Cadmium 1000 µg/ml. Dissolve 1.000 g of cadmium metal in a minimum volume of (1+1) HCl. Dilute to 1 liter with 1% (V/V) HCl.

Operating Parameters

Instruments: ECIL AAS

Wave length: 228.8 nm

Slit setting: 0.5 nm

Light source: Hollow cathode lamp

Flame type: Air-acetylene flame oxidizing (lean, blue)

Sensitivity

For the standard conditions, the sensitivity is about 0.02 µg/ml Cd for 1% absorption. A standard containing 1.5 µg/ml Cd will typically give an absorbance reading of about 0.33 absorbance units (about 53% absorption).

Linear Working Range

For the standard conditions, the working range for Cd is linear up to concentrations of approximately 1.5 μg/ml in aqueous solution.

Other Analytical Lines

Wave Length	Slit	Relative Sensitivity
22.5 nm	0.5 nm	1
326.1 nm	0.5 nm	410

Standard Conditions for Copper (Cu)

Stock Standard Solution

Copper, 1000 μg/ml. Dissolve 1.000 g of copper metal in a minimum volume of (1+1) HNO_3. Dilute to 1 liter with 1% (V/V) HNO_3.

Operating Parameters

Instruments: ECIL AAS

Wave length: 324.7 nm

Slit setting: 0.5 nm

Light source: Hollow cathode lamp

Flame type: Air-acetylene flame oxidizing (lean, blue)

Sensitivity

The sensitivity is about 0.04 μg/ml Cu for 1% absorption. A standard containing 2 μg/ml Cu will typically give an absorbance reading of about 0.22 absorbance units (39% absorption).

Linear Working Range

For the standard conditions, the working range for Cu is linear upto concentrations of approximately 3 μg/ml in aqueous solution.

Other Analytical Lines

Wave Length	Slit	Relative Sensitivity
324.7 nm	0.5 nm	1
222.6 nm	0.2 nm	38
244.2 nm	1.0 nm	280

Lamps

With multi element lamps containing nickel or iron, a 0.2 nm spectral slit width should be used with the copper 324.7 nm line.

Standard Conditions for Iron (Fe)

Stock Standard Solution

Iron, 1000 µg/ml. Dissolve 1.000 g of iron wire in 50 ml of (1+1) HNO_3. Dilute to 1 liter with de-ionized water.

Operating Parameters

Instruments: ECIL AAS

Wave length: 248.3 nm

Slit setting: 0.2 nm

Light source: Hollow cathode lamp

Operating current: 5 mA

Flame type: Air-acetylene flame oxidizing (lean, blue)

Sensitivity

For the standard conditions, the sensitivity is about 0.09 µg/ml Fe for 1% absorption. A standard containing 4.0 µg/ml Fe will typically give an absorbance reading of about 0.19 absorbance units (about 35% absorption).

Linear Working Range

For the standard conditions, the working range for Fe is linear up to concentrations of approximately 4.0 µg/ml in aqueous solution.

Other Analytical Lines

Wave Length	*Slit*	*Relative Sensitivity*
248.3 nm	0.2 nm	1.0
392.0 nm	0.2 nm	270.0

Standard Conditions for Manganese (Mn)

Stock Standard Solution

Manganese, 1000 µg/ml. Dissolve 1.000 g of manganese metal in a minimum volume of (1+1+ HNO_3). Dilute to 1 liter with 1% (V/V) HCl.

Operating Parameters

Instruments: ECIL AAS

Wave length: 279.5 nm

Slit setting: 0.2 nm

Light source: Hollow cathode lamp

Flame type: Air-acetylene flame oxidizing (lean, blue)

Sensitivity

For the standard conditions, the sensitivity is about 0.04 µg/ml Mn for 1% absorption. A standard containing 1 µg/ml Mn will typically give an absorbance reading of about 0.11 absorbance units (about 40% absorption).

Linear Working Range

For the standard conditions, the working range for Mn is linear upto concentrations of approximately 2 µg/ml in aqueous solution.

Other Analytical Lines

Wave Length	*Slit*	*Relative Sensitivity*
279.5 nm	0.2 nm	1.0
403.1 nm	0.2 nm	12.5
321.7 nm	0.2 nm	2750.0

Standard Conditions for Nickel (Ni)

Stock Standard Solution

Nickel, 1000 µg/ml. Dissolve 1.000 g of nickel metal in a minimum volume of (1+1) HNO_3. Dilute to 1 liter with 1% (V/V) HNO_3.

Operating Parameters

Instruments: ECIL AAS

Wave length: 232.0 nm

Slit setting: 0.2 nm

Light source: Hollow cathode lamp

Operating current: 3.5 mA

Flame type: Air-acetylene flame oxidizing (lean, blue)

Sensitivity

The sensitivity is about 0.10 µg/ml Ni for 1% absorption. Standard containing 2.5 µg/ml Ni will typically give an absorbance reading of about 0.11 absorbance units (23% absorption).

Linear Working Range

For the standard conditions, the working range for Ni is linear upto concentrations of approximately 3 µg/ml in aqueous solution.

Other Analytical Lines

Wave Length	*Slit*	*Relative Sensitivity*
232.0 nm	0.2 nm	1.0
352.5 nm	0.5 nm	5.1
351.5 nm	0.5 nm	11.0
362.5 nm	0.5 nm	540.0

Lamps

With multi-element lamps containing iron, interference may occur when using the 232.0 nm nickel line if nickel is being determined in an iron matrix. A secondary nickel line (352.4 or 341.5 nm) should be used.

Standard Conditions for Lead (Pb)

Stock Standard Solution

Lead, 1000 µg/ml. Dissolve 1.598 g of lead nitrate Pb $(NO_3)_2$ 1 liter of 1% (V/V) HNO_3.

Operating Parameters

Instruments: ECIL AAS

Wave length: 217.0 nm

Slit setting: 1.0 nm

Light source: Hollow cathode lamp

Operating current: 5 mA

Flame type: Air-acetylene flame oxidizing (lean, blue)

Sensitivity

The sensitivity is about 0.25 µg/ml Pb for 1% absorption. Standard containing 6 µg/ml Pb will typically give an absorbance reading of about 0.10 absorbance units (about 34% absorption).

Linear Working Range

For the standard conditions, the working range for Pb is linear upto concentrations of approximately 8 µg/ml in aqueous solution.

Other Analytical Lines

Wave Length	*Slit*	*Relative Sensitivity*
217.0 nm	1.0 nm	1.0
283.3 nm	0.5 nm	2.0
261.4 nm	0.5 nm	6.0
205.3 nm	0.5 nm	340.0

Lamps

With multi-element lamps containing copper, the Cu 216.5 resonance line may interfere with lead determinations at the lead 217.0 nm line. The lead 283.3 nm line should be used instead.

Flame Emission

The most sensitive emission wavelength for lead is at 405.8 nm. A nitrous oxide, acetylene flame is recommended. Lead can also be determined at the 368.4, 283.3 and 261.4 nm wavelengths, but with reduced sensitivity. An air acetylene flame may also be used with reduced sensitivity.

Standard Conditions for Zinc (Zn)

Stock Standard Solution

Zinc, 1000 µg/ml. Dissolve 0.500 g of zinc metal in a minimum volume of (1/1) HCl and dilute to 1 liter with 1% (V/V) HCl.

Operating Parameters

Instruments: ECIL AAS
Wave length: 213.9 nm
Slit setting: 1.0 nm
Light source: Hollow cathode lamp
Operating current: 5 mA
Flame type: Air-acetylene flame oxidizing (lean, blue)

Sensitivity

For the standard conditions, the sensitivity is about 0.012 µg/ml Zn for 1% absorption. A standard containing 0.5 µg/ml Zn will typically give an absorbance reading of about 0.18 absorbance units (about 25% absorption).

Linear Working Range

For the standard conditions, the working range for Zn is linear upto concentrations of approximately 1.0 µg/ml in aqueous solution.

Other Analytical Lines

Wave Length	*Slit*	*Relative Sensitivity*
213.9 nm	1.0 nm	1.0
307.6 nm	1.0 nm	8400.0

Some essential knowledge about heavy metals is given below for basic setup and for understanding the sensitivity of each metal studied.

Table 8.1: Standard Criteria for Analyzing Heavy Metals by Atomic Absorption Spectrophotometer (AAS)

Sl.No.	*Name*	*Symbol*	*Wavelength nm*	*Flame Gases*	*Instrument Detection Limits Mg/l*	*Sensitivity Mg/l*	*Optimum Concentration Range Mg/l*
1.	Cadmium	Cd	228.8	A-Ac	0.002	0.025	0.05-2
2.	Copper	Cu	324.7	A-Ac	0.01	0.1	0.02-10
3.	Lead*	Pb	279.5	A-Ac	0.01	0.05	0.1-10
4.	Manganese	Mn	232.0	A-Ac	0.02	0.15	0.3-10
5.	Nickel	Ni	283.3	A-Ac	0.05	0.5	1-20
6.	Zinc	Zn	213.9	A-Ac	0.005	0.02	0.05-2
7.	Iron	Fe	248.3	A-Ac	0.02	0.12	0.3-10

A-Ac = Air-acetylene,

*: The more sensitive 217.0 nm wavelength is recommended for instruments with background correction capabilities (APHA, 1998).

Table 8.2: Periodic Position of Selected Heavy Metals

Sl.No.	Name	Symbol	Atomic Number	Atomic Weight
1.	Cadmium	Cd	48	112.411
2.	Copper	Cu	29	63.546
3.	Lead	Pb	82	207.2
4.	Manganese	Mn	25	54.93805
5.	Nickel	Ni	28	58.6934
6.	Zinc	Zn	30	65.39
7.	Iron	Fe	26	55.845

Source: IUPAC, 1994.

8.8 Significance

Many effects of Cd action results from interactions of various micro and macro elements as it antagonizes to Cu, Zn and Fe and also interferes with Ca absorption. Cadmium found in a sample of Ca is likely in an inorganic form and may be relatively less toxic to flora and fauna, while same amount of Cd when present in zinc or phosphates may be highly toxic to plants and animals, especially in calcium deficiency in soil. The use of contaminated water into irrigation may be increase the cadmium status in agricultural soil (Mani *et al.*, 2005).

Copper is sometimes found in insufficient quantity in soil (Miller and Turk, 2002) but it may be added in to soil system by some anthropogenic activities. Copper may accumulate in living organisms and their various body parts (Kudesia, 1992). High amount if heavy metals like cu and Zn may harm to living organism of existing ecosystem (Aslam *et al.*, 2004).

Iron has more solubility at acidic pH, therefore large quantities of iron are leached out from the soils by acidic waters. In the alkaline medium iron remain comparatively low in soluble phase. Excess calcium can reduced the activity of iron in soil and soil aeration may influence the availability of iron to plants (Miller and Turk, 2002).

Mathess (1974) reported that fresh groundwater constitutes 0.00-0.007 ppm cadmium, WHO (1984) recommended Cd concentration should not exceed maximum of 0.01 ppm in raw drinking water supply, 0.5 ppm in irrigation water. USEPA (1990) recommended maximum permissible Cd concentration as 0.04 and 0.02 ppm to protect aquatic life including fish. Hart (1982) reported a concentration range of Pb 0.0003-0.03 ppm in natural freshwater.

Nickel is one of the second trace elements of the present study after cadmium. As it is very toxic to plants and animals in low concentrations and has a tendency to accumulate in body parts. However Ni was presented in very minor concentrations.

The presence of heavy metals in the aquatic environment has been of great concern to scientists and engineers because of their increased discharge, toxic nature, and other adverse effects on receiving waters (Singh, 2006).

In heavy metals analysis, the total concentrations of the metals are often determined (Okonwo *et al.*, 1999, 2001; Castro Dentros *et al.*, 2003). However, total concentration of trace metals provides no information concerning the fate of the metal in the terms of its interaction with sediments, its mobility, bioavailability, or resultant toxicity (Christie, 1995). It is now widely accepted that measuring total metal concentrations cannot fully assess the role of aquatic sediments as a sink or as a source of pollutants. In addition, determination of total elements does not given an accurate estimate of the likely environmental impact. Instead, it is desirable to have information on the potential availability of metals (whether toxic or essential) to biota under various environmental conditions. Since the mobility of heavy metals, as well as their bioavailability and related eco-toxicity to plants, critically depends upon chemical forms in which, a metal is present in the sediment, considerable interest exists in trace element speciation (Davidson *et al.*, 1994).

Heavy metals are introduced into aquatic system from various anthropogenic sources. Heavy metals constitute a special group of contaminants of aquatic systems and deserve special attention. Since metals are not removed by natural degradation processes, they may become enriched in sediments over time. Metal contamination of sediments is an issue of growing concerns worldwide (NRC, 1989). Both natural processes and anthropogenic activities are responsible for introducing metals in to the aquatic system (Nriagu, 1989). Many contaminants discharged into surface waters rapidly become associated with the particulate matter and incorporated in sediments. Metals in aquatic systems become part of the water-sediment system and their distribution is controlled by a dynamic set of physical-chemical interactions and equilibrium, largely governed by pH and type of legends and chelating agents, oxidation state of the mineral components and the redox conditions of the system. Metal contaminated sediments may release heavy metals back to the overlying water column and, thus, pose risk to aquatic life and ecosystems. Due to their particle reactivity, heavy metals tend to accumulate in sediment as a result may persist in the environment long after their primary sources have been removed (Forstner and Wittman, 1981).

Heavy metals travel from one level to another in the ecological system due to the accumulation in abiotic and biotic components. Heavy metals have a tendency to accumulate and store in a component or trophic levels. The storage of heavy metals has created harmful effects for biotic components. The heavy metals accumulated in sediment and percolated down in to groundwater known as bio-accumulation of metal. From groundwater, heavy metals may turn into two ways; one is though irrigation and second is through drinking by human beings. The accumulation of heavy metals through the food chain is called the biomagnifications. The concentrations of metal increased at every next trophic level, whereas metals can cause various harmful effects on irrigated agricultural soil, human beings and livestock by alteration in some biochemical reaction in body cells (De, 2002).

8.9 A Case Study (Bharti, 2008)*

Abstract

The present chapter deals with the water quality status of Sahastradhara stream by the assessment of heavy metals. A study on Heavy Metals assessment in the water of Sahastradhara hill-stream was conducted with different five sites at significant differences. Heavy Metals were found in fluctuated trend from first upstream to last downstream. The values of almost all Heavy Metals were found in increasing manner especially after the fourth sampling site. After the third sampling station, a solid waste dump site was found. So, there may be a relation between Heavy Metals in stream water and solid waste dumping site. Concentrations of all Heavy Metals at fourth and fifth sampling site were found very high.

Keywords: *Water quality, River ecology, Heavy metal, Solid waste dumping site.*

Introduction

Metals that are naturally introduced into the waterbody come primarily from such sources as rock weathering, soil erosion, or the dissolution of water-soluble salts. Naturally occurring metals move through aquatic environments independently of human activities, usually without any detrimental effects.

Humans consume metallic elements through both water and food. Some metals such as sodium, potassium, magnesium, calcium, and iron are found in living tissue and are essential to human life. Probably less well known is that currently no less than six other heavy metals including molybdenum, manganese, cobalt, copper, and zinc, have been linked to human growth, development, achievement, and reproduction (Vahrenkamp, 1979; Friberg *et al.*, 1979). Even these metals, however, can become toxic or aesthetically undesirable when their concentrations are too great. Several heavy metals, like cadmium, lead, and mercury, are highly toxic at relatively low concentrations, can accumulate in body tissues over long periods of time, and are nonessential for human health.

The toxic heavy metals entering the ecosystem may lead to geo-accumulation, bioaccumulation and biomagnifications. Heavy metals like Fe, Cu, Zn, Ni and other trace elements are important for proper functioning of biological systems and their deficiency or excess could lead to a number of disorders. Food chain contamination by heavy metals has become a burning issue in recent years because of their potential accumulation in biosystems through contaminated water, soil and air.

Therefore, a better understanding of heavy metal sources, their accumulation in the soil and the effect of their presence in water and soil on plant systems seem to be particularly important issues of present-day research on risk assessments (Lokeshwari and Chandrappa, 2006).

---

* (***Reference:*** *Bharti, P.K. (2008): 'Status of water quality and ecotourism enhancement in Sahastradhara stream at Dehradun' in Third Uttarakhand State Science Congress organised by UCOST, Dehradun held on 10-11 November, 2008 at IIT, Roorkee)*

Water is an important substance required by all living organisms and for all anthropogenic activities (Dagaonkar and Saksena, 1992). The problem of environmental pollution due to toxic metals has begun to cause concern now in most major metropolitan cities (Bharti, 2007). Most of our water resources are gradually becoming polluted due to the addition of foreign materials from the surroundings. These include organic matter origin from plant and animal, land surface washing, Industrial and sewage effluents. In some tourist hilly regions, there are not any more industrial pollution, but tourist's anthropogenic activities may alter the water quality and the water quality of lakes of some tourist spot may affect the water quality of that water body.

Methodology

To assess the water quality of Sahastradhara hill-stream, five sampling stations were selected. Water samples were collected in plastic jericanes and analyzed according to APHA (1995) and Trivedi and Goel (1984) with the help of Atomic absorption spectrophotometer.

Results and Discussion

Heavy metals in the water of Sahastradhara hill-stream were detected in very low concentration while upper sites has water free with some metallic contents due to the absence of anthropological activities. However, the area is free from industrial pollution, but due to the increasing tourist activities the water quality is going deteriorate since last few years in a tremendous way. Heavy Metals concentrations are given in Table 8.3 and the increasing trend of Heavy Metals concentrations is indicated by the Figure 8.1.

Heavy Metals were found almost nil or in very low concentrations at all selected site. Heavy Metals like Cadmium, copper, lead were not found in high concentration at all sites during the study period. Cadmium, copper and lead were absolutely

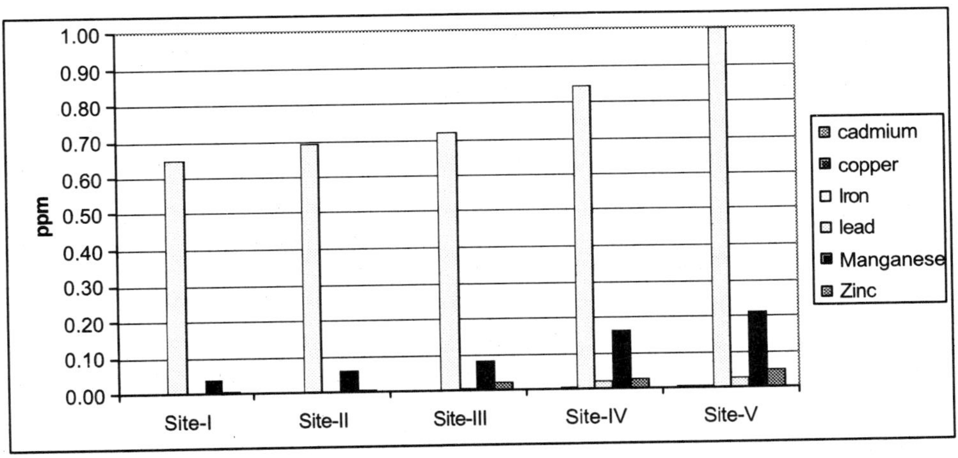

Figure 8.1: Showing the Heavy Metals Concentrations at Various Sampling Stations

absent in upstreams, while Mangenese, Zinz and Iron concentrations were found with in the limit in upstream samples. The concentration of iron was maximum observed 1.0 mg/l at fifth station. Lead was found maximum 0.03 mg/l at last downstream site and Zinc concentration was 0.05 mg/l. Malik *et al.* (2009) described the role of Heavy Metals in the surface water of north India. The results of Bharti *et al.* (2010) were also indicated the relation of Heavy Metals with some biological agents in a north Indian water body.

Table 8.3: Heavy Metals at All Five Locations at Sahastradhara Stream (ppm)

Sl.No.	*Parameter*	*Site–I*	*Site-II*	*Site-III*	*Site-IV*	*Site-V*
1.	Cadmium	0.00	0.00	0.00	0.00	0.01
2.	Copper	0.00	0.00	0.00	0.01	0.01
3.	Iron	0.65	0.69	0.72	0.85	1.00
4.	Lead	0.00	0.00	0.01	0.02	0.03
5.	Manganese	0.04	0.06	0.08	0.16	0.21
6.	Zinc	0.01	0.01	0.02	0.03	0.05

References

APHA, (1995): Standard methods for examination of water and waste water. *American Public Health Association*, 19th edition. Inc, New York, pp: 1170.

Arjariya, Amita (2003): Physico-chemical profile and plankton diversity of Ranital lake, Chhatarpur, M.P., *Nature Env. Poll. Tech.*, 2(3): 327-328.

Bharti, P.K. (2004): Limnological study of Sahastradhara hill-stream, Dehradun, *Dissertation, Gurukula Kangri University, Hardwar*, pp: 102.

Bharti, P.K.; Malik, D.S. and Yadav, R. (2010): Influence of Heavy Metals on Abundance of Cyanophyceae Members in Three Spring-fed Lake in Kempty, Dehradun, In: 'Advances in Aquatic Ecology, Vol-III' ed. by V.B. Sakhare, *Daya Publishing House, New Delhi*, pp: 107-111.

Dagaonkar, A. and Saksena, D.N. (1992): Physico-chemical and biological characterization on tample tank, Kaila Sagar, Gwalior, *J. Hydrobiology*, 8: 11-19.

Lokeshwari, H. and Chandrappa, G.T. (2006): Impact of heavy metal contamination of Bellandur Lake on soil and cultivated vegetation, *Current Science*, 91(9): 622-627.

Malik, D. S. and Bharti, P.K. (2005): Nutrient dynamics in Rhithron zone of Shivalik Himalayan stream Sahastradhara, Dehradun (Uttaranchal)", *Env. Cons. J.* 6 (2): 63-68.

Malik, D.S. ; Bharti, P. K.; Negi, K.S. and Yadav, R. (2009): Distribution of Metals in Water of an Artificial Lake at Mussoorie, Uttarakhand, In: 'Aquatic biology and aquaculture' edited by V.B. Sakhare, Ambajoagi, MS, *Manglam Publication, New Delhi*, pp: 77-95.

Pande, R.K. and Mishra, A. (2000): Water quality study of freshwaters of Dehradun (Sahastradhara stream and Mussoorie lake), *Aquacult*, 1(1): 57-62.

Trivedi, R.K. and Goel, P.K. (1984): Chemical and biological methods for water pollution studies Karad: *Environmental publication*, pp: 1-251.

Chapter 9
Human Activities

Contents

9.1 General

Pollutant sources especially non-point sources of lotic systems are hard to control because they derive, often in small amounts, over a very wide area and enter the system at many locations along its length. Agricultural fields often deliver large quantities of sediments, nutrients, and chemicals like various pesticides to nearby streams and rivers. Urban and residential areas can also add to this pollution when contaminants are accumulated on impervious surfaces such as roads and parking lots that then drain into the system. Elevated nutrient concentrations, especially nitrogen and phosphorus which are key components of fertilizers, can increase periphyton growth, which can be particularly dangerous in slow moving streams (Kushing and Allan, 2001). Another pollutant, acid rain, forms from sulfur dioxide and nitrous oxide emitted from factories and power stations. These substances readily dissolve in atmospheric moisture and enter lotic systems through precipitation. This can lower the pH of these sites, affecting all trophic levels from algae to vertebrates

(Brown 1987). Mean species richness and total species numbers within a system decrease with decreasing pH (Giller and Malmqvist, 1998). While direct pollution of lotic systems has been greatly reduced in the United States under the government's Clean Water Act, contaminants from diffuse, non-point sources, remain a large problem (Kushing and Allan, 2001).

Beside these, few other anthropogenic activities like dams construction alter the flow, temperature, and sediment regime of lotic systems (Giller and Malmqvist, 1998). Additionally, many rivers are dammed at multiple locations, amplifying the impact. Dams can cause enhanced clarity and reduced variability in stream flow, which in turn cause an increase in periphyton abundance. Invertebrates immediately below a dam can show reductions in species richness due to an overall reduction in habitat heterogeneity (Kushing and Allan, 2001). Also, thermal changes can affect insect development, with abnormally warm winter temperatures obscuring cues to break egg diapause and overly cool summer temperatures leaving too few acceptable days to complete growth (Allan, 1995). Finally, dams fragment river systems, isolating previously continuous populations, and preventing the migrations of anadromous and catadromous species (Kushing and Allan, 2001).

9.2 River and Tourism

Rivers always attract to the people especially nature lovers since the ancient times. People feel harmony, peace and internal satisfaction near the springs, streams or rivers. In the recent time, rivers are the part of tourisms. Many tourist places are established near or very closed to the rivers. Rivers or streams have a very old relation with tourisms not only in India but abroad.

A river basin is made up of a mosaic of contrasting and often competing biophysical, economic and social circumstances, and community interests. Only along limited reaches of a river basin is it possible to identify much commonality of attitude or purpose by the inhabitants. More typically, the segmentation of natural and human components of the basin is reflected in conflicting attitudes towards the single unifying element present – the river system.

Those living upstream tend to value the riverine environment primarily for its aesthetic appeal and perhaps its recreational role, rather than its economic function. Further downstream, the value of water for economic purposes becomes paramount to service agricultural, urban and industrial needs. The emphasis is on maximising the quantity of water available, with some level of biophysical degradation acceptable as a trade-off against economic viability and regional development. In the lower reaches of the basin, the riverine environment is degraded further from contaminated effluent, so that aquatic life, wetlands, estuaries, and the coastal zone, are frequently compromised by eutrophication and sedimentation.

Tourism and associated anthropogenic activities may cause effects on water ecosystem and can alter the water quality of that river or stream in many ways. The direct addition or dumping the waste material directly into river water can change many physico-chemical parameters of river water, so that the water quality can degrade drastically after increment in such type of activities and ultimately the entire aquatic ecosystem may disturb. The ecology of river water especially the living organisms of water column may realise the changes in their surrounding environment settings and few of them can show few indication to support or oppose the increasing pollution in the ecosystem. These few species are commonly called as biological indicators of pollution.

During the time of tourist activities especially at hot tourist spots, awareness for environment protection should be increased. Strict rule and regulations should be adopted for all individuals. Anthropogenic activities, which accelerated the rate of pollution or environmental degradation, should be avoided or banned or appropriate alternate should be adopted in those cases.

9.3 Anthropogenic Activities

Water is an important substance required by all living organisms and for all anthropogenic activities. The problem of environmental pollution due to toxic metals has begun to cause concern now in most major metropolitan cities (Bharti, 2007). Most of our water resources are gradually becoming polluted due to the addition of foreign materials from the surroundings. These include organic matter origin from plant and animal, land surface washing, Industrial and sewage effluents.

In some tourist hilly regions, there are not any more industrial pollution, but tourist's anthropogenic activities may alter the water quality and the water quality of lakes of some tourist spot may affect the water quality of that water body.

These are the major human activities which were observed during the study period in Sahastradhara region:

- ☆ Mass bathing
- ☆ Addition of food materials directly into stream water
- ☆ Clothes washing
- ☆ Development of a solid waste dumping site near fourth site
- ☆ Vehicle movement
- ☆ Interference with vegetation composition
- ☆ Dispersion of Polythene wrappers
- ☆ Generation of feacal material.

9.4 Solid Waste Generation

Sahastradhara hill-stream is a fast developing tourist spot of north India. Many restaurants, shops, dhabas and hotels are developed for the needs of tourists. Hotels and restaurants are increasing their number in a tremendous way. Due to the hotels, dhaba and restaurants, a huge amount of solid waste is generated and dumped near fourth sampling site (very closed to Budha temple).

The manual study of solid waste generated at this site was carried out on the basis of percentage composition of materials in soild waste.

Table 9.1: Per cent Composition of Solid Waste for Various Category Waste

Sl.No.	*Material*	*% Composition*
1	Wood products and woody toys	20
2	Plastic and polythene	22
3	Cartoons and papers	28
4	Leaves and straw	8
5	Waste Food materials	10
6	Hairs and bones	5
7	Glass and metals	3
8	Ash	2
9	Others	2

So, the major degradable material was wood products, papers, leaves, waste food and ash and the contribution of degradable materials into total soild waste is 68%. The degradable material will never create a problem in near future, but rest 32 % of undegradable solid waste will certainly harmful for the health of Sahastradhara stream and its water quality also.

Table 9.2: Per cent Composition of Solid Waste

Sl.No.	*Material*	*% Composition*
1.	Degradable	68

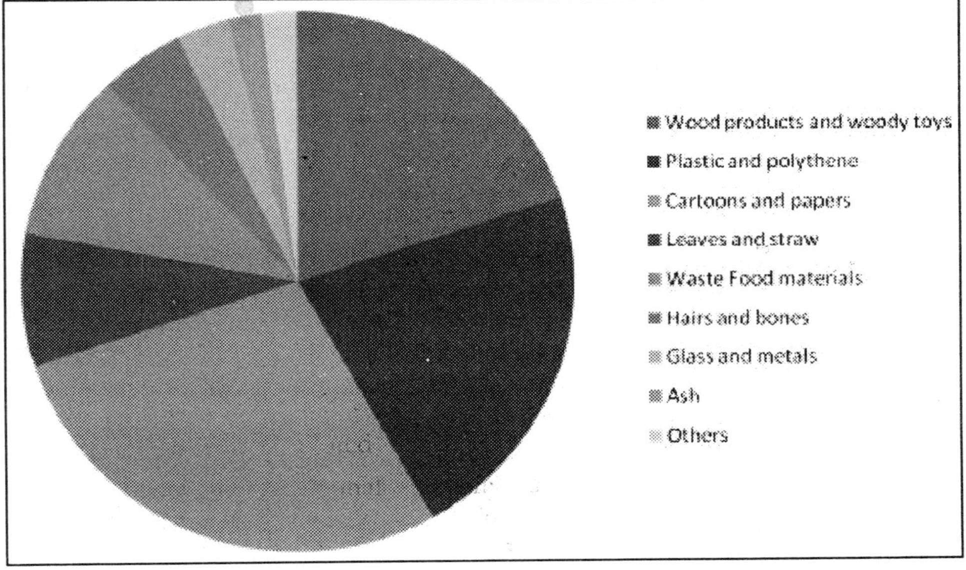

Figure 9.1: Per cent Composition of Solid Waste

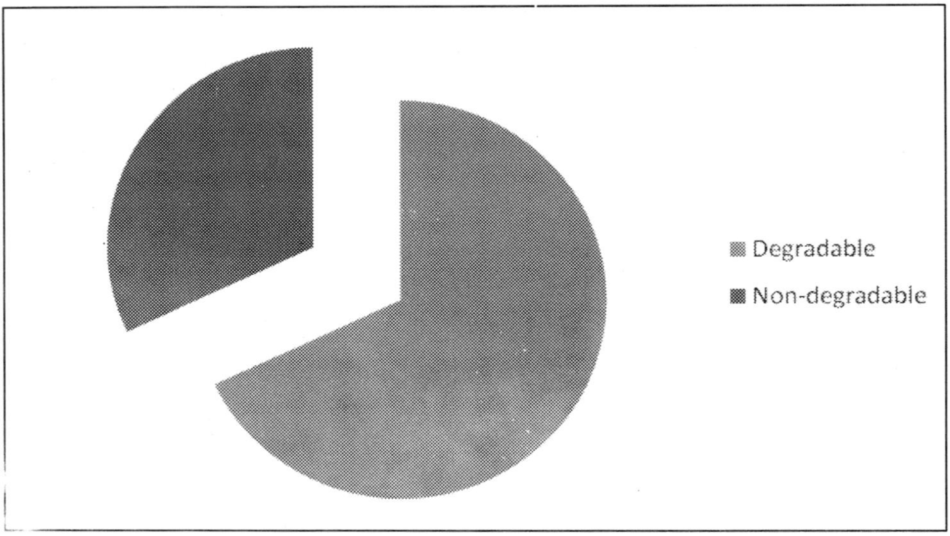

Figure 9.2: Per cent Degradability of Solid Waste

Figure 9.3: A Scene of Mass Bathing in Sahastradhara Hill-stream

Besides the solid waste, the amount of sewage is increasing day by day due to the increasing number of tourist in Sahastradhara region. The major source of drinking water is the Sahastradhara stream and the sewage ultimately going dumped into the same water body into downstream.

Figure 9.4A-F: Few Anthropogenic Activities Near Sahastradhara Hill-stream

9.5 Traffic Volume

The study is a fast developing tourist place near Dehradun. A large number of tourists are visited every year. And this number is going increase every year. Tourist generally used the bus service, but sometimes, they prefer their vehicle for their comfortableness. So, the numbers of vehicle are increasing day by day.

Vehicle plays an important role in this fast going era, so that every person uses the vehicle and contributes to traffic volume density. Expensive and luxury vehicles are the mark of prestigious in the fashionable time. So, few persons are using vehicle only for the purpose.

Vehicle volume is season dependable. A study was conducted for the evaluation of traffic load in dun valley during the day times and nighttime in winter, summer and rainy seasons. A two days based survey was carried out for the assessment of traffic volume density in Sahastradhara Valley. Season-wise data is given for all type of vehicles:

Table 9.3: Traffic Volume Density in Daytime (6.00AM to 6.00 PM)

Sl.No.	*Vehicle Type*	*Winter*	*Summer*	*Rainy*
1.	Trucks and tankers	10	15	8
2.	Buses	10	12	9
3.	Tractors and trailers	8	11	6
4.	JCBs and Earth Moving	5	6	2
5.	Jeeps and Sumo type	10	17	4
6.	Three wheeler	6	11	3
7.	Bikes and scooter	15	23	5
8.	Bicycle	4	7	2

Table 9.4: Traffic Volume Density in Nighttime (6.00PM to 6.00 AM)

Sl.No.	*Vehicle Type*	*Winter*	*Summer*	*Rainy*
1.	Trucks and tankers	1	3	0
2.	Buses	0	1	0
3.	Tractors and trailers	0	2	0
4.	JCBs and Earth Moving	0	1	2
5.	Jeeps and Sumo type	1	2	0
6.	Three wheeler	0	1	0
7.	Bikes and scooter	1	6	0
8.	Bicycle	0	1	0

9.6 Control and Conservation

A huge quantity of solid waste is generated at any tourist place and the study area is not an exceptional case. It has been noticed and examined that the entire

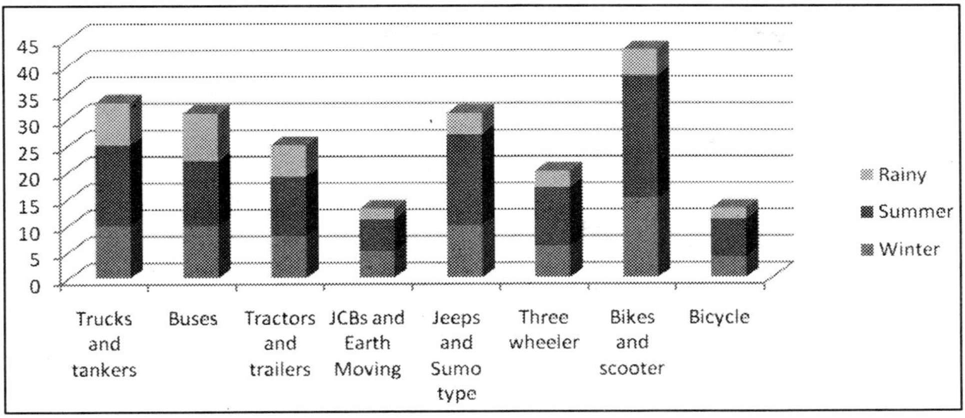

Figure 9.5: Traffic Density in Day Hours

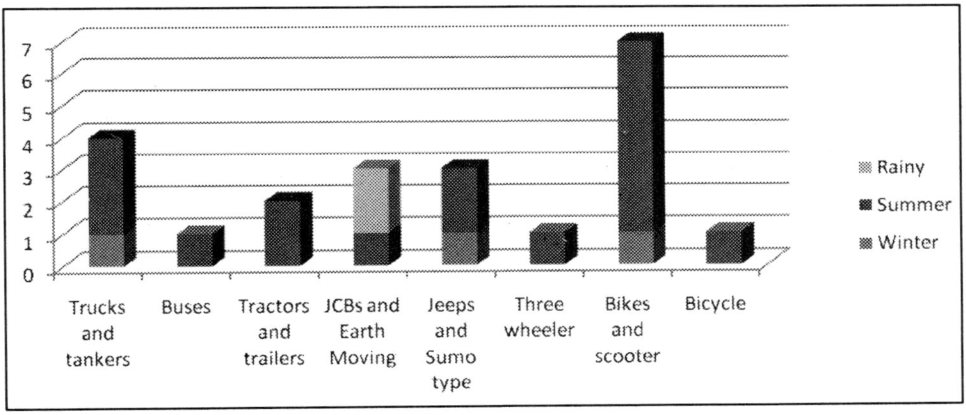

Figure 9.6: Traffic Density in Night Hours

quantity of solid waste generated at Sahastradhara is being dumped near the stream in a very rough manner. This dumped solid waste can cause various environment health hazards. So, the disposal practises for the solid waste should be proper and managed. Even the solid waste should be dumped anywhere very far from the stream basin. It should be keep in the mind that the leaching of pollutants from solid waste dumping site can also impacts on stream environment.

Awareness for environment protection should be increased during the time of tourist activities especially at hot tourist spots. Strict rule and regulations should be adopted for all individuals. Anthropogenic activities, which accelerated the rate of pollution or environmental degradation, should be avoided or banned or appropriate alternate should be adopted in those cases.

9.7 Recommendation

For the protection and conservation of natural habitat and vicinity of Sahastradhara hill-stream tourist place, everyone has to adopt and follow the regulations regarding pollution control. The contribution should be made at every level. Few important recommendations are given below:

- ✰ Don't dump biodegradable as well as non-degradable materials in stream
- ✰ Don't drain community sewage and other liquid waste of hotel shops etc directly in to stream
- ✰ Pollution load should be minimized at personal level too
- ✰ Ban on huge hotel buildings in close vicinity of natural water bodies
- ✰ The water quality should be monitor regularly and emphasized to maintain the better survival of all biotic communities in term of biological productivity
- ✰ Nutrients dynamics and heavy and toxic metal levels should be assessed after a specific period of time.
- ✰ Any disturbance must be prohibited in natural habitat of stream especially regarding bottom structure, biodiversity and macrophytes
- ✰ Different varieties of colored and game fish should be kept for recreation of tourists in the stretch dams of Sahastradhara main spot
- ✰ The endemic fish diversity should be conserved 'in situ' for enhancement the fish angling practices on the upper and lower stretches of Sahastradhara stream
- ✰ Sahastradhara hill-stream should be promoted as 'Pollution free aquatic zone' by Govt. of Uttarakhand state and necessary initiative steps regarding conservation and management of natural springs should be taken on the basis of holistic sustainable aquatic resource management.
- ✰ Ecotourism should be based on sustainable resource utilization and management practices.
- ✰ The awareness programme about "How to conserve and use the natural water bodies for recreations" should be promoted on the spot by Youth conservator groups.
- ✰ *Tal Mitra* or *Sarovar Mitra* should be appointed by the Govt. of Uttarakhand for the protection and conservation of water bodies in different regions.
- ✰ Tourist's numbers should be increased in sustainable way with minimum pollution potential.

9.8 Conclusion

The present chapter described the various pollution sources especially due to the tourist activities and other anthropogenic activities and their effects on the environment in a tourist place. Quantity of solid waste generated at tourist places, traffic density in different seasons, the degradation of organic matter and many other things can contribute to environment pollution significantly. Water quality alterations at various stations of Sahastradhara stream have already been discussed in previous section. These activities can alter the physico-chemical parameters, planktonic and benthic diversity, heavy metal concentration and many other basic characteristics of a natural hill-stream. The diversity of river water may also change their population size, distribution, density and behaviour.

The rate of pollution due to the tourist's activities or other anthropogenic activities should be minimized in a integrated and sustainable ways. Currently, Tourism is one of the hottest industries in India also. On the other hand, environment is also important. So, the pollution abatement should be on top preferences and all the steps should be of eco-friendly manners. Tourisms should be promoted in all regions, but environment conservation is the first priority and above the all aspects.

Both the things can be managed easily with the help of strict regulations and appropriate management practices in the tourisms industry and that is the only way for sustainable development.

Chapter 10
Rivers and Interlinking

Contents

10.1 Rivers of India

A river basin is made up of a mosaic of contrasting and often competing biophysical, economic and social circumstances, and community interests. Only along limited reaches of a river basin is it possible to identify much commonality of attitude or purpose by the inhabitants. More typically, the segmentation of natural and human components of the basin is reflected in conflicting attitudes towards the single unifying element present – the river system.

Rivers take their chemistry from the rocks and dirt beneath them as well as for a great distance around them. The area that a stream drains is called its drainage basin, or catchment area. We also often call it the river's watershed. Water flows downhill (unless it evaporates, freezes, or is taken up by plants). So when it falls as rain, melts from snow or ice, or bubbles up from beneath the earth, it will either flow one direction or another, and always downhill. If you were to stand by a stream at the bottom of a valley, you might look up and see hills all around you. All the land you see that slopes downward toward your river is part of the river's drainage basin.

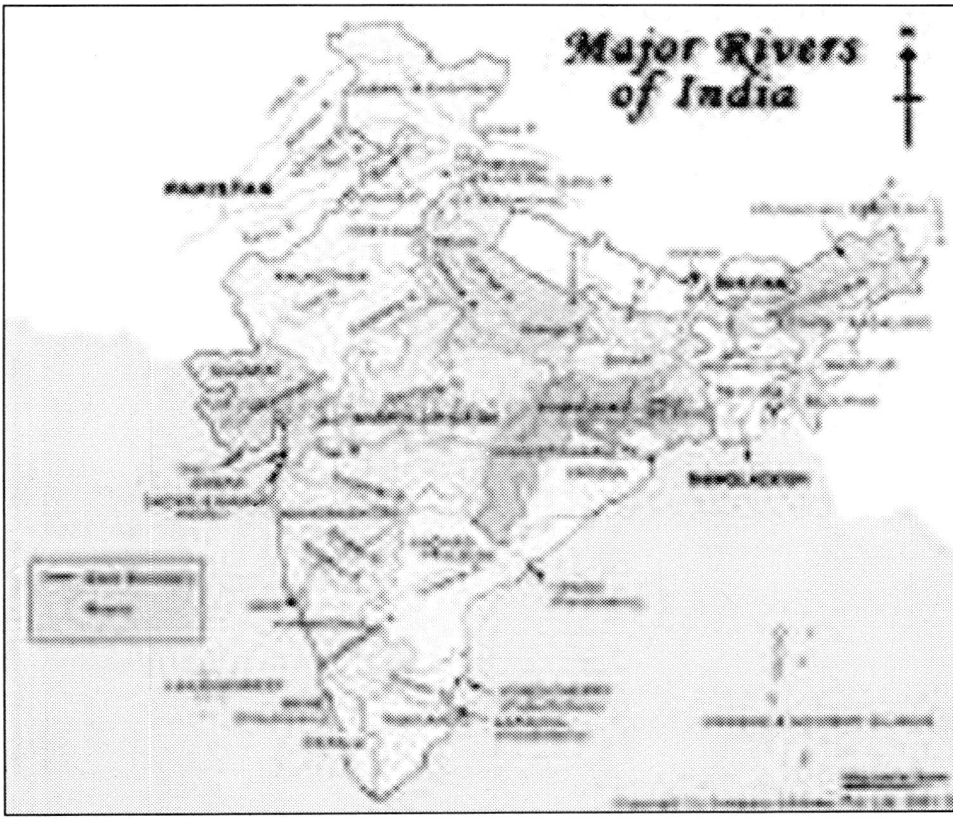

Figure 10.1.1: Major Rivers of India
(*Source*: image.google.com)

Some drainage basins are so unbelievably huge that you can't even see where their downhill flows begin.

Those living upstream tend to value the riverine environment primarily for its aesthetic appeal and perhaps its recreational role, rather than its economic function. Further downstream, the value of water for economic purposes becomes paramount to service agricultural, urban and industrial needs. The emphasis is on maximising the quantity of water available, with some level of biophysical degradation acceptable as a trade-off against economic viability and regional development. In the lower reaches of the basin, the riverine environment is degraded further from contaminated effluent, so that aquatic life, wetlands, estuaries, and the coastal zone, are frequently compromised by eutrophication and sedimentation.

10.2 Rivers and Life

In past three decades, various anthropogenic activities and construction of dam or barrages across on many rivers for hydroelectric power generation, irrigation and

Figure 10.2.1: India and Neighbor Countries
(*Source*: image.google.com)

navigation purposes have interfered with the riverine environment, inevitably affecting the water quality and aquatic resources and biodiversity of the concerned rivers. The existing dam or barrages are posing threat to food and feeding habit, spawning biology and fish migration. They are altering the physico-chemical parameters of river water.

As we know our life depends upon water and man needs water for his drinking and other domestic and industrial processes. With the fast increasing in our industrial civilization, the demand for water is increasing tremendously day by day. Although water pollution is an age old problem but in this modern age, the problems like population increase, sewage disposal, industrial waste, radioactive waste etc. have polluted our water resources so much so that about 70% rivers and streams not only in India but of all the countries contain polluted waters (Kudesia, 1992). The industrial effluents and trade waste of pulp and paper, distillery, fertilizer, electroplating, asbestos, silt, alcohol, detergents, steel, tannery, textile, cane sugar, oils, pesticides and herbicides, radioactive wastes etc., play a significant contribution in pollution of river water.

10.3 Himalaya - The Cradle of Rivers

The Himalayas are one of the greatest physical features of the world. In fact it is a part of a chain of mountains beginning in the west with the Pyrenese and the Alps in Europe and extending right upto the eastern frontiers of India and much beyond into Burma. The Himalayas spread along northern borders of India and have a great impact on the geo-physiography, ethnology, history and cultural heritage of India. In this mountain chain that has a profound influence on the climatic and environmental fronts of Indian sub-continents.

The Himalayas represent the youngest mountain range, having been uplifted about 60–70 million years ago. It is also geologically a very complex range, and its origin is not yet clearly understood. The geology of the Himalaya is also very complex and some parts of it are practically a terra incognita due to the ruggedness of the terrain and the hostile conditions of the climate.

The glacier resources in the Himalayas are vast. The glaciers have their usefulness as water resources. The Himalayan glacier ranging approximately in latitude from 27°N to 36°N and longitude 72°E to 96°E, consists in the greatest part of the cryosphere in the law mid latitude, beside the Antarctica and the North Polar Region. Although,

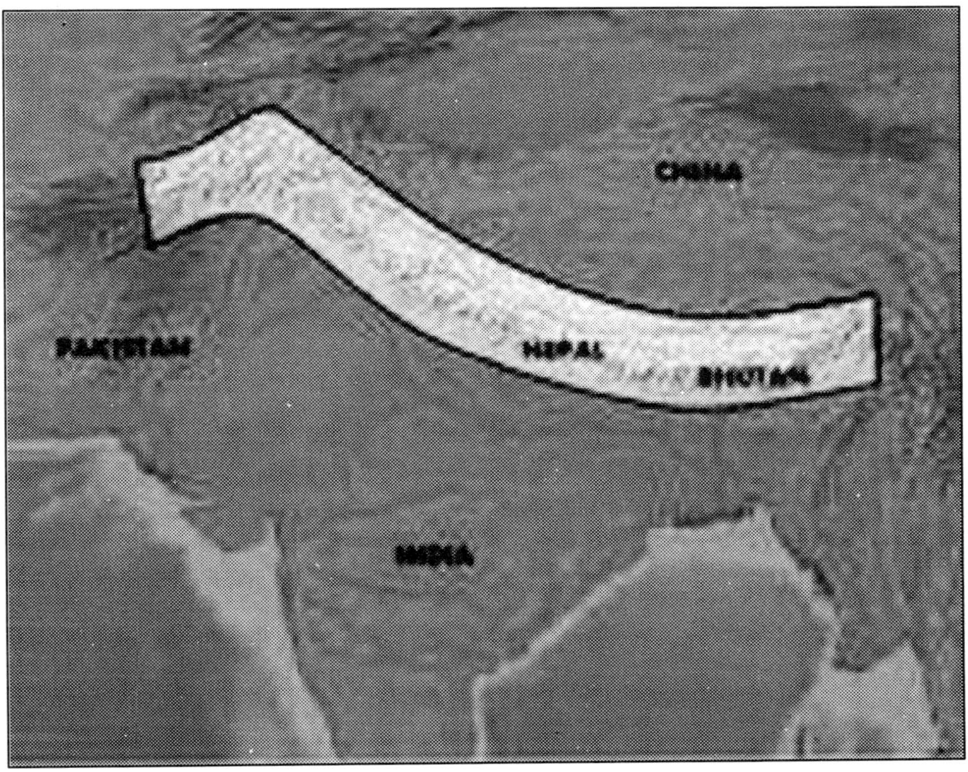

Figure 10.3.1: Map Showing the Himalayan Region
(*Source*: image.google.com)

the Himalayan glacier follows the common properties of the cryosphere, it also takes on significantly the special characteristics as its low-mid latitude position, higher elevation and undergoing the influences of several atmospheric circulation systems. There are 5218 glaciers occurred an area of 38221 sq km, which is 9.04 per cent of the total area of Himalayan zone.

Himalayan glaciers are very important as they are the major factors in controlling the climatic changes in Himalaya and the country. Himalaya can thus be classified into area of:

1. Dominant monsoon precipitation.
2. Equal to sub-euqal monsoon and winter precipitation, and
3. Dominant winter precipitation.

Figure 10.3.2: A View of Himalayan Region
(*Source*: image.google.com)

The region of Mount Everest, Nepal is an example of the first, the area in Ganga basin (equal), in the Beas basin and in parts of the Chenab basin (sub equal) are of the second type, and the regions of Laddakh, Spiti and parts of Tibet are of the third type. Glaciers are also a major source of our water resources as they are feeding nineteen major rivers of north India. Snow melt and glacier melt contribute significantly to the spring season flows in the Himalayan Rivers.

In the mountainous zone of Shiwalik Himalayas a number of tributaries having their sources at high altitudes, join the river Alaknanda *viz.* Dhauli Ganga at

Vishnuprayag, Birahi Ganga between Vishnuprayag and Nandprayag, Nandakini at Nandprayag, Pinder at Karnprayag and Mandakini at Rudraprayag, finally it joins river Bhagirathi at Devprayag. Ganga, the mighty Indian river originates from the snow-clad peaks of Himalayas, is the life line of millions of Indians–From its source to its entry into the Bay of Bengal, it travels a distance of around 2525 km. The river with its well knit tributaries drains the Ganga basin, which encompasses an area of more than a million square kilometers (1060,000 sq km) spread over four countries India, Nepal, Bangladesh and China (Chaphekar and Mhatre, 1983).

10.4 Uttarakhand Scenerio

The Uttarakhand carved out from thirteen northern districts of the Uttar Pradesh was constituted as 27th state of the Indian Republic on) November 9, 2000. The state is spread over a geographical area of 53,204 square kilometres with more than 80 per cent in mountainous region in the central Himalayas. The altitudinal and geographical variation, mountain slopes, expansion of river valleys and vegetation covers results in varying climates in different parts of Uttarakhand State. It is hot an humid (tropical) in the river valleys below 600 msl. At higher elevations, the climate becomes subtropical upto 1200 msl. It has cool temperature upto 1800 msl and cold temperature upto 2500 msl and at still higher altitudes the climate is extremely cold. It receives the highest rainfall in the range from 245 to 260 cm and records low temperature in majority of the regions. But the state is inadequately developed, less accessible thinly populated, nearly urbanized and physically isolated. The state has two main distinct division *viz.*, Garhwal and Kumaon.

Geographically, Garhwal has almost central position in the long Himalayan sweep, it is the most important part of lesser Himalaya, which lies between the

Figure 10.4.1: Major Segments of Uttarakhand
(*Source*: image.google.com)

latitudes 29° 26′ to 31° 28′ N and longtitude 77° 49′ to 80° 06′ E. It has an area of about 30090 sq km, spreading 220 km in east-west and 235km in north-south. On the whole region constitutes about 7.01 per cent of the entire Indian Himalaya. The Tons river separates it from Himachal Pradesh in the west and the district boundaries of Nainital, Almora and Pithoragarh separate it from Kumaon division in the east, starting from the foothills in the south, the region extends upto snow-clad peaks, making the Indo–Tibetan boundary in the north.

The climate of the Garhwal Himalaya very much diversified due to the fact of variation in altitude and physical features. On the southern borders of Garhwal Himalaya 80 to 90 per cent of yearly precipitation falls as rain during the period July to September. While in case of passing towards north, a large portion of annual precipitation fall during winter in the from of snow. The winterly precipitation in the higher ranges of Himalaya might be important in farming the glaciers, out of which the most important rivers originate. These rivers are the most important and common wealth of Uttarakhand state in Himalayan zone.

Nature has endowed Garhwal region with wealth of flora, fauna and large area of water resources. The aquatic resources are present in the form of rivers, serpentine rivulets, streams, beautiful lakes and reservoirs. Some of the most important river systems of northern India owe their origin to the glaciers of the Garhwal Himalaya. The fluvial ecosystem of this region embodies the snow-fed rivers and streams notably Alaknanda, Bhagirathi, Yamuna, Bhilangana, Jar Ganga, Asi Ganga, Mandakini, Nandakini, Pinder etc.; large number of spring fed tributaries and thousands of rivulets, which finally pour into major rivers at various sites. Besides, Garhwal hills are also beautifully dotted with a number of natural ice-cold lakes and small ponds. The nature has gifted a varies and colourfull aquatic flora and fauna in all these water bodies.

In the Garhwal Himalayan region, many big and small hydroelectric Power plants are established for power generation. These power plants are beneficial as well as harmful in many ways for the fragile environment of Himalayan region. Diminishing fossil fuel resources and looming water shortages are focusing alternation on the potential for multi-purpose usage of the national surface, water resources. As the government plans to undertake a large number of runoff the river schemes and storage dams in the near future, it becomes highly necessary that the environmental, social and economic impacts of such project are assessed and highlighted, so the inferences could be drawn for our on-going and future projects.

The Ganga has by far the largest river basin in India (15th in Asia and 29th in World) draining as much as 861404 sq km within the country, covering more than a quarter (26.2 per cent) of Idia's total geographical area. The basin has large surface water and groundwater resources. The annual flow in the basin is 468.7 billion cubic meters, which accounts for 25.2 per cent of India's total water resources. Out of this only 142.6 billion cubic meters is consumed in the basin. Irrigation alone accounts for more than 94 per cent of total basin consumption, whereas domestic and industrial sector use only 2.9 and 2.8 per cent respectively. Due to the much higher intensity of rainfall in the Himalayan region, the streams which join the Ganga from north

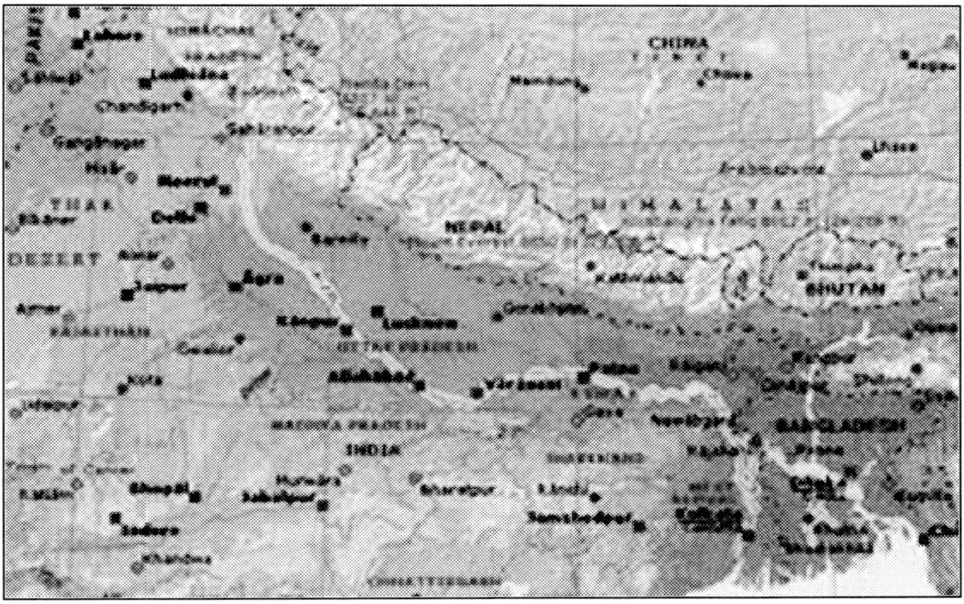

Figure 10.4.2: A Stretch of River Ganga
(*Source*: image.google.com)

contribute more than 60 per cent of the water flowing in the Ganga basin. The peninsular streams contribute the remaining 40 per cent water in southern region.

The main stream of the river Ganga, the Bhagirathi originates from the ice cave of Gaumukh (33° 55′ N, 79° 07′ E) at the snout of Gangotri glacier in the Garhwal portion of western Himalaya, at an elevation of about 4100 meters. The Alaknanda, the sister stream of Bhagirathi rises beyond Mana pass, 8 km away from Badrinath (30° 44 29 N, 79° 29 41 E, 3123 m above msl) joins it at Devprayag. It is below this confluence, the united stream is known as Ganga river. After a run of some 267 km, it emerges into Indo-Gangetic plains at Hardwar (elevations 288 m), where it swells into a mighty system, 750 m wide (approximately).

As a result of many developmental activities and frequently natural ecodisaster, soil erosion and sedimentation in the Ganga basin have become common and serious ecological prepositions. The upland tributaries, Bhagirathi and Alaknanda of Ganga basin are the examples where the coldwater fish habitats, spawning and feeding grounds have been eroded to a great extent by frequent flash floods, land slides and blockade formations. Some important fishes of Ganga basin have shown a sharp depletion in their population.

India is fortunate is possess vast and varied fish germplasm resources distributed widely in vivid aquatic ecosystem. The aqua resources of the country include 2.02 million square kilometer area of Exclusive Economic Zone of surrounding seas, more than 29,000 kilometer length of rivers, about I, 13,000 kilometer of canals, about 1.75 million hectare of existing: water-spread in the form of reservoirs, about one million

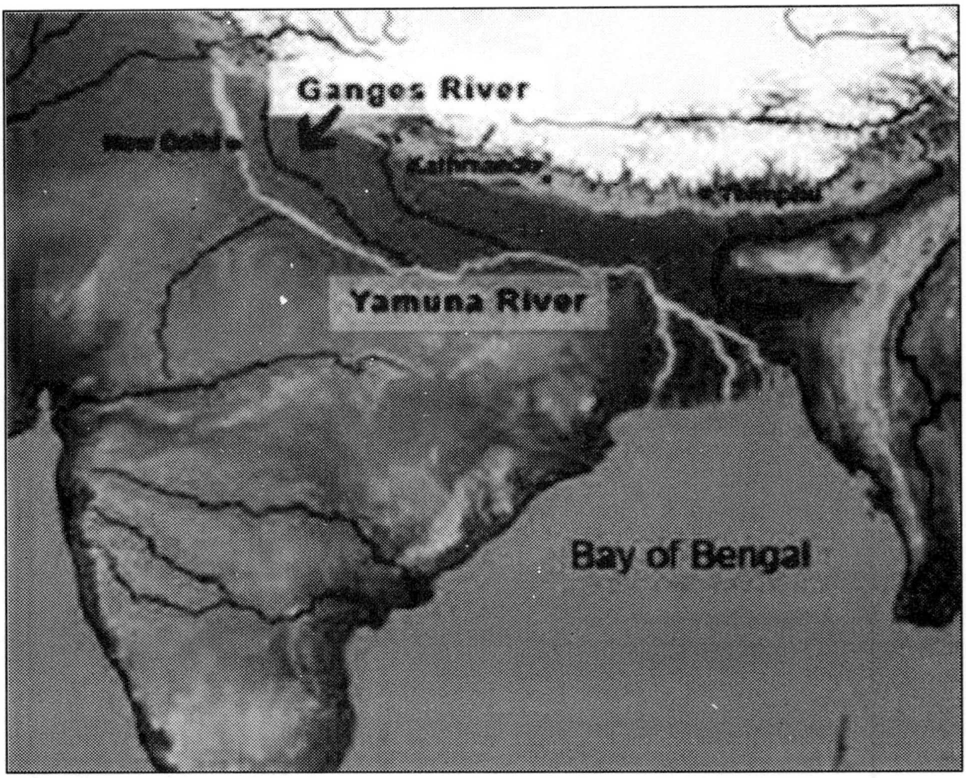

Figure 10.4.3: A Stretch of River Yamuna
(*Source*: image.google.com)

hectare in the form of tanks and ponds and about, 0.6 million hectare of stagnant, derelict, swampy water-spread areas (Jhingran, 1991).

10.5 Interlinking of Rivers

The idea of the 'linking of rivers', dormant for a long time, has acquired new prominence now, particularly in the context of the acute form that the Cauvery dispute took in the course of the year 2002, as well as the drought that afflicted several parts of the country in that year. In response to a public interest writ petition, the Supreme Court has desired that the project for the linking of the rivers of India be accelerated. The Prime Minister has announced the setting up of a task force to consider the modalities of implementing the project, and declared that it would be taken up "on a war footing". The Leader of the Opposition in the Lok Sabha has welcomed this undertaking.

The project has been the subject of much reporting and comment in the media in recent months. It has been presented by the Govt as a major initiative and the definitive answer to the future water problems of the country, and it has been so hailed by some.

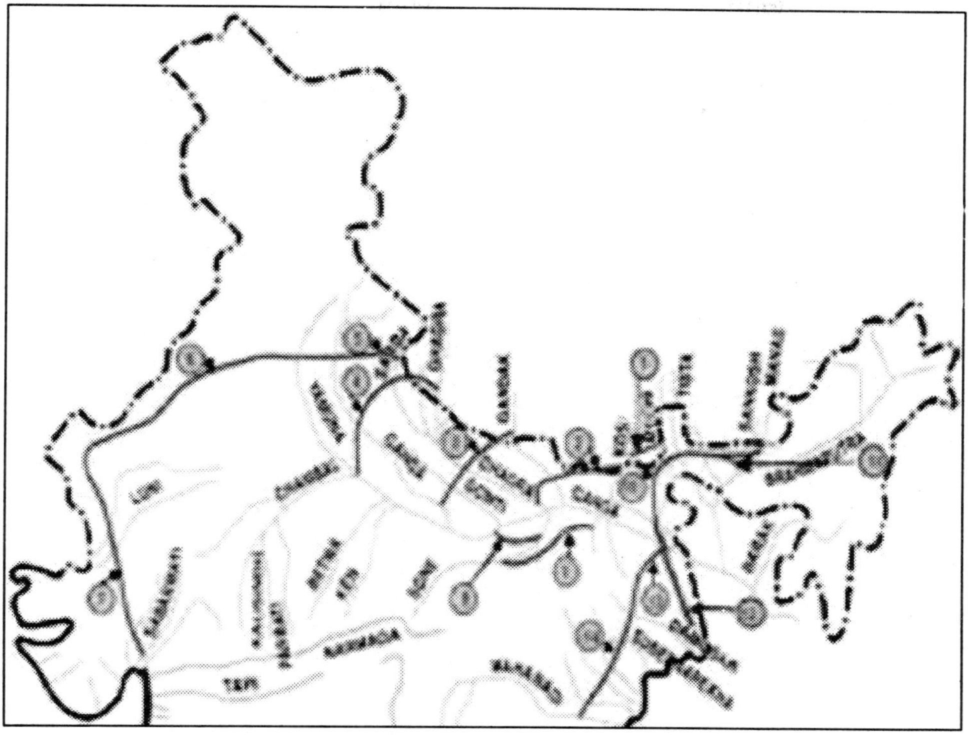

Figure 10.5.1: Planning for Interlinking of Rivers (*Source*: image.google.com)

However, some others have expressed apprehensions. We, the signatories to this memorandum, feel that this decision is fraught with serious consequences, and that the Govt should carefully reconsider it before proceeding further. Without commenting on the Supreme Court's observations in this case, we shall set forth our reasons for urging a reconsideration of the decision by the Govt.

Without going into the history of the idea of the linking of rivers of India, we note that the 'Ganga-Cauvery Link' proposal mooted by Dr. K.L.Rao and the 'Garland Canal' idea put forward by Captain Dinshaw Dastur were examined and found impractical, the former on the grounds of the very large financial and energy costs involved, and the latter because it was technically unsound; and that the proposal now taken up is based on the work that the National Water Development Agency has been doing during the last two decades after its establishment in 1982 in pursuance of the `National Water Perspectives' brought out by the Ministry of Irrigation in 1980. There are two main components in it, namely the Himalayan Rivers component and the Peninsular Rivers component. The Himalayan component envisages a number of links, including some within the Ganga system (Kosi-Ghagra, Gandak-Ganga, Ghagra-Yamuna, Sarda-Yamuna, etc); some between neighbouring rivers in the Brahmaputra system (Manas-Sankosh-Teesta); a couple between those two systems (Teesta-Ganga, and an alternative Brahmaputra-Ganga link); one long link from

Sarda to Sabarmati through the Yamuna and Rajasthan; one from the Ganga to Subernarekha *via* Damodar and then on to Mahanadi; and a few others. The general idea is to transfer waters from `surplus' eastern rivers to `deficit' central, western and southern regions. The Peninsular Rivers component again involves a number of links, of which the most important would be those connecting Mahanadi, Godavari, Krishna, Pennar and Cauvery. The idea is to transfer the surpluses estimated to exist in the Mahanadi and the Godavari to the deficit southern basins (Cauvery, Vaigai). Other links in the Peninsular component would include Ken-Betwa, Parbati-Kalisindh-Chambal, Par-Tapi-Narmada, Damanganga-Pinjal, etc. Another idea is the partial diversion of certain rivers flowing into the Arabian Sea eastwards to link with rivers flowing into the Bay of Bengal (Bedti–Varda, Netravati – Hemavati, Pamba –Achankovil – Vaippar) (Sharma, 2003).

The project appears to have suddenly emerged into prominence. If the Govt had been contemplating a monumental project of this kind, there would have been some indications. There were none. The Ninth Plan made no reference to it. Even the Tenth Plan (which lays special emphasis on water and wishes to be regarded as a 'Water Plan') refers to many important approaches, policies, programmatic initiatives, and so on, but says nothing about any river linking project. The Prime Minister's important Address to the National Water Resources Council (1 April 2002) did not mention it. It seems clear that the Govt were not seriously thinking of any river-linking project. The NWDA's proposals were non-starters for various reasons. The Govt's own initial submissions to the Supreme Court were very cautious and lukewarm. The Supreme Court's direction (if its observations can be so regarded) and the Govt's enthusiastic response to it have changed all that. A project that was not on the anvil has suddenly become the most important undertaking of the Govt. This seems to us to be a bypassing of the planning process (Sharma, 2003).

The average annual precipitation received in the country in the form of rainfall and snow is estimated to be of the order of 4000 km^3. Of this, the average annual run off in the various river basins is of the order of 1869 km^3. The utilisable quantum has been estimated as 690 km^3 for surface water and 432 km^3 for groundwater, making total utilisable as 1122 km^3. Against this, the present utilisation is estimated at about 605 km^3. Balance water could be assumed to be flowing unutilised to the sea mainly in Ganga, Brahmaputra, Mahanadi, Godavari and Narmada (Sharma, 2003).

The mean annual run off in river Ganga in India is estimated to be 501.6 BCM (it became 525 BCM in reply to question no 134 on 181102 in Lok Sabha). Some of the major tributaries of river Ganga are Ramganga, Yamuna, Tons, Gomati, Ghagra, Son, Gandak, Kosi and Mahananda. An assessment of the quantity of Water that can be utilised and the quantity that is being utilised has not been made separately for each tributary of Ganga. For the basin as whole, the quantity of water that can be utilised annually is estimated to be 250 BCM. During the year 2000, the utilisation was estimated to be 150.764 BCM for irrigation 7.9 BCM for domestic use and 5.87 BCM for industrial use (Sharma, 2003).

The Central Water Commission in 1982 had prepared a Feasibility Report on Jogighopa Barrage and Brahmaputra-Ganga Link Canal Project flowing through

Bangladesh by gravity, as the first phase of development/augmentation of the flows of the Ganga during dry season by diversion of Brahmaputra waters to the Ganga. The second phase of the proposal envisages creation of backup storages by construction of two dams on major northern tributaries of the Brahmaputra River, viz., Dihang and Subansiri. The proposal was placed before the Indo-Bangladesh Joint Rivers Commission. However, due to reservations expressed by the Government of the Peoples' Republic of Bangladesh, the proposal was not pursued further.

A familiar phenomenon in human history is the fight to secure natural resources. This essay shall examine how one country, India, is seeking to solve its water problems via the interlinking of all its rivers. River interlinking is a project that is both visionary and controversial in claiming to cure all of the country's water problems. The goal of the project is to interlink all the country's rivers together. This, allegedly, will provide water to all by diverting water from areas that have a 'surplus' to those that don't and "by preventing the unnecessary spillage of water into the sea." Furthermore, such water transfers would also be aimed at flood control during the erratic monsoon season, where floodwaters could simply be diverted away. However, Interlinking at the same time has the potential to become another grand, large-scale project of the sort that creates more problems than it proposes to solve. To assess the risk of this fate, the author provides comparisons with other countries that have undertaken similar projects. These comparisons will show that such large-scale projects typically tend to run into difficulty and usually fail. The goal of this essay is to evaluate why, in spite of these historical precedents against large projects, governments nonetheless tend to follow through with them. Two possible answers come to mind. The first is that governments believe that these are genuinely beneficial projects based on some explicit or implicit calculation of costs and benefits. The second is that government officials are acting self-interestedly, prompted by the influence of special interest groups. The author believes that the answer lies in examining the nature of the benefits and costs involved, and the distribution of these benefits in relation to political power and government self interest. Therefore, in this essay begins with an examination of the cost-benefit procedure, and then examines Interlinking using a qualitative cost-benefit analysis. It follows with possible reasons behind the motivation of Interlinking based on the distribution of costs and benefits and the interests of government leaders, and ends with questioning whether such a project would pass through the legislature regardless (Dev Goel, 2005).

Interlinking of Indian Rivers

India is on the brink of executing a stupendous hydrological phenomenon of inter basin transfer of water, not of one or two river basins as has been done hither to over different parts of the world, but interlinking of all the major rivers *viz.* Ganges and Brahmaputra and connecting them with the southern rivers of Mahanadi, Godavari, Krishna and Kaveri. The scheme, after completion will perhaps be a hydrological marvel of the world.

The project, at an estimated cost of 100 billion US dollars, on completion is expected to contribute significantly to food production, water, energy and transport needs and to mitigate drought and floods in the country.

Many arguments supporting and otherwise of the concept were discussed with scientific basis.

Drinking Water Problems in SAARC Countries

The drinking water problems of SAARC countries were discussed at a special colloquium. The presentations indicate that South Asia remains a region divided-divided between the hopes of the rich and despair of the poor. The rural people in almost all the SAARC countries has still to walk at least 3 – 4 km every day to fetch a pot of drinking water. Contamination from arsenic, fluoride and anthropogenic sources add fuel to fire.

Most of the presentations are focused around a pragmatic approach with peoples' participation on a local scale complemented by proactive government response.

Recommendations

1. While appreciating the existing programmes of water harvesting by government and non-government agencies, it is suggested that a systematic scientific approach should be made mandatory in the selection and the location of the harvesting structures followed by a systematic monitoring of its utility aspects.
2. The persons engaged in watershed management should have an easy access to the data on all aspects of water resources available with government, professional and academic institutions.
3. The basic data may be supplemented with standard field practices, measuring and analysis techniques, models addressed to the local problems.
4. The technocrats have agreed the concept of interlinking of rivers' in principle.

The limitations and impractical propositions raised by the members, as well as the huge costs involved may be subjective for further discussion at governmental level with various sections of people concerned. (www.appliedhydrology.org)

10.6 Demerits

Environmental Impact assessment (EIA) is one of the important methods to determine the negative and positive effects of any proposed project or plan. Many negative effects can be determined in particular region after the EIA study. The impacts on hydrosphere, lithosphere, atmosphere, socio-economic environment and aesthetic values can also determined by EIA study.

The Rs. 4000 crore Ken-Betwa river linking project which includes a dam on the river Ken and a 231 km. canal linking it to the Betwa will submerge significant forest areas including parts of the Panna Tiger Reserve. The feasibility report of the project says that the project will submerge some 100 sq. km. in Panna, Chatarpur and Damoh districts – including 19 villages and about 37.5 sq. km. of forestland as well as 30 km. stretch of the Gangau-Shahpura road in Madhya Pradesh. The agreement for the project was recently signed by the Madhya Pradesh and Uttar Pradesh Chief Ministers, Babulal Gaur and Mulayam Singh Yadav, and Union water resources minister Priya

Ranjan Das Munshi in New Delhi in the presence of Prime Minister Manmohan Singh (PAU, 2005).

It is a common openion of many experts that local weather can be disturbed after adopting the interlinking of rivers. The interlinking project for rivers was stopped immediately just after this statement. Climate change is one of the most important possible negative impacts predicted by the experts.

Chapter 11
Rivers in Vedic Literature

Contents

11.1 General

According to Rigveda, "Water provides a medium for interaction among different compounds water is a great nurture for plants as well as for animals water helps in conducting of energy the form of heat helps in maintaining a soothing climate, water acts as a rejuvenator and medicament it self." The present paper deals with the basic knowledge of water resources conservation and all the aspects of water with special reference to human benefits and utilization on the basis of Vedic literature (ancient history) in India.

In Vedic period (5000 B. C.), many Rishis (spiritually enlightened scientists) studied different aspects of water, and created awareness about the maintenance of water resources and availability of pure water.

इमा आप: प्र भराम्य यक्ष्मा यक्ष्म नाशनीः ।

—अथर्व0 3 / 12 / 9

"Pure water is curable for all diseases, it save us from death. Its precious."

Water is very essential for the survival of all living organism there is a wide variety of beneficial uses of water. Man uses water for many purposes, drinking, irrigation, fisheries, industrial purposes, transportation and waste disposal. The origin of water on the earth is not clear so far. However, the current presumption is that the primordial earth had no oceans and perhaps volatile constituents bound in the earth crust oozing to the surface through volcanoes rock movements and hot springs, condensed to form the ocean and the atmosphere.

In Vedic Literature water is mainly called, as *Apha* we all know that waters is the elixir of life. All living organisms plants and animals are structurally 30-98% water. Besides being a structural component of body water is essential environmentally too. Water is the medium through which nutrients of soil underneath and above on the surface move horizontally as well as vertically water has great power of dissolving most of the inorganic components in mixture form and in the pure elemental and ionic form (Bharti and Malik, 2005).

Water provides a medium for interaction among different compounds water is a great nurture for plants as well as for animals water helps in conducting of energy the form of heat helps in maintaining a soothing climate, water acts as a rejuvenator and medicament it self (Rig 1.23.19).

अपस्वन्तरमृमवमप्सु मेशज्यपायुव प्रयस्ते देवा भवत वाजिनः ।

—ऋग्वेद 1/23/19

There is a main source of water in India by the river by the rivers. In India fourteen major river systems share about 83% of the drainage basis *i.e.* Indian rivers carry about 16,45,000 million cubic meter of water annually (Rao, 1964). The Himalayan rives receive 20-30% of their water from melting of snow and ice during summer and monsoon seasons.

In India all 14 major rivers including Coocum, Ganga, Gomti, Kaveri, Damodar and Mini-Mahi have become polluted. The river Damodar is perhaps the most heavily polluted river. Many parts of river do not seem to have any dissolved oxygen and no wonder that they fail to support the growth of desirable aquatic fauna and flora.

The river Ganga form Haridwar to Calcutta is treated as one unending sewer fit only to carry urban liquid waste, half burnt dead bodies, carrion, pesticides and insecticides. All along Grange's nearly 1,550 miles journey to the sea, some 27 major towns and cities have identified among which hardly a third have any thing resembling a sewage treatment plant of about 312 industrial units dumping their wastes in to the water, only the dozen have effluent treatment facilities. These 27 cities contribute 902 million liters of water to the river each day. The biggest culprits are the cities of Hardwar, Kanpur, Varanasi, Patna and parts of Calcutta form Kanpur alone 270 million liters daily of untreated sewage including 30 x 10^6 liters daily of industrial effluents flow into the river. The water of Ganga affects the health of 250 million of people in northern India.

11.2 Types of Water

The ancient literature described that water can be divided in different types according to their sources. Few examples are given below:

Types of Water in Vedic Literature

(*i*) Water from space:

दिव्याः । ऋ0–4/49/2

(*ii*) Water from rivers-

स्रवन्तिः । ऋ0–4/49/2

(*iii*) Water from groundwater based springs:

स्वसंजा । ऋ0–4/49/2

(*iv*) Water from hill-stream:

हेमवती । अ0–19/2

(*v*) Water from spring:

अस्त्याः । अ0–19/2

(*vi*) Water from river:

सनिष्यदा । अ0–19/2

(*vii*) Water from rain:

वर्ष्याः । अ0–19/2

(*viii*) Water from dugwell:

खनित्रिमाः । अ0–19/2

(*ix*) Water from earthen pot-

कुम्भेभिराभृता । अ0–19/2

11.3 Significance

Neer or Pani or Jala (Water)

Every thing originated in the water and every thing is sustained by water all life on earth depends on water. Water is very essential for the survival of all living organism there is a wide variety of beneficial uses of water. Man uses water for many purposes, drinking, irrigation, fisheries, industrial purposes, transportation and waste disposal. The origin of water on the earth is not clear so far. However, the current presumption is that the primordial earth had no oceans and perhaps volatile constituents bound in the earth crust oozing to the surface through volcanoes rock movements and hot springs, condensed to form the ocean and the atmosphere. This way come into being and eventually become an indispensable component of earth' environment.

आपोहिश्ठा मयोभुवस्ता न अर्जेद्घातन महेरणायं चक्षसे ।

–यजु0 11/50

(जल जीवन का रसायन है, वह ऊर्जा का स्रोत है और जैव विकास व अन्य क्रियाओं का माध्यम भी पृथ्वी पर यही है।)

Water is not only essential for life but predominant inorganic constituent of living mater forming in general nearly three quarters of the weight of living cells. It makes some 5 percent of the body weight of an adult human and can forms as 98 percent of the mass of certain jellyfish. Organisms, which contain relatively small amounts of water, are generally in dormant state or show very slow development; Seeds and certain invertebrates that live in arid environments are examples. On the other high rainfall over a land mass in variably means a large biomass per unit area. It is a common saying that "life is not possible without water". No body can imagine life without water. Water is our basic need even animal and plant can't survive without water. Thus life and water are inseparable faces of the same coin.

इमा आपः प्र भराम्य यक्ष्मा यक्ष्म नाशनीः ।

—अथर्व0 3/12/9

(शुद्ध जल रोग नाशक है। मृत्यु से बचाता है।)

Water is the most Essential commodity for all living creatures. Man needs it for his physiological existence water is the elixir of life It is the source of energy and govern the evaluation and function of the universe on the earth 97.3% of the worlds water *i.e.* 1.4 billion cubic kilometer ocean salty water cannot be used for agriculture domestic and industries purposes. Out of it 2.7% freshwater *i.e.* $73x10^6$ cubic in the form of streams, lakes, wells and tube wells *i.e.* 0.6% 8.5 x $10^{15}m^3$ is groundwater which oceans at the depth of 80 meter below the ground surface (Kataria, 2000).

Chemically water is the mono-oxide of Hydrogen *i.e.* (H.O.H). It freely disassociated into hydrogen and hydroxyl ions. The ionization product (H^+) and (OH^-) is about 10^{-14}. Water is a colourless liquid and possesses a high dielectric constant (81), and there for salts get highly ionized when dissolved in water but not so in the other solvents. Due to this property, water is known as universal solvent present on the earth that is why the natural water contains many salts in dissolved form. On the basis of amount these slats dissolved in the earth only 3% of the total water (approximately 1.4 billion cubic kilometer) is fresh and suitable for human consumption of this, less than 0.01% is associated with rivers and streams (Water Resources 1980).

According to Deming (1975) if the entire ice over of the world would keep flow for 830 years. But now a day due to the various natural and human activities including burning of fossil fuels, natural activities like volcanic eruption, deforestation etc. the earth atmosphere is warming regularly due to the increase in the Co_2 level in the atmosphere.

Modern civilization is dependent on water for irrigation, industry, and domestic needs, shipping and of increasing importance for sanitation and disposal waste. Most of our water bodies such as ponds, lakes, streams and rivers have become polluted and a consequence of increasing industrialization, urbanization and other development activities. Today many of the rivers of the world revives millions of litter of sewage, domestic wastes and industrial and agriculture effluents containing substances varying form simple nutrients to highly toxic substances *viz.* nitrates, selenium, cadmium, mercury, chlorinated hydrocarbons etc. In U.S.A. every major river has become seriously polluted. The great lakes, which furnish the greatest single sources of water to America and Canada, have already been polluted. Massive pollution turned Rhine into a dead river in the heart of Western Europe.

Jalasrota (Water Resources)

These are few types as giving below:

Varsha (Rain)

Rain is the major water resource for earth's total requirements. Besides this, pond, lake, rivers, streams, reservoirs are the other water bodies which provides the water for various purposes. In ancient India, people were aware about the water resources.

Nadi (River)

Rivers are major source of water for various activities in modern India for agriculture, industrial and other purposes. Ganga and Brahmaputra systems are two major river networks of India.

We receive freshwater form the rivers but we also dump our wastes and other things in their water bodies, which has created the problem of water pollution.

नाप्सु मूत्रं पुरीषं वा ष्ठीवनं वा समुत्सृजेत।
अमेध्यलिप्तमन्यद्वा लोहितं वा विषाणु वा।।

—मनु0 156/4

Don't dump the waste into river, never drain urine and other byproducts; otherwise water will be polluted, which may be harmful for living organisms.

The Water of dozens of rivers is rivulets and lakes enhance the rich heritage of this Himalayan State, Among the numerous rivers and streams the Ganga, Yaumna, Alaknanda and Kali are of great religions significance in India the rivers are veritable gifts form mother India it self like her they too are all women and again like her they bear a touch of divinity. River have always been an Inseparable part of Hinduism Ganga to a Hindu is not only the river of life but also at the same time the river of Death for he longs to die beside it or at the very least to have wish ashes after cremation on cash in its water. It is believed that the Holy waters of this rivers washes away the sins and cleanness the soul of lesser mortals same of the facts about the quality of Ganges's water cannot be lightly diseased scientist heaver say they have established how the water will keep for a year in bottles and that cholera grams die in it with in a few hours or even that a tank reputed to be fed from the Ganga has the power of dissolving human bones within there days. Geologists firmly believe that the mineral contents of the water. Also makes the difference a Sanskrit verse that a Hindu recites at the time of taking the dip.

गंगेच यमुने चैंव गोदावरी सरस्वती।
नर्मद सिधुं कावेरी जले अस्मित सनिधम्कुरू।।

—ऋग्वेद (1.23.21)

O Ganga, O Yamuna, and also Godavari and Saraswati and Narmada and Sindhu and Kaveri by your water I purify myself. This hymn to the rivers is also a hymn to the nation.

The Ganga is a holy river of India. Many Indians mainly 'Hindus' worship it like a Goddess. Ganga is known by many names like Bhagarathi Ganga etc. Ganga is one of the four mighty rivers of world. With its tributaries it is largest and very important rivers basin of the country. It is symbol of purity. Alaknanda and Bhagrathi to form the river Ganga. The two parents Strom are snow fed and own their origin to the Himalaya glaciers known as Gomukh. Ganga after traveling a distance of 2525 km falls into Ganga Sagar (West Bengal).

The Ganga joins Ram Ganga at Kannauj and Yamuna at Allahabad. At Rishikesh the Ganga cuts across the Shivalik hills and for the first time enter the plains. Ganga is a holy river and it have a large importance Haridwar is located at the bank of river Ganga. Haridwar has a great Importance for the Ashrams and temples. It is estimated that about 1200 million liters of waste are released in Ganga from about 27 major cities situated at its banks. At Haridwar thousand of pilgrims take bath on every 'Snanparv' like, Bashaki, Sarad purnima, etc. and at the occasion of Kumbh many lacks of pilgrims take bath in the river Ganga.

Kumbha Snaan

The Maha Kumbh Festivals is held once in 12 years at Haridwar, Allahabad, Nasik and Ujjain. There are some fixed days during the period of the Mela for bathing millions of people from all over India assemble at these places of pilgrimage to take advantage of the holy bath. Kumbh is the equivalent of Aquarians, the eleventh sigh in the Zodiac and the Kumbh Mela (Festival) comes every twelth year at a certain combination of Jupiter and the sun Midway between each Maha Kumbh, Purna Kumbh, occurs the Ardha-Kumbh or half Kumbh.

The period during which the sun enters Aries (Mesha) in the zodiac and Jupiter is in Aquarius (Kumbh). The famous MahaKumbh festivals will be observed and celebrated at the scared place of pilgrimages Haridwar, Uttaranchal, India this is a festival which cases of once in 12 year in Haridwar when Jupiter comes to the sign of Aquarius. Tradition has it that drops of the ambrosia of the gods fell in 12 places (8 places in the heaven and 4 places on earth), when it was carried away on the obtaining of the ocean.

According the Kumbh Festivals is held at 4 places in India: at Haridwar at the Junctures of time mentioned above at Prayag (Allahabad) when Jupiter is in Aries (Mesha); at Nasik, where Jupiter is in cancer (Kariatake); and at Ujjain when Jupiter is in Lebra (Tula) Thus in a period of 12 years four Kumbh festivals one held in four different places.

A sacred bath in the holy water of the Ganga at Haridwar at this period is regarded as very auspicious and a great blessing religions leaders, spiritual adepts, yogins, pontiffs and many other persons of mystical and spiritual eminence gather at this time in Haridwar and take their bath in the river Ganga and degrades the quality of its water not only by bathing but also by dumping other things like however ash and garbage so the Ganga water is polluted and that time necessary to check the water quality of Ganga River.

शं नो देवीरभिश्टय आपो भवन्तु पीतये ।

शं योरभी स्रवन्तु नः ।।

—ऋ0 10/9/4

शुद्ध जल हमारे अभीष्ट की प्राप्ति एवं रक्षा के लिये कल्याणकारी हो। जल (प्रदूषण रहित) हम पर सुख समृद्धि की वर्षा करे।

Now it is important that we protect the quality and neutrality of Ganga water, now the time to come to devote more and more time and mind to study the various facts of this pollution.

Sanrakshana (Conservation)

India is a rich country in natural resources. One has to realize the need and importance of water conservation. Conservation and management of water resources was advocated even in ancient times when there was not much pressure on this resource. This is evident from this verse as quoted from the Atharva Veda:

आपो यद् वस्तपस्तेन तं प्रतितपत यो।

स्मान द्वेष्टि यं वयं द्विष्मः ।।

—अथर्व0 2/23/1

i.e. water of river, well, pond etc, if used and managed efficiently will reduced the intensity of drought and water scarcity. Some such strategies of water conservation/ management are described in his pamphlet. Water is used in everything people do; for irrigation, for industry, for power generation, for navigation, drinking, cooling, waste disposal and recreation. The demand for water is continually growing globally at an accelerated pace. The total quantum for water available on the average may be enough to meet all our demands put together. But its availability is highly irregular. It is not available in places where we want it, at times when we want it and in which we want it – hence the need for conservation.

Now it is important that we protect the quality and neutrality of water, now the time to come to devote more and more time and mind to study the various facts of pollution.

According to Rigveda and Yajurveda water can be purified by water purifying air (dissolved oxygen) or any other gas, Sunrays or fire (temperature) and ions.

सवितुर्वः प्रसव उत्पुनाम्यच्छिद्रेण पवित्रेण सूर्यस्य रश्मिभिः ।

—यजु0 01/12

Vedas have the basic principle of modern sciences, including the methods for water purification. According to natural methods passing of sunrays through water purifies it (radiation disinfections in modern science). Kusha grass also purifies the water.

Conservation is defined as preservation against loss of waste. Technically conservation of water implies the same meaning in a much wider perspective. Briefly stated it means putting the water resources of the country for the best beneficial use with all the technologies at our command. In other words, surface water running down to sea should be stored to the maximum extant, evaporation and other losses minimized and benefits spread with the sole criteria of maximum benefit to maximum number having due regard to the properties like drinking, irrigation, industrial use, navigation etc.

Water conservation basically aims at matching demand and supply. The strategies for water conservation may be either demand oriented or supply oriented. The strategies may vary depending upon the field of water use domestic, irrigation or industrial. Some of the supply oriented strategies such as creation of storage; long distance transfer and control of water loss through evaporation are generally common to all the fields of water use, whereas the others may be applicable only to specific field.

Storage of water by construction of various water resources projects has been one of the measures of water conservation. A reference from Vrahat Sanhita (550 A.D.) as quoted below describes utility of ponds for effective storage of water.

पाली प्रागणरायताम्बु सुचिरं धत्ते न याम्योन्तरा।

क्ल्लौलैख दारमेति मरूता सा प्रयषः प्रेरितैः।।

तां चेदिच्छति सारदारूमिरपा सम्पातमावांरयेत,

पाशाणदिभिरेव वा प्रतिचयं क्षुश्णं द्विपा वादिभि।

वृहत संहिता– 54: 118

i.e. a pond laid East to West remains water for a long time while one from North to South is spoilt invariably by the waves raised by the winds. To render it stable the walls have to be lined with timber or with stone and the adjoining soil strengthened by stamping and tramping of elephants, horses etc.

ककुभवगम्रप्लक्ष्कदम्बैः सनिचुलजम्बूवेतसनीपेः।

कुरबकतालाशोकमधूकैर्वकुलविमिश्रेश्चावष्ततीराम।।

वृहत संहिता– 54: 119

i.e. the bank must be shaded by Kakubha, Veta, Amra, Plaksa, Kadamba, Nicula, Jambu, Vetasa, Nipa, Kuravaka, Tala, Ashoka, Madhuka and Bakula Trees.

The scope of storage varies from region to region depending upon water availability, topographic conditions etc. Besides, cost of construction has gone fairly high. On an average the cost of creating irrigation potential by building dams and canals is as much as Rs. 40000 to Rs. 50000 per hectare. The environmental impacts of such storage also need to be examined for developing an environmentally balanced strategy.

Use of groundwater has been practiced from ancient times. Following verses as quoted from Vrahat Sanhita (550 A.D.) will make this aspect clear:

एकेव बर्धेन रसेन चाम्भ्श्च्युतं नमस्तों वसुघाविशेषात।

नानारसत्वं वहुवर्षतां च गने परीक्ष्या क्षितितुल्यमेव।।

वृहत संहिता– 54: 2

i.e. water, which falls from the sky originally has the same colour and same taste, but assumes different colour and taste after coming down on the surface of earth and after percolation.

चिन्हमपि चार्धपुरूषे मन्डूकः पान्डूरोश मृतपीता।

पुत्भेदकश्च तस्मन् प्राषाणो भवति तोयमधः।।

वृहत संहिता– 54: 2

i. e. on digging if we will get yellow frog at a depth of half Purusha, then yellow soil, then rocks, certainly then we will get ample amount of water beneath.

11.4 Vedic Mantras

India has a strong base of science according to our ancient literature. The description of use of water, water resources and conservation of these resources are given in Vedic literature in the form of Mantras. Some of the mantras are given here:

आपो वै रक्षोघ्नीः। तै0 सं0– 3/2/3/12

जालाषमग्रभेषजं। अ0– 6/57/2

(वेदों में जल की महिमा है।)

अप्स्वन्तरमृतमप्सु भेषजम्। ऋ0– 1/23/9

जीवा स्थ। अ0–19/69/1

(जल में अमृत है, यह जीवन है और परम औषध है।)

आप्सु मे सोमो अब्रवीदन्तर्विश्वानि भेषजा। ऋ0–1/23/20

आप पृणीत भेषजम् वरूथं तन्वे मम। ऋ0–1/23/21

(इसमें अनेक औषध शक्ति है, यह शरीर में पोषक तत्व उत्पन्न करके बल को बढाता है।)

मनो मे तर्पयत वांच में तर्पयत। यजु0– 6/31

(यह ज्ञानेन्द्रियों व मानसिक शक्ति को बढाता है।)

तं मा संसृज वर्चसा। ऋ0–1/23/23

विश्वेदेवा यासूर्ज मदन्ति। ऋ0–6/49/4

(जल में अग्नि तत्व है। इससे शरीर में बल उत्पन्न होता है।)

इदं रूदस्य भेषजम्। अ0–6 / 57 / 1

(जल विद्युत से उत्पन्न होता है।)

शतशल्यामपाब्रवत्। अ0–6 / 57 / 1

(जल घाव, चोट व व्रणों को ठीक करता है।)

मा च नः किचनामयत्। अ0–6 / 57 / 3

(जल रोगों से शरीर को बचाता है।)

अयक्ष्मं करणीरपः। अ0–19 / 2 / 5

(जल रोगनाशक होता है।)

शुचयः पावकास्ता आपः देवीरिह मामवन्तु। ऋ0–7 / 49 / 2

(शुद्ध व पवित्र जल शरीर की रक्षा करता है।)

अयक्ष्मा अनमीबा अनागसः। यजु0–4 / 12

(गंदा जल शरीर की रक्षा नही करता।)

Mantras

अप्स्वन्तरमृततप्सु भेषजमपामुत प्रशस्यते। देवा भवत वाजिनः।। ऋ0–1 / 23 / 19

अप्सु मे सोमो अब्रतीदन्तर्विश्वानि भेषजा।

अग्निं च विश्वशभुंवमापश्च विश्वभेषजीः।। ऋ0–1 / 23 / 20

आपः पृणीत भेषजम् वरूथं तन्वे कम। च्योक् च सूर्य द्दशे।। ऋ0–1 / 23 / 21

आपो अद्यान्वचारिषं रसेन समत्रस्महि।

प्यस्वानग्न आगहि तं मा संसृज वर्चसा।। ऋ0–1 / 23 / 23

(जल में अमष्त व औषधी है।)

या आपो दिव्या उत वा स्रवन्ति खनित्रिमा उत वा या स्वयंजाः।

समुद्रार्था या सुचयः पावकास्ता आपो देवीरिह मामवन्तु।। ऋ0–7 / 49 / 2

यासु राजा वरूणो यासु सोमो विश्वे देवा यासूर्ज मदन्ति।

वैश्वानरो या स्वाग्निः प्रविष्टस्ता आपो देवीरिह मामवन्तु।। ऋ0–7 / 49 / 4

(जल हमारी रक्षा करे।)

आपो हिष्ठा मयोभुवस्ता न ऊर्जे दधातन।

महे रणाय चक्षसे।। ऋ0– 10 / 9 / 1

(हे जल! हमारे लिए कल्याणकारी बनो।)

यो वः शिवतमो रसस्तस्य भाजयतेह नः।
उशतीरिव मातरः।। ऋ0– 10/9/2
(जल हमारे लिएएक परमकल्याणकारी रस है।)
ईशाना वार्याणां क्षयन्तीश्चर्षणीनाम्।
अपो याचामि भेषजम्। ऋ0– 10/9/5
मनो मे तपर्यत वाचं मे तपर्यत चक्षुर्मे तपर्यत।
श्रोतं में तपर्यतात्मानं में तपर्यत।। यजु0– 6/31/31
(हे जल! हमारी आत्मा को तष्प्त करो।)
यासां देवा दिवि कष्ण्वन्ति भक्षं या अंतरिक्षे बहुधा भवन्ति।
या अग्निं गर्भं दधिरे सुवर्णास्ता न आपः शं स्योना भवन्तु।। अ0– 1/33
(जल हमारे लिए सुख व कल्याणकारी हो।)
इदमिद् वा उ भेषजमिदं रूदस्य भेषजम्।
येनेसुमेकतेजनां शतशल्यामपव्रवत।। अ0– 6/57/1
जालाषेणभि षिञ्चत जालाषेणोप सिञ्चत।
जालाषमुग्रं भेषजं तेन नो मृड जीव से।। अ0– 6/57/2
(जल जख्मों को ठीक करता है।)
शं त आपो हैमवतीः शमु ते सन्तूत्स्याः।
शं ते शनिष्यदा आपः शमु ते सन्तु वर्ष्याः।। अ0– 19/2/1
शं त आपोधन्वन्याः शं ते सन्त्वनूप्याः।
शं ते खनित्रिमा आपः शं याः कुम्भेभिरामृताः।। अ0– 19/2/2
अनभ्रयः खनमाना विप्रा गम्भीरे अपसः।
भिषग्भ्यो भिषक्तरा आपो अच्छा वदामसि।। अ0– 19/2/3
(जल जीवों के लिए कल्याणकारी है।)
अपामह दिव्यानामपां स्रोतस्यानाम।
अपामह प्रणेजनेऽश्वा भवथ वाजिनः।। अ0– 19/2/4
ता अपः शिवा अपोऽयक्ष्मंकरणीरपः।
यथैव तृप्यते मयस्तास्त आ दत्त भेषजीः।। अ0– 19/2/5
(निरोगता के लिए जल आवश्यक है।)

Chapter 12
National Water Policy

Contents

12.1 General

Land, water and energy are the basic need for any development of the region. Out of this water has become the matter of concern in almost all the countries. The central theme in the "decade of 80" was water, because of the major droughts faced by many countries. This period has paradoxically coincided with the International Decade of drinking water. The rapidity with which the water crisis occupied the center stage of Indian planning warns that water resources should not be taken for granted any more.

Water is not automatically available because the ecological process that gives stability to the water cycle governs its renewability. The seasonal rains in most parts of India, lasting hardly for 90 days, have made the agriculture and social life adapt to seasonability. Frequent droughts have made it necessary to employ various water conservation methods, including traditional ones.

The water logging and subsequent salinity problems which have become common phenomenon in most of the surface irrigation project, the increasing concentration of nitrates, phosphates, fluoride and potash in intensely cultivated areas and major urban areas point out that groundwater management and conservation of groundwater as a precious national resources should be taken up seriously by the planners and by the general public. Otherwise, the unplanned exploitation coupled with contamination and salinity ingress would cause damage to the entire groundwater system. Such damage has already been noticed in certain coastal areas and in parts of the Lakshadweep and Andman-Nicobar Islands in the Arabian Sea and Bay of Bengal Islands respectively.

12.2 Water Demand

India is the wettest country in the world, should consider itself singularly blessed as it is one of the few countries which is self sufficient in water resources. It receives an average yearly rainfall of 1170 mm while central west America which is supposed to be the food bowl of the world, gets a more 200 mm annual rainfall.

It is estimated that in our country about 19 million kiloliters of freshwater is tappable but we utilize only fraction of this amount. It is estimated that by the turn of the 21st century, we will be able to utilize only about 10.9 million kiloliters of water, that is, just a little more than half the amount available. Out of this available supply, 79.59 per cent will be used for irrigation, 13.75 per cent for the production for electric power, 3.2 per cent in industries and 3.47 percent for domestic purposes.

In our country, piped or organized water supply was given a thrust in 1970s and in the beginning three metropolitan cities "Calcutta, Bombay and Madras (now Kolkata, Mumbai, and Chennai) were covered". Still by 1991, about 44 per cent of the population had access to piped water supply. Out of the beneficiaries so covered 71 per cent live in the urban areas and 29 per cent in rural areas. If the current trend continues for another three years, India will suffer an acute drinking water crisis. The present crisis is due to mismanagement in the storage of rainwater. At present India utilizes only about 10 per cent of the available rainfall and, according to some projections at the current rate we will use a maximum of 25 per cent of available annual rainfall in the next 30 years. About one-third of the villages in the country have been declared water deficient, the main reason for within is rapid industrialization. In the last 10 years, the urban population has risen by 46.2 per cent.

Today, India is not the only country which is facing crisis but there are 26 another countries, collectively home of 230 million people, in this category. The lack of water becomes a severe constraint in food production, economic development and protection of natural systems. In many reasons as demand continue to rise and water supply projects get more difficult to built, water budgets are becoming badly imbalanced. Water that is reliably available to the human population is about 9000 cubic kilometers per year or about 1800 cubic meters per person. This may sound like a lot of water but the available resource are neither distributed evenly nor used efficiently. More than 600 million people live in the world arid and semi-arid areas where they face chronic water scarcity. It is a serious problem in these areas because about 47 per cent of rain fed crop land is affected by desertification.

Africa has the largest number of water scare countries *i.e.*. eleven and the Middle East is the world's worst affected region, with nine of its 14 countries facing shortages.

Chine with 2 per cent of the world's people and just 8 per cent of its freshwater faces severe constraints. Water labels beneath Beijing have been dropping one of two meters a year, and a third of its wells have gone dry. Some 100 Chinese cities and town, in the northern and coastal regions, have suffered severe shortage in the last few years. Paris of Mexico, Thailand and the western United States also suffer from a declining water table.

12.3 Need of Policy

Water is a prime natural resource, a basic human need and a precious national asset. Planning and development of water resources must take into account interalia, the national water resource position and financial and material aspects of exploitation and sustenance of water resources under an integrated national prospective.

It has been estimated that out of the total precipitation of around 400 million hectare meters in the country, the surface water availability is about 178 million hectare meters. Out of this, about 50% can be put to beneficial use because of topographical and other constraints. In addition, there is a groundwater potential of about 42 million hectare meters. The availability of water is highly uneven in terms of both space and time. Precipitation is confined to only about three or four months in the year and varies from 10 cm in the western parts of Rajasthan to over 1000 cm at Cherrapunji in Meghalaya. Further, water does not respect state boundaries. Not merely rivers but even underground aquifers often cut across state boundaries. Water as a resource is one and indivisible: rainfall, river waters, surface ponds and lakes and groundwater are all part of one system. Similarly, water is also a part of a large ecological system.

Flood sand droughts affect vast areas of the country, transcending state boundaries. Almost one third of the country is drought-prone. Floods affect an average area of around 9 million hectares per year. According to the National Commission on Floods, the area susceptible to floods is around 40 million hectares. The approach to the management of drought and floods has to be coordinated and guided at the national level. Even the planning and implementation of individual irrigation of multi-purpose projects, though done at the State level, involve a number of aspects and issues such as environmental protection, rehabilitation of project affected people and livestock, public health consequences of water impoundment, dam safety, etc.

On these matters integrated approaches and guidelines are necessary. Moreover certain problems and weaknesses have affected a large number of projects all over the country. There have been substantial time and cost overruns on projects. In some irrigation commands, problems of water-logging and soil salinity have emerged, leading to the degradation of good agriculture land. There are also complex problems of equity and social justice in regard to water distribution. The development and exploitation of the country's groundwater resources also give rise to questions of judicious and scientific resource management and conservation. All these question need to be tackled on the basis of common policies and strategies. The growth process and the expansion of economic activities inevitably lead to increasing demands for water for diverse purposes like domestic, industrial, agricultural, hydro-power, navigational and recreational use.

Domestic and industrial water needs have largely been concentrated in or near the principal cities, but the demand from rural society his expected to increase substantially as the development programme improve economic conditions in the rural areas. The demand for water for hydro and thermal power generation and for other industrial uses is also likely to increase substantially. As a result water which is already a scare resource will become even most scare in future.

The emphasized the need for the utmost efficiency in water utilization and a public awareness of the importance of its conservation. Another important aspect is water quality. Improvements in existing strategies and the innovation of new techniques based on strong research and developmental activities in science and technology will be needed to eliminate the pollution of surface and groundwater resources, to improve water quality and to set up the recycling and re-use of water. Science and technology and training have also important roles to play in water resources development in general.

Water is one of the most crucial elements in developmental planning. The need for a national water policy is thus abundantly clear that water is a source and precious national resource to be planned, developed and conserved on an integrated and environmentally sustainable basis, keeping in view the needs of the states concerned.

12.4 National Water Policy

As it is necessary to plan and develop this prime natural resource carefully under the given national perspectives, the Ministry of Water Resources drafted the National Water Policy in 1987. a brief outline of the chief contents of the policy is as follows:

1. A standard national information system should be established with a network of data banks to collect information about resource's availability and their utilization.
2. Comprehensive and reliable projections of future demands for water for diverse purposes.
3. Maximum utilization of water resources with the help of conservation augmentation and prevention of losses.
4. Establishment of organizational set up for the planned development and management of a river basin as a whole with the help of appropriate legislations.
5. Transfers of surplus water from one river basin in other having shortage of the same.
6. Recycling and reuse of water.
7. Water resources projects should be multipurpose projects with priority for drinking water use, the other uses being irrigation flood control, power generation, navigational, piscicultural, industrial and recreational.
8. Study of environmental socio-economic impacts of the projects during construction and later stages should be an essential component of project planning. The adverse impact if any should be minimized and off-set by adequate compensatory measures.

9. Integrated multi-disciplinary approach with more attention to needs of tribal and scheduled castes or weaker sections of the populations.
10. Appropriate provision should be made for periodic maintenance of the systems and structures created.
11. Continuous surveillance and monitoring of the system created.
12. Periodic reassessment of groundwater resources.
13. Periodic quality monitoring in case of surface water and groundwater.
14. Strict control on groundwater exploitation to ensure social equity and to avoid adverse effects like salinity ingress.
15. Integrated and co-ordinated development of surface and groundwater their conjunctive use.
16. Water rates should be such as to convey the scarcity value of the resources to the users and to foster the motivation for economy in water use.
17. Efforts should be made to involve people in various aspects of management especially distribution of water and collection water rates.
18. Water zoning: Industrial, agricultural and urban development should be planned on the basis of water availability in a particular zone.
19. Drought prone areas should be made less vulnerable to nature's vagaries through:
    (*a*) Soil moisture conservation measures;
    (*b*) Rain water harvesting;
    (*c*) Minimization of evaporation losses; and
    (*d*) Full development of groundwater and surface water potential.
20. Adequate training facilities for personnel engaged/involved in the discipline of water management.

Base on the National Water Policy document, the conference of "State Secretaries connected with groundwater exploitation work and concerned officials from the Government of India", gave recommendations as follows (June 1989, New Delhi):

1. Establishment of block wise and district wise computerized data storage and retrieval system.
2. Periodic assessment of groundwater potential.
3. Continuous monitoring of water quality and mapping of protection zones were considered to be of paramount importance for urban, industrial and agricultural areas with intensive chemical inputs. The States should arrange follow up action in areas identified as potentially hazardous from groundwater pollution angle.
4. The designs of groundwater structures should be on the basis of the recommendations of the District Development Plans prepared by Central Groundwater Board (which is the apex Government organization in the field of groundwater management commonly known as CGWB), so that they could withstand the vagaries of the monsoon.

5. Based on predicted level of the monsoon rainfall, management of the total resource would be worked out to ensure fulfillment of the needs of domestic water supply followed by needs of agricultural production.
6. Area specific methodologies would be developed for artificial recharge of groundwater. These projects would be prioritized and implemented in a phased manner.

12.5 National Water Policy 2002 (MWR-GoI)

National water policy, which is given here, is as given by Ministry of Water Resources, Government of India in 2002. The full version is given below:

Need for a National Water Policy

1.1 Water is a prime natural resource, a basic human need and a precious national asset. Planning, development and management of water resources need to be governed by national perspectives.

1.2 As per the latest assessment (1993), out of the total precipitation, including snowfall, of around 4000 billion cubic metre in the country, the availability from surface water and replenishable groundwater is put at 1869 billion cubic metre. Because of topographical and other constraints, about 60% of this *i.e.* 690 billion cubic metre from surface water and 432 billion cubic metre from groundwater, can be put to beneficial use. Availability of water is highly uneven in both space and time. Precipitation is confined to only about three or four months in a year and varies from 100 mm in the western parts of Rajasthan to over 10000 mm at Cherrapunji in Meghalaya. Rivers and under ground aquifers often cut across state boundaries. Water, as a resource is one and indivisible: rainfall, river waters, surface ponds and lakes and groundwater are all part of one system.

1.3 Water is part of a larger ecological system. Realising the importance and scarcity attached to the freshwater, it has to be treated as an essential environment for sustaining all life forms.

1.4 Water is a scarce and precious national resource to be planned, developed, conserved and managed as such, and on an integrated and environmentally sound basis, keeping in view the socio-economic aspects and needs of the States. It is one of the most crucial elements in developmental planning. As the country has entered the 21st century, efforts to develop, conserve, utilise and manage this important resource in a sustainable manner, have to be guided by the national perspective.

1.5 Floods and droughts affect vast areas of the country, transcending state boundaries. One-sixth area of the country is drought-prone. Out of 40 million hectare of the flood prone area in the country, on an average, floods affect an area of around 7.5 million hectare per year. Approach to management of droughts and floods has to be co-ordinated and guided at the national level.

1.6 Planning and implementation of water resources projects involve a number of socio-economic aspects and issues such as environmental sustainability, appropriate resettlement and rehabilitation of project-affected people and livestock, public health concerns of water impoundment, dam safety etc. Common approaches and guidelines are necessary on these matters. Moreover, certain problems and weaknesses have affected a large number of water resources projects all over the country. There have been substantial time and cost overruns on projects. Problems of water logging and soil salinity have emerged in some irrigation commands, leading to the degradation of agricultural land. Complex issues of equity and social justice in regard to water distribution are required to be addressed. The development, and overexploitation of groundwater resources in certain parts of the country have raised the concern and need for judicious and scientific resource management and conservation. All these concerns need to be addressed on the basis of common policies and strategies.

1.7 Growth process and the expansion of economic activities inevitably lead to increasing demands for water for diverse purposes: domestic, industrial, agricultural, hydro-power, thermal-power, navigation, recreation, etc. So far, the major consumptive use of water has been for irrigation. While the gross irrigation potential is estimated to have increased from 19.5 million hectare at the time of independence to about 95 million hectare by the end of the Year 1999-2000, further development of a substantial order is necessary if the food and fiber needs of our growing population are to be met with. The country's population which is over 1027 million (2001 AD) at present is expected to reach a level of around 1390 million by 2025 AD.

1.8 Production of food grains has increased from around 50 million tonnes in the fifties to about 208 million tonnes in the Year 1999-2000. This will have to be raised to around 350 million tonnes by the year 2025 AD. The drinking water needs of people and livestock have also to be met. Domestic and industrial water needs have largely been concentrated in or near major cities. However, the demand in rural areas is expected to increase sharply as the development programmes improve economic conditions of the rural masses. Demand for water for hydro and thermal power generation and for other industrial uses is also increasing substantially. As a result, water, which is already a scarce resource, will become even scarcer in future. This underscores the need for the utmost efficiency in water utilisation and a public awareness of the importance of its conservation.

1.9 Another important aspect is water quality. Improvements in existing strategies, innovation of new techniques resting on a strong science and technology base are needed to eliminate the pollution of surface and groundwater resources, to improve water quality. Science and technology and training have to play important roles in water resources development and management in general.

1.10 National Water Policy was adopted in September, 1987. Since then, a number of issues and challenges have emerged in the development and management of the water resources. Therefore, the National Water Policy (1987) has been reviewed and updated.

Information System

2.1 A well developed information system, for water related data in its entirety, at the national/state level, is a prime requisite for resource planning. A standardised national information system should be established with a network of data banks and data bases, integrating and strengthening the existing Central and State level agencies and improving the quality of data and the processing capabilities.

2.2 Standards for coding, classification, processing of data and methods/procedures for its collection should be adopted. Advances in information technology must be introduced to create a modern information system promoting free exchange of data among various agencies. Special efforts should be made to develop and continuously upgrade technological capability to collect, process and disseminate reliable data in the desired time frame.

2.3 Apart from the data regarding water availability and actual water use, the system should also include comprehensive and reliable projections of future demands of water for diverse purposes.

Water Resources Planning

3.1 Water resources available to the country should be brought within the category of utilisable resources to the maximum possible extent.

3.2 Non-conventional methods for utilisation of water such as through inter-basin transfers, artificial recharge of groundwater and desalination of brackish or sea water as well as traditional water conservation practices like rainwater harvesting, including roof-top rainwater harvesting, need to be practiced to further increase the utilisable water resources. Promotion of frontier research and development, in a focused manner, for these techniques is necessary.

3.3 Water resources development and management will have to be planned for a hydrological unit such as drainage basin as a whole or for a sub-basin, multi-sectorally, taking into account surface and groundwater for sustainable use incorporating quantity and quality aspects as well as environmental considerations. All individual developmental projects and proposals should be formulated and considered within the framework of such an overall plan keeping in view the existing agreements/awards for a basin or a subbasin so that the best possible combination of options can be selected and sustained.

3.4 Watershed management through extensive soil conservation, catchment-area treatment, preservation of forests and increasing the forest cover and the construction of check-dams should be promoted. Efforts shall be to conserve the water in the catchment.

3.5 Water should be made available to water short areas by transfer from other areas including transfers from one river basin to another, based on a national perspective, after taking into account the requirements of the areas/basins.

Institutional Mechanism

4.1 With a view to give effect to the planning, development and management of the water resources on a hydrological unit basis, along with a multi-sectoral, multi-disciplinary and participatory approach as well as integrating quality, quantity and the environmental aspects, the existing institutions at various levels under the water resources sector will have to be appropriately reoriented/reorganised and even created, wherever necessary. As maintenance of water resource schemes is under non-plan budget, it is generally being neglected. The institutional arrangements should be such that this vital aspect is given importance equal or even more than that of new constructions.

4.2 Appropriate river basin organisations should be established for the planned development and management of a river basin as a whole or sub-basins, wherever necessary. Special multi-disciplinary units should be set up to prepare comprehensive plans taking into account not only the needs of irrigation but also harmonising various other water uses, so that the available water resources are determined and put to optimum use having regard to existing agreements or awards of Tribunals under the relevant laws. The scope and powers of the river basin organisations shall be decided by the basin states themselves.

Water Allocation Priorities

5. In the planning and operation of systems, water allocation priorities should be broadly as follows:

- ☆ Drinking water
- ☆ Irrigation
- ☆ Hydro-power
- ☆ Ecology
- ☆ Agro-industries and non-agricultural industries
- ☆ Navigation and other uses.

However, the priorities could be modified or added if warranted by the area/region specific considerations.

Project Planning

6.1 Water resource development projects should as far as possible be planned and developed as multipurpose projects. Provision for drinking water should be a primary consideration.

6.2 The study of the likely impact of a project during construction and later on human lives, settlements, occupations, socio-economic, environment and other aspects shall form an essential component of project planning.

6.3 In the planning, implementation and operation of a project, the preservation of the quality of environment and the ecological balance should be a primary consideration. The adverse impact on the environment, if any, should be minimised and should be offset by adequate compensatory measures. The project should, nevertheless, be sustainable.

6.4 There should be an integrated and multi-disciplinary approach to the planning, formulation, clearance and implementation of projects, including catchment area treatment and management, environmental and ecological aspects, the rehabilitation of affected people and command area development. The planning of projects in hilly areas should take into account the need to provide assured drinking water, possibilities of hydro-power development and the proper approach to irrigation in such areas, in the context of physical features and constraints of the basin such as steep slopes, rapid run-off and the incidence of soil erosion. The economic evaluation of projects in such areas should also take these factors into account.

6.5 Special efforts should be made to investigate and formulate projects either in, or for the benefit of, areas inhabited by tribal or other specially disadvantaged groups such as socially weak, scheduled castes and scheduled tribes. In other areas also, project planning should pay special attention to the needs of scheduled castes and scheduled tribes and other weaker sections of the society. The economic evaluation of projects benefiting such disadvantaged sections should also take these factors into account.

6.6 The drainage system should form an integral part of any irrigation project right from the planning stage.

6.7 Time and cost overruns and deficient realisation of benefits characterising most water related projects should be overcome by upgrading the quality of project preparation and management. The inadequate funding of projects should be obviated by an optimal allocation of resources on the basis of prioritisation, having regard to the early completion of on-going projects as well as the need to reduce regional imbalances.

6.8 The involvement and participation of beneficiaries and other stakeholders should be encouraged right from the project planning stage itself.

Groundwater Development

7.1 There should be a periodical reassessment of the groundwater potential on a scientific basis, taking into consideration the qualit y of the water available and economic viability of its extraction.

7.2 Exploitation of groundwater resources should be so regulated as not to exceed the recharging possibilities, as also to ensure social equity. The detrimental environmental consequences of overexploitation of groundwater need to be effectively prevented by the Central and State Governments. Groundwater recharge projects should be developed and implemented for improving both the quality and availability of groundwater resource.

7.3 Integrated and coordinated development of surface water and groundwater resources and their conjunctive use, should be envisaged right from the project planning stage and should form an integral part of the project implementation.

7.4 Over exploitation of groundwater should be avoided especially near the coast to prevent ingress of seawater into sweet water aquifers.

Drinking Water

8. Adequate safe drinking water facilities should be provided to the entire population both in urban and in rural areas. Irrigation and multipurpose projects should invariably include a drinking water component, wherever there is no alternative source of drinking water. Drinking water needs of human beings and animals should be the first charge on any available water.

Irrigation

9.1 Irrigation planning either in an individual project or in a basin as a whole should take into account the irrigability of land, cost-effective irrigation options possible from all available sources of water and appropriate irrigation techniques for optimising water use efficiency. Irrigation intensity should be such as to extend the benefits of irrigation to as large a number of farm families as possible, keeping in view the need to maximise production.

9.2 There should be a close integration of water-use and land-use policies.

9.3 Water allocation in an irrigation system should be done with due regard to equity and social justice. Disparities in the availability of water between head-reach and tail-end farms and between large and small farms should be obviated by adoption of a rotational water distribution system and supply of water on a volumetric basis subject to certain ceilings and rational pricing.

9.4 Concerted efforts should be made to ensure that the irrigation potential created is fully utilised. For this purpose, the command area development approach should be adopted in all irrigation projects.

9.5 Irrigation being the largest consumer of freshwater, the aim should be to get optimal productivity per unit of water. Scientific water management, farm practices and sprinkler and drip system of irrigation should be adopted wherever feasible.

9.6 Reclamation of water logged/saline affected land by scientific and cost-effective methods should form a part of command area development programme.

Resettlement and Rehabilitation

10. Optimal use of water resources necessitates construction of storages and the consequent resettlement and rehabilitation of population. A skeletal national policy in this regard needs to be formulated so that the project affected persons share the benefits through proper rehabilitation. States should accordingly evolve their own detailed resettlement and rehabilitation policies for the sector, taking into account the local conditions. Careful planning is necessary to ensure that the construction and rehabilitation activities proceed simultaneously and smoothly.

Financial and Physical Sustainability

11. Besides creating additional water resources facilities for various uses, adequate emphasis needs to be given to the physical and financial sustainability of existing facilities. There is, therefore, a need to ensure that the water charges for various uses should be fixed in such a way that they cover at least the operation and maintenance charges of providing the service initially and a part of the capital costs subsequently. These rates should be linked directly to the quality of service provided. The subsidy on water rates to the disadvantaged and poorer sections of the society should be well targeted and transparent.

Participatory Approach to Water Resources Management

12. Management of the water resources for diverse uses should incorporate a participatory approach; by involving not only the various governmental agencies but also the users and other stakeholders, in an effective and decisive manner, in various aspects of planning, design, development and management of the water resources schemes. Necessary legal and institutional changes should be made at various levels for the purpose, duly ensuring appropr iate role for women. Water Users' Associations and the local bodies such as municipalities and *gram panchayats* should particularly be involved in the operation, maintenance and management of water infrastructures/facilities at appropriate levels progressively, with a view to eventually transfer the management of such facilities to the user groups/local bodies.

Private Sector Participation

13. Private sector participation should be encouraged in planning, development and management of water resources projects for diverse uses, wherever feasible. Private sector participation may help in introducing innovative ideas, generating financial resources and introducing corporate management and improving service efficiency and accountability to users. Depending upon the specific situations, various combinations of private sector participation, in building, owning, operating, leasing and transferring of water resources facilities, may be considered.

Water Quality

14.1 Both surface water and groundwater should be regularly monitored for quality. A phased programme should be undertaken for improvements in water quality.

14.2 Effluents should be treated to acceptable levels and standards before discharging them into natural streams.

14.3 Minimum flow should be ensured in the perennial streams for maintaining ecology and social considerations.

14.4 Principle of 'polluter pays' should be followed in management of polluted water.

14.5 Necessary legislation is to be made for preservation of existing water bodies by preventing encroachment and deterioration of water quality.

Water Zoning

15. Economic development and activities including agricultural, industrial and urban development, should be planned with due regard to the constraints imposed by the configuration of water availability. There should be a water zoning of the country and the economic activities should be guided and regulated in accordance with such zoning.

Conservation of Water

16.1 Efficiency of utilisation in all the diverse uses of water should be optimised and an awareness of water as a scarce resource should be fostered. Conservation consciousness should be promoted through education, regulation, incentives and disincentives.

16.2 The resources should be conserved and the availability augmented by maximising retention, eliminating pollution and minimising losses. For this, measures like selective linings in the conveyance system, modernisation and rehabilitation of existing systems including tanks, recycling and re-use of treated effluents and adoption of traditional techniques like mulching or pitcher irrigation and new techniques like drip and sprinkler may be promoted, wherever feasible.

Flood Control and Management

17.1 There should be a master plan for flood control and management for each flood prone basin.

17.2 Adequate flood-cushion should be provided in water storage projects, wherever feasible, to facilitate better flood management. In highly flood prone areas, flood control should be given overriding consideration in reservoir regulation policy even at the cost of sacrificing some irrigation or power benefits.

17.3 While physical flood protection works like embankments and dykes will continue to be necessary, increased emphasis should be laid on non-structural measures such as flood forecasting and warning, flood plain zoning and flood proofing for the minimisation of losses and to reduce the recurring expenditure on flood relief.

17.4 There should be strict regulation of settlements and economic activity in the flood plain zones along with flood proofing, to minimise the loss of life and property on account of floods.

17.5 The flood forecasting activities should be modernised, value added and extended to other uncovered areas. Inflow forecasting to reservoirs should be instituted for their effective regulation.

Land Erosion by Sea or River

18.1 The erosion of land, whether by the sea in coastal areas or by river waters inland, should be minimised by suitable cost-effective measures. The States and Union Territories should also undertake all requisite steps to ensure that indiscriminate occupation and exploitation of coastal strips of land are discouraged and that the location of economic activities in areas adjacent to the sea is regulated.

18.2 Each coastal State should prepare a comprehensive coastal land management plan, keeping in view the environmental and ecological impacts, and regulate the developmental activities accordingly.

Drought-prone Area Development

19.1 Drought-prone areas should be made less vulnerable to drought-associated problems through soil moisture conservation measures, water harvesting practices, minimisation of evaporation losses, development of the groundwater potential including recharging and the transfer of surface water from surplus areas where feasible and appropriate. Pastures, forestry or other modes of development which are relatively less water demanding should be encouraged. In planning water resource development projects, the needs of drought-prone areas should be given priority.

19.2 Relief works undertaken for providing employment to drought-stricken population should preferably be for drought proofing.

Monitoring of Projects

20.1 A close monitoring of projects to identify bottlenecks and to adopt timely measures to obviate time and cost overrun should form part of project planning and execution.

20.2 There should be a system to monitor and evaluate the performance and socio-economic impact of the project.

Water Sharing/Distribution amongst the States

21.1 The water sharing/distribution amongst the states should be guided by a national perspective with due regard to water resources availability and needs within the river basin. Necessary guidelines, including for water short states even outside the basin, need to be evolved for facilitating future agreements amongst the basin states.

21.2 The Inter-State Water Disputes Act of 1956 may be suitably reviewed and amended for timely adjudication of water disputes referred to the Tribunal.

Performance Improvement

22. There is an urgent need of paradigm shift in the emphasis in the management of water resources sector. From the present emphasis on the creation and expansion of water resources infrastructures for diverse uses, there is now a need to give greater emphasis on the improvement of the performance of the existing water resources facilities. Therefore, allocation of funds under the water resources sector should be re-prioritised to ensure that the needs for development as well as operation and maintenance of the facilities are met.

Maintenance and Modernisation

23.1 Structures and systems created through massive investments should be properly maintained in good health. Appropriate annual provisions should be made for this purpose in the budgets.

23.2 There should be a regular monitoring of structures and systems and necessary rehabilitation and modernisation programmes should be undertaken.

23.3 Formation of Water Users' Association with authority and responsibility should be encouraged to facilitate the management including maintenance of irrigation system in a time bound manner.

Safety of Structures

24. There should be proper organisational arrangements at the national and state levels for ensuring the safety of storage dams and other water-related structures consisting of specialists in investigation, design, construction, hydrology, geology, etc. A dam safety legislation may be enacted to ensure proper inspection, maintenance and surveillance of existing dams and also to ensure proper planning, investigation, design and construction for safety of new dams. The Guidelines on the subject should be periodically updated and reformulated. There should be a system of continuous surveillance and regular visits by experts.

Science and Technology

25. For effective and economical management of our water resources, the frontiers of knowledge need to be pushed forward in several directions by intensifying research efforts in various areas, including the following:

- ☆ Hydrometeorology
- ☆ Snow and lake hydrology

- Surface and groundwater hydrology
- River morphology and hydraulics
- Assessment of water resources
- Water harvesting and groundwater recharge
- Water quality
- Water conservation
- Evaporation and seepage losses
- Recycling and re-use
- Better water management practices and improvements in operational technology
- Crops and cropping systems
- Soils and material research
- New construction materials and technology (with particular reference to roller compacted concrete, fiber reinforced concrete, new methodologies in tunneling technologies, instrumentation, advanced numerical analysis in structures and back analysis)
- Seismology and seismic design of structures;
- The safety and longevity of water-related structures
- Economical designs for water resource projects
- Risk analysis and disaster management
- Use of remote sensing techniques in development and management
- Use of static groundwater resource as a crisis management measure
- Sedimentation of reservoirs
- Use of sea water resources
- Prevention of salinity ingress
- Prevention of water logging and soil salinity
- Reclamation of water logged and saline lands
- Environmental impact
- Regional equity.

Training

26. A perspective plan for standardised training should be an integral part of water resource development. It should cover training in information systems, sectoral planning, project planning and formulation, project management, operation of projects and their physical structures and systems and the management of the water distribution systems. The training should extend to all the categories of personnel involved in these activities as also the farmers.

Conclusion

27. In view of the vital importance of water for human and animal life, for maintaining ecological balance and for economic and developmental activities of all kinds, and considering its increasing scarcity, the planning and management of this resource and its optimal, economical and equitable use has become a matter of the utmost urgency. Concerns of the community need to be taken into account for water resources development and management. The success of the National Water Policy will depend entirely on evolving and maintaining a national consensus and commitment to its underlying principles and objectives. To achieve the desired objectives, State Water Policy backed with an operational action plan shall be formulated in a time bound manner say in two years. National Water Policy may be revised periodically as and when need arises.

Chapter 13

Water Quality Index and Standards

Contents

13.1 General

The water quality index is a guideline-driven tool that allows the user to distil large amounts of water quality data from a monitoring site into a single number, or index value. The index was developed after a review of water quality reporting in jurisdictions in Canada and elsewhere, and the final approach was based on work done in British Columbia (Rocchini and Swain, 1995).

Different forms of the index have been used for water quality reporting by several jurisdictions, including British Columbia, Alberta (Alberta Ministry of the Environment, 2001), the City of Edmonton (City of Edmonton, 2003), Newfoundland (NF, 2001), and the Toronto Region Conservation Authority (Forester, D.L. 2000). Recently, there has been an attempt at cross-jurisdictional application in Atlantic Canada (EC, 2003) and Alberta (Glozer *et al.*, 2004).

13.2 Quality Index

The formulation of the water quality index is based on three measures of compliance or deviation from established water quality guidelines.

The first component of the index is referred to as *scope,* and it measures the number of parameters out of compliance with objectives as a percentage of the total number of parameters measured.

The second component is referred to as *frequency,* and measures how often a water quality objective is exceeded.

The final component is referred to as *magnitude* and measures by how many the objectives are exceeded.

The three components are assembled into a unit less number scaled from 0 to 100. Higher index numbers reflect higher water quality, while lower numbers reflect poorer water quality.

There are three factors in the water quality index, each of which has been scaled to range between 0 and 100. The values of the three measures of variance from selected objectives for water quality are combined to create a vector in an imaginary 'objective exceedance' space. The length of the vector is then scaled to range between zero and 100, and subtracted from 100 to produce an index which is 0 or close to 0 for very poor water quality, and close to 100 for excellent water quality. Since the index is designed to measure water quality, it was felt that the index should produce higher numbers for better water quality (CCME, 2006).

The WQI score is a number between 1 and 100, with 100 being obtained when no data for any variables are above guideline values. This score can be further simplified by assigning it to one of five descriptive categories. These categories are as follows:

- **Excellent**: (CCME WQI Value 95-100)–water quality is protected with a virtual absence of threat or impairment; conditions very close to natural or pristine levels. These index values can only be obtained if all measurements are within objectives virtually all of the time.
- **Good**: (CCME WQI Value 80-94)–water quality is protected with only a minor degree of threat or impairment; conditions rarely depart from natural or desirable levels.
- **Fair**: (CCME WQI Value 65-79)–water quality is usually protected but occasionally threatened or impaired; conditions sometimes depart from natural or desirable levels.
- **Marginal**: (CCME WQI Value 45-64)–water quality is frequently threatened or impaired; conditions often depart from natural or desirable levels.
- **Poor**: (CCME WQI Value 0-44)–water quality is almost always threatened or impaired; conditions usually depart from natural or desirable levels.

The WQI score can be used to look at trends in the water quality of a river. For example, the WQI score for a river might slowly increase from 75 to 90 over a ten year period; this would be evidence that the water quality of this river is improving.

13.3 Significance

The purpose of the Water Quality Index (WQI) is to summarize large amounts of water quality data for a specific river into simple terms (*i.e.* one number and a statement such as "good"). This makes it easily understandable for communities in the watershed and for watershed management, as well as creates a consistent system for reporting throughout Canada. The WQI was created by the Canadian Council of Ministers of the Environment (CCME) based on the previous work developed by British Columbia. The WQI is now used nationally in all provinces and territories. The WQI is based on the protection of aquatic life, not on human health (CCME, 2006).

13.4 How to Calculate WQI

13.4.1 Choose the Variables

Five to fifteen variables (such as dissolved oxygen, acidity, lead) are chosen for each monitoring site, that best characterizes the water quality or are a concern for the local aquatic life. These variables usually depend on the land use practices in the watershed, whether the variable has been high at any point in the past, and whether there is an increasing trend for the variable. For example, if there is agriculture in the watershed, nitrogen and phosphorus would likely be chosen as variables. This same site might have had a couple events of high cadmium ten years ago, as well as a long term increase of temperature of water, therefore cadmium and water temperature would also be chosen as variables.

13.4.2 Choose the Guidelines

Once variables have been selected, the guidelines for each of these variables have to be chosen. The CCME has published guidelines for many water quality variables, and most often these guidelines are used to calculate the WQI (CCME, 2006). But other times, these guidelines are not applicable; for example, if the natural state of a river has aluminium levels higher than the CCME guidelines because of a glacier that feeds the river, a higher guideline higher than the CCME one would be chosen. Over the past couple of decades, variable and guidelines have been developed with respect to specific water bodies, taking into consideration the physical and biological characteristics of the water body and watershed; these are science-based and called site-specific guidelines, and should be developed for the river before the index is calculated.

13.4.3 Calculate WQI Score

After the variables and guidelines are chosen, this information and the appropriate water quality data are inputted into a computer program that calculates the WQI. Some variables also require additional information (*i.e.* modifying factors) in order for the score to be calculated. For example, the guidelines for several metals are dependent on water hardness, therefore hardness values must also be included for the WQI to be calculated.

The guidelines are intended to provide protection to aquatic life from human-caused stressors, both physical (*e.g.* water temperature) and chemical (*e.g.* nitrate).

The guidelines were based on the most current toxicological data available for each variable. Note that the WQI is based only on the protection of aquatic life, not on the protection of water for drinking or agriculture or any other use (CCME, 2006).

The program uses the inputted guidelines and data to base the calculation on three functions relating to site specific water quality guidelines:

- **Scope**–How many guidelines have been exceeded?–The number of water quality variables that do not meet guidelines in at least one sample during the time period under consideration, relative to the total number of variables measured.
- **Frequency**–How often has the data exceeded guidelines?–The number of individual measurements that do not meet guidelines, relative to the total number of measurements made in all samples for the time period of interest.
- **Amplitude**–How much has the data exceeded guidelines?–The amount by which measurements which do not meet the guidelines depart from those guidelines.

13.4.4 WQI Calculation and Formulas

The CCME Water Quality Index takes the form in the following formula (CCME, 2006):

$$WQI = 100 - \left(\frac{\sqrt{F_1^2 + F_2^2 + F_3^2}}{1.732} \right) \qquad (1)$$

where, *F1* represents the percentage of variables that depart from their objectives at least once, relative to the total number of variables measured:

$$F_1 = \left(\frac{\text{Number of failed variables}}{\text{Total number of variables}} \right) \times 100 \qquad (2)$$

F2 represents the percentage of failed individual tests:

$$F_2 = \left(\frac{\text{Number of failed tests}}{\text{Total number of tests}} \right) \times 100 \qquad (3)$$

and *F3* is an asymptotic capping function that scales the normalized sum of the excursions from objectives (*nse*) to yield a range between 0 and 100.

$$F_3 = \left(\frac{nse}{0.01nse + 0.01} \right) \qquad (4)$$

The collective amount by which individual tests are out of compliance is calculated by summing the departures of individual tests from their objectives and dividing by the total number of tests (both those meeting objectives and those departing from objectives). The *nse* variable is expressed as (CCME, 2006):

$$nse = \frac{\sum_{i=1}^{n} departure_i}{\#\ of\ tests} \tag{5}$$

For the cases in which the test value must not exceed the objective:

$$departure_i = \left(\frac{FailedTest_i}{Objective_j}\right) - 1 \tag{6}$$

For the cases in which the test value must not fall below the objective:

$$departure_i = \left(\frac{Objective_j}{FailedTest_i}\right) - 1 \tag{7}$$

For the cases in which the objective is zero,

$$departure_i = Failed\ Test_i \tag{8}$$

Departures are equivalent to the number of times by which a concentration is greater than (or less than) the objective.

A sensitivity analysis is a study of the response of an output variable to variations in the input variables. In the case of the CWQI, there are a number of input variables whose influence on the output can be assessed. These are:

- The selection of inputs – both the number of the inputs and the actual parameters.
- The number of sampling occasions for the index period.
- The selection of the water quality objectives against which the index is being calculated.

An examination of the sensitivity of the CWQI to varying some of these inputs has been conducted on a large set of water quality data from Ontario (Painter and Waltho, 2003). Their major conclusions were:

- The Index computed with ten parameters provided more stable scores than with six parameters. Using nine parameters resulted in 14% of the Index scores ranked differently when compared to the Index with 10 parameters. If only 5 rather than 6 parameters had been used, then 30% of the scores were ranked differently. The Index was less likely to incorrectly rank a site when more variables were included in the calculation.
- When the parameters tested were increased beyond 10 and included other water quality parameters that were still relevant to the sites but passed, the Index scores predictably improved. The scores improved when 21 parameters were tested and marginally improved when 32 were included.
- Guideline selection influenced the results. Care needs to be exercised when making comparisons between sites that have used guidelines from various

sources. The protection level and beneficial use of the guidelines should be equivalent for comparisons to be valid.

- ☆ The stability of the Index improved when at least 3 years of data were included in the calculation. The inclusion of data from several years would ensure a more complete representation of the environmental condition. However, inclusion of too many years would dampen the responsiveness of the Index.
- ☆ In this exercise, aquatic life protection guidelines were used so the dataset should reflect the environmental exposure or the risk associated with the guideline. For example, the interim PWQO phosphorus objective is designed to protect streams from excessive aquatic plant growth. Hence, the relevant dataset would be the spring, summer and fall growing season for that parameter.
- ☆ Based on this sensitivity analysis, the performance of the Index was reasonable when at least 10 or more variables were included and at least 30 observations over a period of at least 3 years were used in the calculation.

These conclusions have limited relevance to many applications of the CWQI. There are few jurisdictions that routinely sample for as many as 32 parameters at water quality stations (CCME, 2006). Most water quality assessment programs have much smaller suites of chemical analyses available, so recommendations for inclusion of large numbers of parameters cannot be achieved in most jurisdictions.

13.5 Sensitivity

13.5.1 Number of Parameters

The first variable to be evaluated was the number of parameters that are fed into the index. This evaluation was conducted on the Environment Canada data set from Alberta. There were eleven variables available for index calculation, and there were twenty assessments of the impact of parameter removal. In the two cases presented in detail, parameters were removed in a different order. The CWQI output stayed relatively stable (within 5 – 10% of the value calculated with all parameters) in both instances until the parameters dropped below 7. Based on this assessment, and an examination of the mean CWQI calculated on the twenty parameter removal trials, it would appear that 7 or more parameters are required in order to use the CWQI.

In a separate assessment of the CWQI, ten or more parameters were recommended for CWQI calculation (Painter and Waltho, 2003). However, it is not just the number of parameters that influences the CWQI – it is the selection of parameters. In the Alberta data set used for this evaluation, nutrients are the water quality parameters of most concern, and the parameters for which most exceedances were observed. Removing or retaining those parameters and cadmium (a metal with relatively frequent guideline exceedances) had more of an impact than removing or selecting metals that had fewer exceedances (CCME, 2006).

13.5.2 Parameter Selection

The CWQI is intrinsically sensitive to which parameters are selected. This somewhat confounds the observations made above regarding the number of parameters used to calculate the index. It is also difficult to formulate recommendations regarding the parameters to select, because they will be highly dependent on the site at which the CWQI will be calculated. In the evaluation conducted in this study, the CWQI output was measured by the number of sites in various water quality ranges as a function of selectively removing specific parameters. In the Quebec data set used, feacal coliform was the parameter that had most influence on the index value. Removal of that parameter had a significant impact on the distribution of index values, while the index somewhat more stable to the inclusion or exclusion of the other parameters.

If the index is to be used to assess the impact of mine drainage on a Boreal Shield site, then parameters associated with that water quality impact should be included. Adding large numbers of parameters related to organochlorine pesticides and eutrophication related parameters will "dilute" the index and artificially increase the CWQI values. Similarly, an evaluation of agricultural runoff should include nutrients, dissolved oxygen, and microbial parameters as index inputs. Adding large numbers of metals or acidification-related parameters will necessarily increase index values (CCME, 2006).

Painter and Waltho (2003) made similar conclusions by adding 30 or more parameters to the index calculation. The CWQI will produce output indicating improved water quality if the index is "diluted" by adding parameters that are not relevant to the water quality issues at the site. It is difficult to formulate a "rule of thumb" that encapsulates these observations. Basically, the user of the CWQI should select parameters that are relevant to the water quality issues that are perceived to be a problem at a given site.

13.5.3 Number of Measurements

The sensitivity of the index to the number of measurements was evaluated by examining two sites for which there were ten-year water quality data sets. The CWQI values measured by averaging yearly data (calculated on 6-12 samples per year) were compared to CWQI values measured on all samples (70 – 110 samples. In general, the results were similar for the sites considered. The averages of the annual measurements were within 5 – 10% of the CWQI values calculated based on all measurements. Of course, annual measurements can be expected to vary based on differences in hydrologic factors and pollutant inputs. Calculating the index based on longer-term data sets will dampen these effects. Painter and Waltho (2003) recommended three or more years of monthly measurements to produce a relatively stable index value. This may be a reasonable recommendation if the user wants to produce a single index value for a site.

It is generally recognized that water quality may vary significantly from year to year, and within the year from season to season. Climatic variables like sunlight and rainfall may have significant impacts on water quality, and can be reflected either in annual or seasonal variation. The design of normal monitoring programs should not have to be altered to fit the requirements of the CWQI (CCME, 2006).

13.5.4 Objective Selection

Since the CWQI is based on the frequency, scope, and amplitude of objectives exceedance, its sensitivity to the selection of different objectives is inevitable. This aspect of index sensitivity was not evaluated quantitatively. As noted above, CWQI users are encouraged to select objectives relevant to the site being evaluated.

13.6 WQI: A Case Study (Malik *et al.*, 2009)*

Abstract

Hydrochemistry of groundwater (pH, Conductivity, DO, COD, TDS, TSS, Turbidity, Alkalinity, T. Hardness, Ca, Mg, Chloride, Iron and Sodium) around four industrial zone (Textile, Oil refinery, Thermal power plant, Sugar industry) of district Panipat, were selected to assess the drinking water quality of groundwater. Analytical techniques as described in the standard methods for examination of water and waste water (APHA, 1998) were adopted for physico-chemical analysis of groundwater samples and results compared with the standards given by WHO and BIS guidelines for drinking water. Water quality index (WQI) was calculated for quality standard of groundwater to determine the suitability of drinking water. The present study revealed that water quality is highly contaminated due to excessive concentration of nine to ten water quality parameters such as conductivity, TDS, TSS, Turbidity, Alkalinity, Hardness, Ca-Hardness, Mg-Hardness, COD and Iron. WQI were ranged (35.05-59.45) and showed marginal or poor category *i.e.* water quality is frequently or almost always threatened or impaired; conditions often or usually depart from natural or desirable level.

Keywords: *Groundwater quality, Industrial pollution, Water quality index.*

Introduction

Panipat is famous city of handloom business in India and international level the new industrial state have been established and promoted through new economic policies. The major industries in Panipat industrial region industrial regions are textile (hand loom, power loom), dyes, Indian Oil refinery, Natural fertilizer limited, Thermal power, Sugar and chemical industries located in close vicinity of city. These industries have exploited the large amount of freshwater indifferent units and discharged their wastewater in the form of effluents into any freshwater body *viz.* pond, streams, or any seasonal drain as in the open land and ultimately contaminated or degraded the quality of groundwater.

Groundwater is used for domestic, industries and agriculture in most part of world as it is a replensible resource. There has been a tremendous increase in demand of freshwater due to growth of population, advanced agricultural practices and industrial applications (Bachmet, 1994). The impact of leachates of industrial effluents

---

* (***Reference***- *Malik, D.S.; Kumar, P.; Bharti, P. K. and Bharti, U.* (2009): *Assessment of groundwater quality in industrial area at Panipat* (*Haryana*), *J. Natcon, 21* (2): 267-273.)

on groundwater has attracted a lot of attention worldwide because of its overwhelming environmental significance as high deteriorating risk to groundwater resources.

Water quality index (WQI) has provided an assessment of water quality trends for management purpose even though it *i.e.* not meant especially as an absolute measure of the degree of pollution or the actual water quality (Anonymous, 1997). The water quality index system is well known method of expressing water quality that offers a simple, stable and reproducing unit of measure, which responds to change in the physical and chemical characteristics of water (Brown, *et al.*, 1972).

In the present study, the main objective was to assess the extent of industrial effluents on the groundwater quality in the rural and urban adjoining areas of industrial region of Panipat city. The present extensive research efforts lead to accumulation of considerable indexing criterion to quantify the assessment of groundwater in term of drinking water quality, which is being utilized continuously for the drinking and other domestic purposes by the local inhabitants of Panipat region.

Materials and Methods

Panipat is situated on the bank of river Yamuna, lies in between 29° 09°50″ and 29′50′ North latitude and 76′ 31′ 15″ and 77° 12′ 45″ East longitudes on the height of 255 meters above sea level. Panipat city was selected on the basis of existence of large members of textile industries its subsidiary dye houses and other different industrial units. The following sampling areas were selected on the basis of particular industrial zone as:

- ✰ Sampling site-I: located in Jatal road in textile and dye houses industrial area.
- ✰ Sampling site-II: located in Indian oil refinery industrial area.
- ✰ Sampling site-III: located in adjoining parts of sugar industry.
- ✰ Sampling site-IV: located in thermal power station area.

The groundwater samples were collected from the different stations of all sampling site from the hand pumps of rural and urban areas of Panipat industrial regions. The water samples were analyzed for physico-chemical parameters as standard methods described by APHA, (1995) and compared with the drinking water standards given by WHO (2004) and Bureau of Indian standard BIS (1991).

The CCME Water Quality Index: The CCME-WQI produces a measure of the derivation of water quality from water quality guidelines from described in (CCME-WQI, 2001).

$$WQI = 100 - \left(\frac{\sqrt{F_1^2 + F_2^2 + F_3^2}}{1.732} \right) \quad (1)$$

where,

F_1: Number of failed variables/Total number of variables×100

F_2: Number of failed test/Total number of test×100

F_3: (nse/001nse+0.01)

The divisor 1.732 normalizes the resultant values range between 0 and 100, where 0 represents the "worst" water quality and 100 represents the "best" water quality.

Once WQI value has been determined, water quality is ranked by relating it to one of the following categories:

Rank	*CCME-WQI*	*Description*
Excellent	95-100	Water quality is protected with a virtual absence of threat or impairment; conditions very close to natural or pristine levels; these index values can only be obtained if all measurements are within objectives virtually all of the time.
Good	80-94	Water quality is protected with only a minor degree of threat or impairment; conditions rarely depart from natural or desirable levels.
Fair	65-79	Water quality is usually protected but occasionally threatened or impaired; conditions sometimes depart from natural or desirable levels.
Marginal	45-64	Water quality is frequently threatened or impaired; conditions often depart from natural or desirable levels.
Poor	0-44	Water quality is almost always threatened or impaired; conditions usually depart from natural or desirable levels.

Table 1: Drinking Water Quality Standards given by WHO and BIS

Parameters	*Unit*	*WHO*	*BIS*
pH	–	6.5–8.5	–
Conductivity	µmho/cm	400	–
TDS	mgL^{-1}	500	–
TSS	mgL^{-1}	5	–
Turbidity	NTU	5	–
Alkalinity	mgL^{-1}	–	200
T. Hardness	mgL^{-1}	–	300
Ca	mgL^{-1}	–	75
Mg	mgL^{-1}	–	30
DO	mgL^{-1}	3	–
COD	mgL^{-1}	10	–
Chloride	mgL^{-1}	–	250
Iron	mgL^{-1}	0.3	–
Sodium	mgL^{-1}	200	–

Discussion

In present study, the four different sampling zones were selected in the vicinity of four different types of industry located in the industrial area at Panipat. The receiving source of drinking water for the labour resides in suburban localities near to particular sampling zones through shallow bored hand pumps. Such groundwater

Table 2: Seasonal Variations in Water Quality Parameter of Groundwater in Industrial Area at Panipat

Parameters	*Unit*	*Site–I*			*Site–II*			*Site–III*			*Site–IV*		
		Summer	*Monsoon*	*Winter*	*Summer*	*Monsoon*	*Winter*	*Summer*	*Monsoon*	*Winter*	*Summer*	*Monsoon*	*Winter*
pH	–	6.7	6.9	7.1	7.4	7.8	7.5	7.6	7.9	7.1	7.6	7.9	7.1
Conductivity	μmho/cm	1270	1420	1190	1210	1340	1130	1280	1332	1188	1280	1332	1188
TDS	mgL^{-1}	806	937	885	794	884	766	844	897	784	864	879	784
TSS	mgL^{-1}	7	10	6	7	9	8	6	7	5	6	7	5
Turbidity	NTU	17	21	16	15	17	14	14	18	12	14	18	12
Alkalinity	mgL^{-1}	323	328	340	328	352	308	338	344	324	338	348	324
T. Hardness	mgL^{-1}	281	309	296	271	302	258	278	284	252	378	284	352
Ca	mgL^{-1}	192	201	178	178	194	170	188	175	170	188	185	180
Mg	mgL^{-1}	89	108	118	93	108	88	90	109	82	90	109	82
DO	mgL^{-1}	3.2	3.8	4.1	5.5	3.8	4.1	5.7	3.1	3.8	5.7	3.1	3.8
COD	mgL^{-1}	10.1	12.8	11.2	9.1	9.8	10.2	8.8	9.2	8.1	7.4	8.8	8.2
Chloride	mgL^{-1}	48.2	51.3	39.3	32.3	35.3	28.5	34.0	37.4	35.9	34.0	37.4	35.9
Iron	mgL^{-1}	0.51	0.58	0.41	0.45	0.51	0.42	0.32	0.38	0.30	0.32	0.38	0.24
Sodium	mgL^{-1}	72.5	57.5	140.2	70.2	52.9	130.5	68.4	47.8	125.7	66.2	48.5	115.8

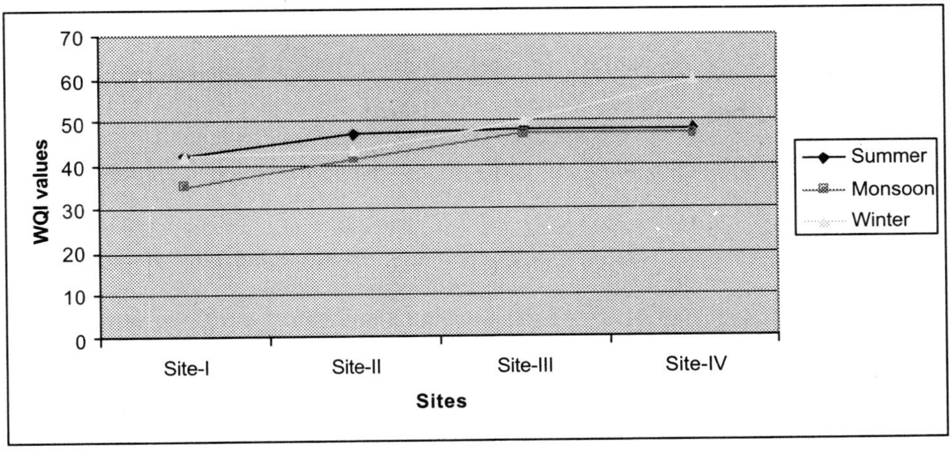

Figure 1: CCME WQI Rating at Different Sites and in Different Seasons

has been extensively utilized by labour class people because of its easy assessness of drinking water from shallow strata of water table.

pH values in groundwater were ranged 6.7-7.9 as lowest and highest value of pH recorded at site-I and site-II during summer and monsoon season respectively. Electrical Conductivity is the most important parameter in determining the suitability of water for drinking purpose. Electrical conductivity with regards to water quality referred to the amount of salts in the water and an approximate indicator of total dissolved ions such as heavy metals to determining the pollution load (Nasrullah, *et al.*, 2006). Conductivity of all groundwater samples of all sites were recorded in the range between 1188 to 1420 µmho/cm. The values of electrical conductivity have showed higher trend with comparison than standard value (400 mg/l) given by WHO. Total dissolved solids exhibited turbid condition of water pollution strength. TDS values of groundwater samples were recorded in the range between 766 to 937 mg/l, as lowest at site-II and highest at site-I during winter season respectively. Water with high total dissolved solids generally is inferior potability and may induce an unfavorable physiological reaction in the transient consumer and gastrointestinal infections. Kulshrestha, *et al.* (2002) also observed the same range of total dissolved solids in groundwater depending on depth of water table. Total suspended solids in groundwater samples of all sites were found in the range between 5-9 mg/l, as lowest and highest values were recorded at site-IV and site-II during winter and monsoon season respectively. Turbidity in groundwater samples of all sites were recorded ranged from 5-21 mg/l, as lowest and highest values of turbidity recorded at site-III and site-I during winter and monsoon season respectively. Alkalinity of water is strongly correlated with pH value, if pH of drinking water is high than alkalinity also showed higher trends. The values of alkalinity in groundwater samples were observed in the range between 308-352 mg/l, but lowest value found at site-II during winter and highest values recorded site-II during monsoon season. Alkalinity of groundwater samples have showed higher trend with comparison than standard value (200 mg/l) given by BIS.

The high degree of hardness can definitely be attributed to the disposal of untreated and improperly treated sewage and industrial wastes (Shanker, *et al.*, 2008). The lowest and highest values of total hardness in groundwater samples were recorded as 252-309 mg/l at site-IV and site-I during winter and monsoon season respectively. Total Hardness of groundwater samples at site-I and site-II during monsoon season showed higher trend with comparison than standard value (300 mg/l) given by BIS. The lowest and highest values of Ca-hardness in groundwater were recorded as 170-201 mg/l at site-II and site-I during winter and monsoon season respectively. The similar trend of calcium hardness occurred in groundwater also reported by Ramakrishnaiah, *et al.* (2009). The lowest and highest values of Mg-hardness in groundwater were recorded as 82-118 mg/l at site-VI and site-I during winter season respectively. Chemical oxygen demand represent the amount of required for microbial decomposition of organic matter. The values of COD of groundwater samples were ranged 7.4-12.8 mg/l, lowest and highest value of COD recorded at site-VI and site-I during winter and monsoon season respectively. The values of COD of groundwater have showed higher trend at site-I with comparison than standard value (10 mg/l) given by WHO. Similar trend of COD values in groundwater also recorded by Ahamad *et al.* (2008).

Iron content in groundwater samples were varied from 0.24 to 0.58 mg/l, lowest and highest value of iron recorded at site-IV and site-I during winter and monsoon season respectively. The values of iron content in groundwater have showed higher trend with comparison than standard value (0.30 mg/l) given by WHO except site-VI during winter season. The concentrations of chloride in groundwater samples ranged 28.5-51.3 mg/l, lowest and highest were recorded at site-II and site-I during winter and monsoon season respectively. Excessive chloride imparts bitter taste to water and corrode steel and may cause cardio-vascular problem. The lowest and highest values of sodium in groundwater were recorded as 47.8-140.2 mg/l at site-III and site-I during monsoon and winter season respectively. Same range of sodium in groundwater also reported by Ramakrishnaiah *et al.* (2009).

Water quality ratings were ranged 35.05-42.08, lowest and highest values of water quality ratings recorded at site-I during Monsoon and winter season respectively. All the values of WQI ratings at site-I in all three seasons recorded under the poor category. Lowest and highest value water quality ratings were measured as 41.20-46.73, at site-II during monsoon and summer season respectively. Water quality ratings at site-II were recorded in poor category in monsoon and winter seasons and marginal in summer season. Lowest and highest values of water quality ratings were recorded as 46.84-49.57 at site-III during monsoon and winter season respectively. The values of water quality rating at site-III recorded under marginal category. Lowest and highest values of water quality ratings were measured as 46.93-59.45 at site-IV during monsoon and winter season respectively. All the values of water quality ratings at all sites recorded under marginal or poor category (35.05-59.45) *i.e.* water quality is frequently or almost always threatened or impaired; conditions often or usually depart from natural or desirable level.

Deleterious level of groundwater pollution caused severe diseases in primary stage and slowly created a potential health hazards to the inhabitants of affected area. The overall observation of present study indicated deterioration trend of groundwater quality in the available water table on sampling areas due to lack of waste water treatment facilities in all industries These industries have not fulfilled the norms of pollution controlling authorities such as central pollution control board, New Delhi and state pollution control board. This problem is coming by lack of environmental ethics, lack of financial resources and non-adoption of environmental laws at the corporate level. The groundwater resources must be non-contaminated, purified and treated efficiently on sustainable basis at point and non point sources of pollution level. The drinking water quality should be properly maintained and be available for healthy human society to get longer life.

References

Anonymous (1997): A Hach Water Analysis Handbook. 3rd Edn USA: Hach Company.

Ahamad, M.; Ahamad, S.; Waleed. S and Hammad (2008): Industrial effluent quality, pollution monitoring and environmental management. *Environ. Monit. Assess.* 147: 297-306.

APHA (1995): Standard methods for the examination of wastewater, *American Public Health Association, Washington, D.C.* pp: 1190.

Bachmet, Y. (1994): Groundwater as part of the water system. In Groundwater contamination and control. *Ed. V. Zoller. Marcel Dekker, Inc, New York,* pp: 1-560.

BIS (1991): Bureau of Indian Standards IS: 10500, Manak Bhavan, New Delhi, India.

Brown, R. M., McLelland, N., Deininger, R. A. and O'Connor, M. F. (1972): A water quality index, crashing the psychological barrier. *Indicators of Environmental Quality.*

Nasrullah., Naz, R.; Bibi, H.; Iqbal, M. and Durrani, M. I. (2006): Pollution load in industrial effluent and groundwater of Gadoon Amazai Industrial Estate (GAIE) Swabi, NWFP. *Journal of Agriculture and Biological Science,* 1(**3**):18-24.

Ramakrishnaiah, C. R., Sadashivaiah, C. and Ranganna, G. (2009): Assessment of Water Quality Index for the groundwater in Tumukpur Taluk Karnataka State, India. *E. J. of Chem.*6 (**2**):523-530.

Shanker, B.S.; Balasubramanya, N. and Reddy, M. T. M. (2008): Impact of industrialization on groundwater quality- a case study of Peenya industrial area, Bangalore, India. *Environ. Monit. Assess.* **142**:263-268.

WHO (2004): Guidelines for Drinking Water Quality. Vol.1-4, Geneva, pp: 515.

13.7 Water Quality Standards

Water–the most abundant and vital natural resource is extremely essential for survival of all living organisms, but today clean water has become a precious commodity and its quality is threatened by numerous sources of pollution, Water pollution creates physical, chemical and biological changes in the water, and further affects the water quality for a long time of period. As the heavy metals enter in the food chains of aquatic ecosystem, ultimately affect the health of higher animals of

Table 13.7.1: WHO's Guidelines for Drinking Water Quality, 2006, are the International Reference Point for Standard Setting and Drinking Water Safety

Element/Substance	*Symbol/ Formula*	*Normally Found in Freshwater/Surface Water/Groundwater*	*Health Based Guideline by the WHO*
Aluminium	Al		0.2 mg/l
Ammonia	NH_4	< 0.2 mg/l (up to 0.3 mg/l in anaerobic waters)	No guideline
Antimony	Sb	< 4 μg/l	0.02 mg/l
Arsenic	As		0.01 mg/l
Asbestos			No guideline
Barium	Ba		0.7 mg/l
Beryllium	Be	< 1 μg/l	No guideline
Boron	B	< 1 mg/l	0.5 mg/l
Cadmium	Cd	< 1 μg/l	0.003 mg/l
Chloride	Cl		No guideline
Chromium	Cr^{+3}, Cr^{+6}	< 2 μg/l	0.05 mg/l
Colour			Not mentioned
Copper	Cu		2 mg/l
Cyanide	CN^-		0.07 mg/l
Dissolved oxygen	O_2		No guideline
Fluoride	F	< 1.5 mg/l (up to 10)	1.5 mg/l
Hardness	mg/l $CaCO_3$		No guideline
Hydrogen sulfide	H_2S		No guideline
Iron	Fe	0.5–50 mg/l	No guideline
Lead	Pb		0.01 mg/l
Manganese	Mn		0.4 mg/l
Mercury	Hg	< 0.5 μg/l	0.006 mg/l
Molybdenum	Mb	< 0.01 mg/l	0.07 mg/l
Nickel	Ni	< 0.02 mg/l	0.07 mg/l
Nitrate and nitrite	NO_3, NO_2		50 mg/l and 3 mg/l
Turbidity			Not mentioned
pH			No guideline
Selenium	Se	< 0.01 mg/l	0.01 mg/l
Silver	Ag	5 – 50 μg/l	No guideline
Sodium	Na	< 20 mg/l	No guideline
Sulfate	SO_4		No guideline
Inorganic tin	Sn		Not mentioned
TDS			No guideline
Uranium	U		0.015 mg/l
Zinc	Zn		No guideline

(*Source*: www.who.in)

that particular ecosystem. Different heavy metals like Mercury, Lead, Chromium, and Nickel, Cadmium etc. release from various sources like agriculture, urban and industrial uses, and these factors degrade the water quality.

Table 13.7.2: Drinking Water Quality Standards

Parameters	*BIS*	*CPCB*	*UPPCB*	*WHO*
Temperature	40 ºC	±5ºC than receiving water	40 ºC	–
SS	100 mg/l	100 mg/l	100 mg/l	5–25 mg/l
pH	5.5–9.0	5.5–9.0	5.5–9.0	7.0–8.5
BOD_5 at 20ºC	30 mg/l	30 mg/l	30 mg/l	–
COD	250 mg/l	250 mg/l	250 mg/l	–
Cl	–	–	–	75–200 mg/l
Ca	–	–	–	75–200 mg/l
Mg	–	–	–	30–150 mg/l
Cd	2.0 mg/l	2.0 mg/l	2.0 mg/l	0.1 mg/l
Cu	3.0 mg/l	3.0 mg/l	3.0 mg/l	0.05–1.5 mg/l
Fe	–	3.0 mg/l	–	0.1–1.0 mg/l
Pb	0.1 mg/l	0.1 mg/l	0.1 mg/l	0.1 mg/l
Mn	–	2.0 mg/l	–	0.05–0.5 mg/l
Ni	2.0 mg/l	3.0 mg/l	2.0 mg/l	–
Zn	5.0 mg/l	5.0 mg/l	5.0 mg/l	5–15.0 mg/l

Table 13.7.3: Recent Standards for Heavy Metals (in mg/l)

	Inland Surface Water		*Drinking Water*		
	BIS/CPCB	*WHO*	*WHO, 1993*	*WHO, 2006*	
			Drinking Water	*Normal*	*Health Based*
Cd	2.0	0.1	0.003–0.005	<1µg/l	0.003
Cu	3.0	0.05–1.5	2.0	–	2.0
Fe	3.0	0.1–1.0	0.2	0.5–50	–
Mn	2.0	0.05–0.5	0.5–0.05	–	0.4
Ni	2.0	–	0.02	0.02	0.07
Pb	0.1	0.1	0.01	–	0.01
Zn	5.0	5.0–15.0	3.0	<20	–

Source: www.lenntech.com.

To minimize the pollution load of water bodies various guidelines, quality standards and maximum permissible limits of pollutants have been set up in different countries. However, WHO standards are being applied in most countries of the world as they are considered as ideal. The Indian standards (BIS) or CPCB standards show relatively high deviation from the WHO standards for environmental quality. Maximum permissible limits for some water quality parameters are different than those of WHO. Limits for toxic metals (Cd, Cu, Hg, Mn, Ni, Pb, Zn) in drinking water are high in BIS or CPCB standards compared to WHO standards. Heavy metals are highly toxic and cause various health problems in humans and also affect cattle and vegetation. Thus, it is essential to control their migration to the unpolluted environment for the safety of human health and livestock (Bharti, 2007).

The first sets of standards were published as Indian Standard, 2490 in 1963. These standards set the tolerance limits for Industrial Effluent discharged into inland surface water. The Indian Standard 2296 was also published in 1963, which set the tolerance limits for inland surface water subject to pollution.

The first attempts of water pollution control thus approached the problem using two independent concepts, one dealt with the control of pollution through specification of various parameters and their maximum concentration in the effluent itself. These could be referred to as 'Effluent Standards'. The other approach was to set standards for the receiving water body presumply after a reasonable opportunity for dilution. These standards could be called 'Receiving Water Body Standards' and were related to identified beneficial use to the receiving water body. It is extremely significant that the very first attempt of control of water pollution was through setting of standards simultaneously adopting the above two approaches.

Around 1976, the CPCB developed the concept of evolving industry specific effluent standards based on a comprehensive study of the problems of that particular industry relevant polluting parameters, their pollution potential, best pollution control technology available in the country and the cost of such a technology.

From these, comprehensive documentation evolved the idea of Minimal National Standards (MINAS). These standards were considered to be the minimum standards for specified industries. In the Environmental Protection Act (EPA), 1986, some of these standards were incorporated. Since these are the Minimal National Standards, the State Boards are only permitted to make them more stringent and in no case can relax them. It is essential that effluent standards satisfy three basic criteria namely Necessity, Implement ability and Enforceability. The stipulation of standards for a specific parameter is necessary when the effect of the parameters on the environment were thoroughly studied and established. No compromise, therefore, can be made with regard to concentration of toxic pollutants. By implement ability it should mean that with best pollution control technology currently available in this country, these parameters could be brought down to the specified limits. Enforceability means either the industry or the concerned authorities have the expertise to analyze, to monitor the wastewater discharged from the industry. Each of the parameters included in the MINAS must satisfy each of these three fundamental criteria. At the same time, the set of parameters chosen must ensure the primary objective of protection of environment. Keeping in mind the basic criteria, major polluting parameters from the industries and the performance of the treatment plants, the standards are evolved.

Glossary

Asexual reproduction: Asexual means having no sex or sex organs, therefore asexual reproduction would be reproducing by means other than sex.

Benthic: Benthos and benthic refers to living on or under the substrate at the bottom of aquatic environments including lakes, ponds, rivers and streams, and oceans.

- ☆ Sessile–means the organism is attached to the substrate.
- ☆ Pelagic- refers to living in the water above the bottom. Pelagic organisms usually have some ability to move around.

Brackish: Water that is neither fresh nor saltwater, but is somewhere in between. In nature this occurs at the mouths of rivers and swamps near the sea. Brackish water should have enough salt added to reach a specific gravity in the range of 1.002 to 1.008. Since brackish water is generally a mixture of freshwater and saltwater, a high quality saltwater mix works best but pure rock salt will work in a pinch. A hydrometer is needed to measure salinity but be sure that the one used will measure the necessary range. Most hydrometers found in aquarium stores are made for measuring pure saltwater so they will not measure the lower salinity needed for brackish.

Carnivore: Animals who hunt and eat other animals; meat eater. Sharks are a good example.

Carapace: A bony or hard shell that covers part or all of an animal. Turtles, crabs, and boxfish are good examples.

Caudal: The single fin mounted vertically at the rear of the fish. The tail fin.

Coelenterate: An aquatic animal of the Phylum Coelenterata which is characterized by a central mouth usually surrounded by tentacles bearing stinging cells, and no anus; includes sea anemones, corals, and jellyfishes.

Commensalism: One of several types of symbiotic relationships between the individuals of two (or more) different species In a comensal relationship one species benefits while the other does not (see symbiosis).

Competition: One of several types of symbiotic relationships between the individuals of two (or more) different species. In a competitive relationship neither species benefits (see symbiosis).

Conspecific: Refers to animals of the same species.

Corallivores: species that feed on corals/coral polyps

Cryptocaryon: Cryptocaryon irritans is a parasitic infection where white spots appear on the body and fins. Fish will scratch themselves against rocks and breathing may become rapid if gills are affected. Treatment can be done by copper or other anti-parasite remedies, but this is incompatible with inverts. Cleaner shrimps and wrasses will remove the parasites, but may not keep up with a major infestation. Cryptocaryon is often referred to as the marine equivalent of the freshwater white spot disease, Ichthyophthirius, or Ick.

Cyanobacteria: Cyanobacteria is commonly referred to as red slime algae by hobbyists although it is not really an algae. It is a bacteria. Poor water quality with excessive nutrients are the usual causes. To combat, do frequent water changes, siphon out detritus, and use a good protein skimmer.

Demersal: Sinking to or lying on the bottom; living on or near the bottom and feeding on benthic organisms.

Detritus: Grayish piles of organic compounds that accumulate in the aquarium. Commonly will contain fish wastes, fragments of rock, leftover food, among other things. Usually detritus will accumulate in low water flow areas, sumps, etc.

Detrivores: Animals that eat detritus. Common detritvores are urchins, stars, hermits, etc.

Diatom: A diatom is any of a class of microscopic one-celled algae having walls of silica consisting of two interlocking valves.

Dinoflagellates: Any of numerous minute, chiefly marine protozoans.

Diurnal: An organism that is active during the day, and sleeping at night.

Dorsal fin: The fin directly on the top of the body (it's the fin that sticks out of the water when you see a shark). Some fish have two dorsal fins one directly behind the other.

Endemic: Restricted to a particular place. Means the animal lives in a certain place and nowhere else.

Facultative: Capable of living in varying conditions, ie. facultative cleaners do not rely strictly on parasites for food (compare to obligatory).

Genus: In the taxonomy classification, the genus is the category ranking below a family and above a species.

Gonopodium: Particular to the Live-bearing tooth carps, the gonopodium is the pelvic fins of male fish that have been converted into genital organs.

Herbivore: Animals whose diet consists mainly of vegetable matter.

Hermaphrodite: Refers to both male and female in the same organism. This occurs either at the same time (synchronous hermaphrodite) or at different times (successive hermaphrodite). When the female form occurs first, this is referred to as protogynous hermaphroditism, otherwise protandrous hermaphroditism.

Heterospecific: Refers to animals of different species. If two or more animals are heterospecific, it means they are not the same species.

Hydrometer: A Hydrometer is an instrument used to determine the specific gravity of a fluid. Hobbyist grade hydrometers are temperature corrected to read the specific gravity at around 77°F (25°C) because specific gravity is temperature dependent.

Invertebrate: Commonly called inverts by many in the hobby. Invertebrates are animals without backbones like anemones, corals, shrimps, snails, and crabs.

Larvae: The first stage of development after hatching for many fish and invertebrates.

Lateral line: The lateral line is a line of perforated scales along the flanks of a fish which lead to a pressure-sensitive nervous system. This enables the fish to detect vibrations in the surrounding water caused by other fish and their own reflected vibrations against obstacles.

Littoral: Pertaining to the edge of the lake, near the shore.

Mutualism: One of several types of symbiotic relationships between the individuals of two (or more) different species. In a mutualistic relationship both species benefit (see symbiosis).

Neutralism: One of several types of symbiotic relationships between the individuals of two (or more) different species. In a neutral relationship both species are unaffected (see symbiosis).

Obligatory: Obligate or required: ie. an obligatory cleaner fish relies entirely on this feeding mode to obtain nutrients (compared to facultative).

Octocoral: Octocorals have eight tentacles on each polyp. There are many different forms which may be soft, leathery, or even those producing hard skeletons.

Omnivore: Animals who eat both meat and vegetables like marine angelfish.

Ocellus: A marking that resembles an eye, eye-like colored spot; an eyespot.

Oviparous: Producing eggs which are fertilized, develop and hatch outside the body.

Parasitism: Oone of several types of symbiotic relationships between the individuals of two (or more) different species In a parasitic relationship one species benefits, the other is harmed (see symbiosis).

Pinnate: Feather like. The 'pinnules' which are found on many octocorals are small side branches of the polyp tentacle which give it a 'pinnate' appearance.

Pelagic: Refers to living in the water of the ocean above the bottom. Pelagic organisms have the ability to swim around or move in some fashion. "Pelagic" is also used to refer (usually) to eggs that are basically at the mercy of the ocean currents. Benthos and benthic refers to living on or under substrate at the bottom of the ocean. Sessile means the organism is attached to the substrate.

Pectoral fins: The anterior or dorsalmost paired fins of fishes. They correspond to the anterior limbs of the higher vertebrates.

Photosynthetic: The process by which organisms, usually plants, use the energy contained in light, usually sunlight.

Phytoplankton: Microscopic free-floating aquatic plants, mainly algae. It lives suspended in bodies of water and drifts about. See plankton.

Piscivore: Habitually feeding on fish; fish-eating

Planktivore: A general term to describe an organism adapted to feed and survive from eating mostly plankton.

Plankton: Plankton are the drifters of the sea. Although they may have some form of locomotion they are mostly carried by water currents. Plankton is divided into macroplankton (jellyfish, sargassum weed) and microplankton, organisms that can only be seen by a microscope. The microplankton is divided into zooplankton, tiny marine animals, and phytoplankton, or plants. Most fish start their lives as small animals in the plankton.

Polyp: A polyp is the living unit of a coral.

Predaceous: This means the animal will hunt and eat other animals. The old rule comes to mind, big fish eat little fish!

Protozoan: A protozoan is a single-celled, microscopic (usually) organism. For example, an amoeba.

Red Slime: see cyanobacteria.

Sessile: Sessile means the organism is attached to the substrate at the bottom of the ocean and therefore cannot move around. Pelagic refers to living in the water of the ocean above the bottom. Pelagic organisms have the ability to move around. Benthos and benthic refers to living near or under substrate at the bottom of the ocean.

Specific gravity: As a hobbyist definition, specific gravity is the amount of salt in the water. See the hydrometer definition above for more information. Specific Gravity of seawater ranges from 1.022 to 1.030.

Symbiotic: A relationship where two or more different kinds of animals live together and both benefit in some way from the other's company. The most famous example is the clownfish and the anemone.

Siphon: The inhalent and exhalent siphons of tridacnid clams are used to allow for gas exchange and to expel wastes.

Symbiosis: A close ecological relationship between the individuals of two (or more) different species. Sometimes a symbiotic relationship benefits both species, sometimes one species benefits at the other's expense, and in other cases neither species benefits.

Taxonomy: The classification of organisms in an ordered system that indicates natural relationships.

Ultraviolet (UV) light: Ultraviolet is a high energy, short wavelength of light. It is shorter than violet in the visible spectrum and on the border of the x-ray region.

UV sterilizer: A UV Sterilizer is a device that uses ultraviolet light to make the water treated with it free of microorganisms which may cause disease.

Weber's apparatus: Described in 1820 by E. H. Weber, the Weber's apparatus connects the hearing organ with the swim bladder where it operates as a sounding board thus amplifying sounds.

Zooplankton: Small, usually microscopic animals; includes tiny waterborne crustaceans and fish larvae, also includes corals, rotifers, sea anemones, and jellyfish.–See plankton.

Zooxanthellae algae: (zo-zan-thel-ee) Zooxanthellae algae are tiny plants called dinoflagellates (single-celled microscopic organisms which belong to the Protista kingdom) that live symbiotically with corals, tridacnid clams, and some sponges. The algae provides food for the host and in return gets the nitrogen, phosphorous, and carbon dioxide it needs to grow. The scientific name is *Symbiodinium* spp.

Bibliography

Abbas, N. and Subramanian, V. (1984): Erosion and sediment transport in the Ganges river basin. *J.Hydrol*, 69: 173-182.

Adefemi, O.S.; Asaolu, S.S. and Olaofe, O. (2007): Assessment of the Physico-Chemical Status of Water Samples from Major Dams in Ekiti State, Nigeria, *Pakistan Journal of Nutrition*, 6 (6): 657-659,

Adwant, M.P. (1989): Limnological Studies on Godavari basin at Nanded (M.S.), Ph.D. Thesis, *Marathavada University Aurangabed.*

Agbaire, P.O. and Obi, C.G. (2009): Seasonal Variations of Some Physico-Chemical Properties of River Ethiope Water in Abraka, Nigeria. *J. Appl. Sci. Environ. Manage.*, 13(1): 55-57.

Ahamed, S. and Hasnain, S.I. (2001): Snow and stream water chemistry of the Ganga headwater basin, Garhwal Himalaya, India, *Hydrological Sciences Journal*, 46(1): 103-111.

Ahica Ajakane (1995): Ecological characteristics of the benthic macro-invertebrates of high altitude streams (Morocco). pp: 537-543.

Ahmed, I.; Rashid, H. and Rahman, Z.U. (2009): Study on heavy metals in some environmental samples. *Environmental Monitoring and Assessment*, 158 (1-4): 139-144.

Alam, J.B.; Islam, M. R.; Muyen, Z.; Mamun, M. and Islam, S. (2007): Water quality parameters along rivers. *Int. J. Environ. Sci. Tech.*, 4 (1): 159-167.

Allan, J.D. (1995): Stream Ecology: structure and function of running waters. *Chapman and Hall, London*. pp: 388.

Allen, W.E. (1920): A quantitative and statistical study of the plankton of the San Joaquin River and its tributaries in a near Stockton California in 1913. *Univ. Calif. Publ. Zool.* 22(1): 1-24.

Altin, A.; Filiz, Z. and Iscen, C.F. (2009): Assessment of seasonal variations of surface water quality charecteristics for Porsuk stream. *Environmental Monitoring and Assessment*, 158 (1-4): 51-65.

AME (2003): Alberta Ministry of the Environment, Annual Report, 2001-2002.

Amita Arjariya (2003): Physico-chemcial profile and plankton diversity of Ranital Lake, Chhatarpur, M.P. *Nature env. and Pollution Technology*, Vol-2, No-3: 327-328.

Angelier, E. (2003): Ecology of Streams and Rivers. *Science Publishers, Inc., Enfield*. pp: 215.

Anita Jhajhria (2002): Limnobiotic studies of Shekhawat pond, Jodhpur with special reference to plankton. *J. Natcon*, 14 (2): 215-224.

APHA (1980): Ecological methods for the examination of water. *American Public Health Association*, 1015 fifteen street NW, Washington, 15:1-1134.

Asaolu, S.S. (1998): Chemical Pollution Studies of Coastal Waters of Ondo State. Ph.D, Thesis, Federal University of Technology, Akure. (Unpublished).

B.C. Ministry of Environment, Land and Parks (1996): British Columbia Water Quality Status Report. pp: 181.

B.C. Ministry of Environment, Land and Parks (2001): Environmental Indicator 2000: Water Quality in British Columbia. Online available.

http://wlapwww.gov.bc.ca/soerpt/files_to_link/2000tecdocs/07-waterquality-techdoc.pdf

Badola, S.P. and Singh, H.R. (1981): Hydrobiology of the river Alaknanda of Garhwal Himalaya *Indian J. Ecol.*, 8(2): 269-276.

Baron, J. and Bricker, O.P. (1990): Hydrological and chemical flux in Loch Vale watershed, Rocky Mountain National Park. In: Biogeochemistry of major rivers. SCOPE 42. *Wiley and sons, New York*, USA.

Bernatowicz, W.; Weib, A. and Matschullat, J. (2009): Linking biological and physic-chemical water quality. *Environmental Monitoring and Assessment*, 159 (1-4): 311-330.

Berndtsson, R. (1990): Transport and sedimentation of pollutants in a river reach: a chemical mass balance approach. *Wat. Resour. Res.* 26 (7): 1549-1558.

Bharti, P.K. (2004): Limnological study of Sahastradhara hill-stream, Dehradun, M.Sc. *Dissertation, Gurukula Kangri University, Hardwar*, pp: 102.

Bharti, P.K. (2007a): Why are Indian standards not so strict?, *Current Science*, 93(9): 1202.

Bharti, P.K. (2007b): Where is Environmental science going in India? *Current Science*, 92 (4): 414.

Bharti, P.K. (2007c): Any means to save Lalita river?, *Down To Earth*, 15(17): 3.

Bharti, P.K. (2007d): Effect of textile industrial effluents on groundwater and soil quality in Panipat region (Haryana); Ph. D. thesis, *Gurukula Kangri University, Hardwar*. pp: 191.

Bharti, P.K. (2010): Sandushan- (Eutrophication), *Vigyan Pragati*, January 2010, pp: 29-31.

Bharti, P.K. and Malik, D.S. (2005): Significance of rivers in Vedic literature, *Gurukula Shodha Bharti*, Vol- 4, pp: 217-221.

Bharti, P.K. and Malik, D.S. (2005b): Sahastradhara Nadi ke vibhinna sthhano par machhliyon ke anukool vaas sthhano ke liye upyukt dashaayen, in proceedings of (in Hindi) National Symposium: Uttaranchal me Maatyasyki ki bhaavi sambhaavnaye' organized by department of zoology, H.N.B. Garhwal University, Srinagar on 28-29 October 2005, pp: 84-87.

Bharti, P.K.; Malik, D. S. and Yadav, R. (2008): Influence of Heavy Metals on Abundance of Cyanophyceae Members in Three Spring-fed Lake in Kempty, Dehradun, *Journal of Ecology and Fisheries*, 1(1): 35-38.

Bhatt, S.D. and Pathak, J.K. (1992): Himalayan Environment: water quality of the drainage basin. *Shree Almora Book Depot, Almora*, India. pp: 150.

Bhutiani, R. and Khanna, D.R. (2005): Water in Vedas, *Gurukula Shodha Bharti*, 3: 225-231.

Bond, H.W. (1979): Nutrient concentrations patterns in a stream draining a montane ecosystem in Utah. *Ecology* 60(6): 1184-1196.

Boyer, D.G. and G.C. Pasquarell (1995): Nitrate concentrations in Karst spring in an extensively grazed area. *Water resources Bulletin*, 31(4): 729-736.

Boyer, D.G. and G.C. Pasquarell (1996): Agricultural land use effects on Nitrate concentrations in a mature Karst Aquifer. *Water resources Bulletin*, 32 (3): 565-573.

Brenner,F.J. and J.J. Mondok, (1995): Non-point source pollution potential in an agricultural in watershed in Northwestern Pennsylvania. *Water resources Bulletin*, 31(6): 1101-1112.

Caine, N. and Thurman, E. M. (1990): Temporal and spatial variations in the solute content of an alpine stream, Colorado Front range, *Geomorphology*, 4:55-72.

Cameron,E.M. (1996): Hydrogeo-chemistry of the Fraser river British Columbia: seasonal variation in major and minor components. *Journal of hydrology*, Vol-182 No-1-4: 209-225.

CCME (2001): Canadian Council of Ministers of the Environment, Canadian water quality guidelines for the protection of aquatic life: CCME Water Quality Index 1.0, Technical Report. In: Canadian environmental quality guidelines, 1999, Canadian Council of Ministers of the Environment, Winnipeg. *http://www.ccme.ca/assets/pdf/wqi_techrprtfctsht_e.pdf*

CCME (2006): A sensitivity analysis of the Canadian water quality index, A Report for CCME Prepared by *Gartner Lee Limited*, 140 Renfrew Drive, Suite 102, Markham, Ontario, L3R 6B3, pp: 38.

Chatterjee, S.; Chattopadhyay, B. and Mukhopadhyay, S.K. (2010): Monitoring waste metal pollution at Ganga estuary via the east Calcutta wetlands areas. *Environmental Monitoring and Assessment*, 170 (1-4): 23-31.

Chauhan. D.S and Hasnain, S.I. (1993): Chemical characteristics, should and suspended sediment loads in the melt waters draining from Satopanth and Bhagirath Kharak glaciers, Ganga basin, India. In: *Snow and Glacier Hydrology* (ed. by G. J young) Proc. Kathmandu symp., November (1992), 403-410, IAHS Pub. No-218.

Chopra, A.K., Patrick, Nirmal, J. (1994): Effect of domestic sewage on self-purification of Ganga water at Rishikesh. *A. Bio.science.* 13(11): 75-82.

City of Edmonton (2003): Office of the Environment Edmonton's Environment: A Snapshot 2002. Online available.

http://www.gov.edmonton.ab.ca/am_pw/office_of_the_environment/stateofenv.pdf

Collins R., Jenkins A. and Boorman D. (1998): Stream water acidification in Response to anthropogenic pollution inputs of forested and cultivated catchments in the middle hills, Nepal. (Editor: Suresh, R.C.) International conferences on ecohydrology of high mountain areas. Institute of hydrology, *Wallingford, Oxon, U.K.*- pp: 245-263.

Collins, R. and A. Jenkins, (1996): The impact of agricultural land used on stream chemistry in the middle hills of the Himalayas, Nepal. *Journal of Hydrology* 185: 71-86.

Cooper, D.M., Morris, E.M., and Smith, C.J. (1987): Precipitation and stream water chemistry in a sub-Arctic Scotish catchment. *J. Hydrol.* 93: 221-240.

Correll, D.L, Jordon, T.E. and Weller, D.E. (1994): The Chespeake Bay watershed: Effects of land use and geology on dissolved nitrogen concentrations. In: Toward a sustainable coastal watershed: The Chesapeake experiment, Proceedings of a conference. *Chesapeake Research consortium, Pub.* No.-149: 639-648.

CPCB (2006): Water quality status of Yamuna river (1999-2005). *Technical Report, Central Pollution Control Board*, pp: 136.

Cushing, C.E. and Allan, J.D. (2001): Streams: their ecology and life. *Academic Press, San Diego.* pp: 366.

D' Elia, C.F; Sanders, J.G. and Boynton, W.R. (1986): Nutrient enrichment studies in a coastal plain estuary, phytoplankton growth in large scale, continuous cultures. *Canadian Journal of fisheries and aquatic sciences.* 43: 397-406.

Dai, Z.; Du, J.; Zhang, X.; Su, N. and Li, J.(2011): Variation of Riverine Material Loads and Environmental Consequences on the Changjiang (Yangtze) Estuary in Recent Decades (1955-2008). *Environ. Sci. Technol.*, 45: 223–227.

Das, S.M. and Pathani, S.S. (1978): A study on the effect of lake ecology on production of Mahaseer (*Tor tor and T. putitora*) in Kumaon lake. *Indian Matsya*. 4: 25-31.

Das, S.M. and Srivastava, V.K. (1956): Studies of freshwater plankton II correlation between plankton and hydro-biological factors *Proc. Nat. Acad. Sci. India*, (13) 26: 243-253.

Deming, H.G. (1975): Water the fundamentals of opportunity. *Oxford University Press, New York*. pp: 942.

Dev Goel, (2005): A Political-Economic Analysis of India's River Interlinking Project. (August 30, 2005) *Florida State University D-Scholarship Repository*, Article #132. (http://dscholarship.lib.fsu.edu/undergrad/132)

Dezuane, J. (1979): Handbook of drinking water quality. Indiana University Press, pp: 3-17.

Diez, I.; Seceila, A.; Santolaria, A. and Gorostiaga, J.M. (2009): Ecological monitoring of intertidal phytobenthic communities of the Basque coast (N. Spain) following the Prestige Oil spill. *Environmental Monitoring and Assessment*, 159 (1-4): 555-575.

Dobriyal, A.K. (1985): Ecology of limnofauna in the small streams and their importance to the village life in Garhwal Himalaya. *Uttar Pradesh J. Zool*. 5 (2): 139-144.

Dolan, D.M. and El-Shaarrawi, A.H. (1989): Inferences about point source loadings form Upstream/downstream River monitoring data. *Environmental Monitoring and Assessment*. 12: 343-357.

Doyle, M.W. and Bernhardts, E.S. (2011): What is a stream? *Environ. Sci. Technol.*, 45: 354-359.

Dragun, Z.; Roje, V.; Mikac, N. and Raspor, B. (2009): Preliminary assessment of total dissolved trace metal concentrations in Sara river water. *Environmental Monitoring and Assessment*, 159 (1-4): 99-110.

Duran, M. and Suicmez, M. (2007): Utilization of both benthic macroinvertebrates and physicochemical parameters for evaluating water quality of the stream Cekerek (Tokat, Turkey). *J. Environ. Biol.*, 28, 231-236.

Dutta, S.P.S., Malhotra, Y.R.; Sharma, K.K. and Sinha, K. (1997): Diel variations in physico-chemical characterstics of water and macrobenthic invertebrates in river Tawi, near Nagrota bypass, Jammu. *Him. J. Env. Zool*, Vol-11: 45-50.

EC (2003): Environment Canada, CCME National Water Quality Index Workshop: A Path Forward for Consistent Implementation and Reporting. November 24 – 25, 2003. Halifax, Nova Scotia. Workshop Proceedings. 81 pp. available online. http://www.ccme.ca/assets/pdf/wqi_wkshp_rpt_nov_2003_e.pdf

Eddy, S. (1934): A study of freshwater plankton communities. *Illinois Biol. Monogr*. 12 (4): 1-93.

Ferro, W. (1982): Limnology of Pokhara valley lakes and its implications for fishery and fish culture. *J. Nepal Res. Center*, 5/6: 27-52.

Fokmare, A.K. and Musaddiq, M. (2002): A study on physico- chemical characteristics of Kapshi lake and Purna river waters in Akola district of Maharashtra (India). *Nature Env. And pollution technology*, 1 (3): 261-263.

Forester, D.L. (2000): Water Quality in the Credit River: 1964 to 1998, M.A. 2000, Deborah Lynn Forester, Department of Geography / Institute for Environmental Studies, University of Toronto. *http://www.utoronto.ca/env/ies/debfor/*

Forstner, U. and G.T.W. Wittman, (1979): Metal Pollution in the Aquatic Environment. Berlin, Spring-Verlag, pp: 486.

Friberg, L., Nordberg, G.F., and Vouk, V.B. (Eds.) (1979): *Handbook on the Toxicology of Metals.* Elsevier / North–Holland Biomedical Press, Amsterdam, pp: 709.

Fulazzaky, M.A. (2009): Water quality evaluation system to assess the Brantes river water. *Wat. Res. Management*, 23 (14): 3019-3033.

Fulazzaky, M.A.; Seong, T.W. and Masirin, I.M. (2010): Assessment of Water Quality Status for the Selangor River in Malaysia. *Water Air Soil Poll.*, 205:63–77

Galloway, J.N. (1989): Atmospheric acidification: Projection for the future. *Ambio*, 18: 161-166.

Ghavzan, N. J.; Gunale, V. R. and Trivedy, R. K. (2006): Limnological evaluation of an urban freshwater river with special reference to phytoplankton. *Pollution Research*, 25(2): 259-268.

Giller, S. and Malmqvist, B. (1998): The Biology of Streams and Rivers. *Oxford University Press, Oxford*. pp: 296.

Glozier, N.E., R.W. Crosley, L.A. Mottle and D.B. Donald (2004): Water Quality Characteristics and Trends for Banff and Jasper National Parks: 1973 – 2002. Environmental Conservation Branch, Environment Canada, August 2004. pp: 86.

Goldberg, E.D., Hodge, V.; Koide, M.; Griffin, J.; O.P. Bricker, G. Matisoff, G.R. Holdren, (1978): A pollution history of Chesapeake Bay. *Goechem. Cosmochem. Acta* 42: 1413-1425.

Gomes, L.; Troiani, E.P. and Nozaki, J. (2011): Analysis of environmental impacts on a stream: is only tannery to blame? *Environmental Monitoring and Assessment*, 173 (1-4): 489-498.

Graening, G.O and Brown, A.V. (2003): Ecosystem dynamics and pollution effects in an Ozark cave stream, *Journal of American Water Resources Association. (JAWRA)*, Vol-39 (6): 1497-1507.

Green, W.J. and Canfield, D.E. (1984): Geochemistry of the Onyx River (Wright valley, Antarctica) and its role in the chemical evolution of Lake Yanda. *Geochim. Cosmochim. Acta*, 48: 2457-2467.

Gu Wei-Zu (1995): A neutron activation study of the geochemistry of natural water in Lhasa. Tibet, Xian University of technology, China. pp-573-577.

Hall, K.J., Schreier, H. and Brown, S.J. (1991): Water quality in the Fraser River basin. In: A.H.J. Dorcey and J.R. Griggs (Editors). Water in Sustainable Development: Exploring our Common Future in the Fraser River Basin. *West water Research Centre, University of British Columbia, Vancouver*, pp. 41-75.

Hallberg, G.R. (1986): From Hoes to Herbicides: Agriculture and groundwater quality. *J. Soil and water Conser.* 41: 357-364.

Handa. B.K. (1992): Geochemistry of Ganges river water. *Indian Geohydrol.* 8: 71-78.

Hartig, J.H.; Zarulla, M.A.; Ciborowski, J.J.H.; Gannon, J.E.; Wilks, E.; Norwood, G. and Vincent, A.N. (2009): Long term ecosystem monitoring and assessment of the Detroit river and western Lake Erie. *Environmental Monitoring and Assessment*, 158 (1-4): 87-104.

Hasnain, S.I. and Renoj. J.T. (1960): Sediment transport and solute variation in meltwaters of Dokriani glacier (Bamak). Garhwal Himalaya. *J. Geol. Soc. India* 47: 731-739.

Hasnain, S.I. and Thayyen, R.J. (1999a:. Discharge and suspended sediment concentration of melt waters draining from Dokriani glaciar, Garhwal Himalaya. *India. J. Hydrol.* 218: 191-198.

Hasnain, S.I. and Thayyen, R.J. (1999b): Solute acquisition processes in glacier basin of southern slope of Himalaya, *India. J. Glaciol.* 45: 191-198.

Hasnain. S.I., Subramanian, V and Dhanpal, K (1989): Chemical characteristics of meltwaters from a Himalaya Glacier India, *J. Hydrol.* 106: 98-106.

Helgesen, J.O., Zelt, R.B. and Stamer, J.K. (1994): Nitrogen and Phosphorus in water as related to environmental science Nebraska. *Water resources Bulletin* 30 (5): 809-822.

http://audit.ea.gov.au/ANRA/agriculture/docs/national/Agriculture_Contents.html

http://www.dnr.maryland.gov/streams/mbss/mbss_volun.html

http://www.finance.gov.ab.ca/publications/measuring/annrept02/environment.pdf

Hu, M.H. Stallard, R.F. and Edmond, J. M. (1982): Major ion chemistry of some large Chinese rivers. *Nature*, 298: 550-553.

Hutchinson, G.C. (1957): A treatise on limnology, geography, physical and chemical, Vol.-I, New York: *John Wiley and Sons, Inc.*, pp: 1-1015.

Hynes, H.B.N. (1970): The ecology of running waters. *Liverpool University Press, Liverpool, 4th impression*: 1-555.

Ingrid Juttner, Heike Rothfritz and Steve J. Ormerod (1995): Diatom Communities in Himalayan hill-streams. *University of Wales, Cardiff, CFI 3TL UK*- pp-589-597.

Iqbal, F.; Ali, M.; Salam, A.; Khan, B.A.; Ahmad, S.; Qamar, M. and Umer, K. (2004): Seasonal Variations of Physico-Chemical Characteristics of River Soan Water at Dhoak Pathan Bridge (Chakwal), Pakistan. *International Journal of Agriculture and Biology*, 6(1): 89-92.

Jain, C.K. (1992): Effect of waste disposals on quality of water of River Kali (Uttar Pradesh). Tech, Report no. TR-148, *National Institutute of Hydrology*, Roorkee, India.

Jain, C.K. (1996): Application of chemical mass balance approach to Upstream/ downstream River monitoring data. *J. Hydrol* 182: 105-115.

Jain, C.K. (2001): Application of chemical mass balance approach to determine nutrient loading" *"Hydrological sciences Journal* Vol-45, No-1-4: 577-587.

Jain, C.K., Bhatia, K.K.S. and Seth, S.M. (1997): Characterization of waste disposals and their impact on the water quality of River Kali, *Indian J. Environ. Rat.* 17 (4): 287-295.

Jain, C.K., Bhatia, K.K.S. and Seth, S.M. (1998): Assessment of point and non-point sources of pollution using a chemical mass balance approach. *Hydrol. Sci. J.* 43(3): 379-390.

Jenkins, A., Sloan W.T. and Cosby, B.J. (1995): Stream chemistry is the middle hills and high mountain of the Himalaya, Nepal. *Journal of Hydrology*. Vol-166, No-1-4: 61-79.

Jindal, R. and Sharma, Chetan (2011): Studies on water quality of Sutlej river around Ludhiana with reference to physic-chemical parameters. *Environmental Monitoring and Assessment*, 174 (1-4): 417-425.

Jones, J.R., Knowlton, M.F. and Swar, D.B. (1989): Limnological reconnaissance of water bodies in central and southern Nepal. *Hydrobio.* 184: 171-189.

Joshi, B.D. (1996): Hydro-biological profile of River Sutlej in its middle stretch in Western Himalayas. *U.P.I. Zool.*, 16(2): 9-103.

Joshi, B.D. and Bisht, R.E. (1993): Some aspects of physico-chemical characteristics of western Ganga canal near Jwalapur Hardwar, *Himalayan, J.Env.* 7(1): 76-82.

Joshi, B.D. and Bisht, R.E. (1993): Some aspects of physico-chemical characteristics of western Ganga canal near Jwalapur Haridwar, *Himalyan. J.Env.* 7(1): 76-82.

Joshi, B.D. and Kathait, R.S. (1998): Limnlogical characteristics of three tributaries of river Ganga between Devprayag and Rishikesh. *Him. J. Env. Zool.* Vol-12: 225-243.

Joshi, B.D. and Rajendra Singh (1997): Phytoplanktonic population in relation to certain physiochemical characteristics of river Ganga at Rishikesh. *Him. J. Env. Zool.*, Vol-11: 61-64.

Joshi, B.D., Bisht, R.C.S. and Semval, V.P. (1995): Primary productivity in western Ganga Canal at Hardwar. *Indian J.Ecol.* 22(2): 123-126.

Juahir, H.; Zain, S.M.; Yusoff, M.K.; Hanidza, T.I.T.; Armi, A.S.M.; Toriman, M.E. and Mokhtar, M. (2011): Spatial water quality assessment of Langat River Basin (Malaysia) using environmetric techniques. *Environmental Monitoring and Assessment*, 173: 625–641.

Kamble, S.M.; Jadhav, M.J. and Chavan, A.M. (2011): Seasonal variations in algal population of Ajanta water–fall. *Recent Research in Science and Technology*, 3(5): 40-41.

Kannel, P.R.; Kanel, S.R.; Lee, S. and Lee, Y.S. (2011): Chemometrics in assessment of seasonal variation of water quality in freshwater systems. *Environmental Monitoring and Assessment*, 174 (1-4): 529-545.

Kapsikar, G.B.; Khajure, P.V. and Rathod, J.L. (2011): Physico-chemical features of Kali river, Karwar,west coast of India. *Recent Research in Science and Technology*, 3(4): 12-14.

Karbassi, A.R.; Monavari, S.M.; Bidhendi, Gh. R.N.; Nouri, J. And Nemetpour, K. (2008): Metal pollution assessment of sediment and water in the Shur river. *Environmental Monitoring and Assessment*, 147 (1-3): 107-116.

Kataria, H.C. (2000): Preliminary study on the drinking water of Piparea Township. *Enviromedia.* Poll Res 19(4). 645-649.

Kaul, V. (1977): Limnological survey of Kashmire lakes with reference to trophic status and conservation. *Int. J. Ecol. Environ. Sci.* 3: 19-44.

Kavitha, R. and Elangovan, K. (2010): Groundwater quality characteristics at Erode district, Tamilnadu India. *International Journal of Environmental Sciences*, 1(2): 144-150.

Khan, A.A. and Siddiqui, A. (1971): *Hydrobiologia*, 37:447.

Khanna, D.R and Singh. R.K. (2000): Seasonal fluctuations in the plankton of Suswa River at Raiwala Dehradun. *Env. Conservations J.* 1(2 and 3): 89-92.

Khanna, D.R. and Rakesh Bhutiani (2003): Limnolgical status of Satikund pond at Hardwar (U.A) *Indian Journal of Env. Science*, 7(2): 131-136.

Khanna, D.R., Ashutosh Gautom, Tarun Chugh and Praveen Sarkaar (2000): Impact of abiotic factors on the phytoplanktonic population of a pond. *Env. Conservation J.*, 1(1): 41-46.

Khanna, D.R., Badola, S.P., Sing, H.R. and Dobriyal, K., Anoop (1992): Observations on seasonal trends in diatomic diversity in the river Ganga at Sapt-sarover, Hardwar. Recent research in cold water: Fisheries, ed. by K.L. Sehgal, Today and Tomarrow printers and publishers, New Delhi: 99-107.

Khanna, D.R., Malik, D.S. and Rana, D.S. (1998): Phytoplanktonic communities in relation to certain physico-chemical parameters of Ganga canal at Hardwar. *Him. J. Env. Zool.*, Vol-12: 193-197.

Khanna, D.R.and Rakesh Bhutiani (2003): Limnological characteristics of the river Ganga at Hardwar (U.A.). *Uttar Pradesh J. Zool.* Vol-23 No.3:179-183.

Khanna, D.R; (1993): Ecology and pollution of Ganga River. *Ashish Publishing House*, New Delhi. pp: 1-241.

Koloutsou, S. and Chinta, V.I. (2011): Multilateral environmental agreements for wastes and chemicals: 40 years of global negotiations. *Environ. Sci. Technol.*, 45: 10–15.

Krokhin, E.M. (1959): Energy flows in the ecosystem of the Dalni lake pelagic zone (Kamchatka). *Dokl. Akad. Nank SSSR* 189: 1118-1121.

Kumar, B.V.; Khajure, P.V. and Roopa, S.V. (2011): Aquachemistry, Zooplankton and bacterial diversity in three ponds of Karwar district, Karnataka. *Recent Research in Science and Technology*, 3(4): 39-48.

Kumar, S.K.; Rammohan, V.; Sahayam, J.D. and Jeevanandam, M. (2009): Assessment of groundwater quality and hydrogeochemistry of Manimuktha river basin, Tamilnadu, India. *Environmental Monitoring and Assessment*, 159 (1-4): 341-351.

Lakshminarayana and R.K. Someshekar (2001): Ecology of polluted water by Arvind Kumar Vol-1, chapter II, pp. 51-60, *APH Pub. Corp.* New Delhi-110002.

Lamontagne, S, (2002): Groundwater delivery rate of nitrate and predicted change in nitrate concentration in Blue Lake, South Australia. *Marine and Freshwater Research*, 53: 1129-1142.

Lamontagne, S; Herczeg AL, Dighton JC, Pritchard JL, Jiwan JS, Ullman WJ, (2003): Groundwater-surface water interactions between streams and alluvial aquifers: Results from the Wollombi Brook (NSW) study (Part II–Biogeochemical processes), *CSIRO Technical Report* 42/03.

Latimer, J.S., Carey, C.G., Hoffman, E.J. and Quinn, J.G. (1988): Water quality in the Pawtuxet River: metal monitoring and Geochemistry. *Wat. Resour. Bull.* 24(4): 791-800.

Lawrence, C.R. (1983): Nitrate-rich groundwaters of Australia. *Australian Water Resources Council Technical Paper* No. 79.

Leland, H.V. (1995): Distribution of phytobenthos in the Yakima River basin, Washington, in relation to geology, land use, and other environmental factors. In: *Can. Journal Fish. Aquat. Sci.* 52: 1108-1129.

Linderfelt, W.R. and Turner, J.V. (2001): Interaction between shallow groundwater, saline surface water and nutrient discharge in a seasonal estuary: The Swan-Canning system. *Hydrological Processes*, 15: 2631-2653.

Lobo, E.A; Katoh, K., and Aruga, Y. (1995): Response of epilithic diatom assemblages to water pollution in rivers in the Tokyo metropolitan area, Japan. *In Freshwater Biol.* 34: 191-204.

Lohmann, K., Jones. J.R., Knowlton. M. F., Swar. D.B., Pamperi. M.A. and Brazos, B.J. (1988): Pre- and post monsoon limno-logical characteristics of lakes in the Pokhara and Kathmandu valleys, Nepal. Verh. *Int. Ver. Limnol.* 23: 558-565.

Madhu, N.V.; Balachandran, K.K.; Martin, G.D.; Jyothibabu, R.; Thottathil, S.D.; Nair, M.; Joseph, T. and Kusum, K.K. (2010): Short term variability of water quality and implication on phytoplanktons production in a tropical estuary (Cochin backwaters-India). *Environmental Monitoring and Assessment*, 170 (1-4): 287-300.

Malik, D. S. and Bharti, P.K. (2005a): Nutrient dynamics in Rhithron zone of Shivalik Himalayan stream Sahastradhara, Dehradun (Uttaranchal), *Env. Cons. J.* 6 (2): 63-68.

Malik, D. S. and Bharti, P.K. (2005b): Fluctuation in planktonic population of Sahastradhara hill-stream at Dehradun (Uttaranchal), *Aquacult.* 6 (2): 191-198.

Malik, D. S. and Bharti, P.K. (2005c): Primary production efficiency of Sahstradhara hill-stream, Dehradun, *Env. Cons. J.* 6 (3): 117-121.

Malik, D. S. and Bharti, P.K. (2007a): Water resources conservation in Vedas, *Gurukula Shodha Bharati,* Vol-7, pp: 231-235.

Malik, D. S. and Bharti, P.K. (2007b): Macro-zoobanthos as pollution indicator in river Saung at Dehradun (Uttaranchal), *J. Exp. Zool. India,* 10 (1): 221-222.

Malik, D. S. and Bharti, P.K. (2007c): Soil quality of irrigated agricultural fields in textile industrial area of Panipat city, *Asian J. Exp. Sciences,* 21 (2): 445-451.

Malik, D. S. and Bharti, P.K. (2007d): Ecology of Sahastradhara Hill-stream at Dehradun (Uttaranchal), In: 'Advances in Aquatic Ecology, Vol-I' ed. by V.B. Sakhare, *Daya Publishing House, New Delhi,* pp: 1-11.

Malik, D. S.; Bharti, P.K. and Grover, S. (2006): Alteration in surface water quality near textile industries at Panipat (Haryana), *Environment Conservation J.,* 7(2): 65-68.

Malik, D. S.; Bharti, P.K. and Yadav, R. (2006): Role of *Eichhornia crassipes* (Water hyacinth) in remediation of sewage water pollutants, *Exp. J. Zool.* 9(1): 117-124.

Malik, D. S.; Bharti, P.K. and Yadav, R.; Kumar, P. and Chauhan, P. (2008): Dispersion of heavy metals in textile effluent and pond environment in Panipat industrial area, *Env. Cons. J.* 9 (3): 77-81.

Malik, D. S.; Bharti, P.K.; Kamboj, N. and Yadav, R. (2007): Quantification of heavy metals migration in groundwater regime due to discharge of textile industrial effluents in Panipat area, Haryana, *Pollution Research,* 26 (4): 725-727.

Malik, D. S.; Bharti, P.K.; Yadav, R. and Deepmala (2008): Distribution of heavy metals in pond sediment in textile industrial area at Panipat (Haryana), *Journal of Ecology and Fisheries,* 1(1): 39-44.

Malik, D. S.; Yadav, R. and Bharti, P.K. (2004): Accumulation of heavy metals in crop plants through irrigation of contaminated groundwater in Panipat region, *Env. Cons. J.* 5 (1-3): 101-104

Malik, D. S.; Yadav, R. and Bharti, P.K. (2009): Role of aquatic macrophytes in the remediation of metal pollutants, In: 'Aquatic Ecology II', *Narendra Publishing House, New Delhi,* pp: 145-158.

Malik, D.S. and Bharti, P.K. (2006): Sahastradhara me Matasya vinod evam paryatan, in proceeding of national seminar on 'Meethajal matsyiki' organized by Rashtriya matsya anuvanshik sansadhan bureau, Lucknow.

Malik, D.S.; Bharti, P. K.; Negi, K.S. and Yadav, R. (2009): Distribution of Metals in Water of an Artificial Lake at Mussoorie, Uttarakhand, In: 'Aquatic biology and aquaculture' edited by V.B. Sakhare, Ambajoagi, MS, *Manglam Publication, New Delhi,* pp: 77-95.

Mayewski, P.A., Lyons. W.B., Spencer, M.J. and Spencer, J.L. (1986): Snow chemistry form Xixabangama Peak, Tibet. *J. Glaciol.*, 30: 112-142.

Miller, C.V., Denis, J.M., Ator, S.W., and Brakebill, J.W. (1997): Nutrients in stream during baseflow in selected environmental settings of the Potomac river Basin, *Journal of the American Water Resources Association*, Vol-33 (6): 1155-1171.

Naidu, P.T., Narashimha Rao, K.L., and Prasad, K.S.S. (1989): Hydrochemistry of Polar river basin Chittor district. Andhra Pradesh, *Asian Environ.* 11: 3-11.

Nautiyal, P. (1982): Some aspects of bio ecology of Tor putitora in relation to hydrobiology of some Garhwal hill-stream. *D. Phill. Thesis;* Garhwal University.

Negi, K.S.; Malik, D.S. and Bharti, P.K. (2006): Impact of river flow regulation on the planktonic population in Ganga river at Rishikesh (Uttaranchal), *Environment Conservation J.*, 7(1): 55-58.

NF (2001): Newfoundland Department of Environment, Water Resources Management Division, "Water Quality Index applied to the Exploits River Watershed" 24 pp. *http://www.gov.nf.ca/env/Env/waterres/Surfacewater/WQI/Exploits-WQI-study.pdf*

Nijampurkar, V.N., Sarin, M.M and Rao, D.K. (1993): Chemical composition of snow and ice from Chhota Shigri glacier, Central Himalaya. *J. Hydrol.* 151: 19-34.

Odum, E.P. (1971): Fundamentals of Ecology. New York. *W.B. Saunders and Co.*

Officer C.B., Biggs, R.B.; Taft, J.; L.E. Cronin, M.A. Tyler, and W. Boynton (1984). Chesapeake Bay Anoxia: Origin, development and significance. *Science*, 223: 23-27.

Ogbonna, D.N. (2010): Seasonal dynamics of microbial population and physicochemical characteristics of a water body receiving industrial pollutants in Port Harcourt, Nigeria. *Agriculture and Biology Journal of North America*, 1(6): 1333-1339.

Ohimain,E.I.; Imoobe, T.O. and Bawo, D.D.S. (2008): Changes in Water Physico-Chemical Properties Following the Dredging of an Oil Well Access Canal in the Niger Delta. *World Journal of Agricultural Sciences*, 4 (6): 752-758.

Ormerod, S.J. and Juttner, I. (1996): Catchment sustainability and river biodiversity in Asia. A case study form Nepal. In Harper, D. and Brown, T. (eds.), Sustainable management in tropical catchments. Chichester: *John Wiley and Sons,.*

Ormerod, S.J.; Buckton, S.T.; Brewin, P.A.; Juttner, I. (1997): University of *Wales, Cardiff, U.K.*- 'Biodiversity, chemistry and structure in stream of the Nepal/Himalaya: Developing biological indicators of change. pp: 631-640.

Osibanjo, O. and Adie, G. U. (2007): Impact of effluent from Bodija abattoir on the physico-chemical parameters of Oshunkaye stream in Ibadan city, Nigeria. *African J. Biotechnol.*, 6(15): 1806-1811.

Otokunefor, T. V. and Obiukwu, C. (2005): Impact of refinery effluent on the physicochemical properties of a water body in the Niger Delta. *Appl. Biol. and Environ. Research*, 3 (1): 61-72.

Pahwa, D.V. and Malhotra, S.N. (1966). *Proc. Nat. Acad. Sci.* 49:212.

Painter, S. and J. Waltho (2003): "Taking the Canada Water Quality Index for a Test Drive". Presented at the CCME National Water Quality Index Workshop, Halifax, Nova Scotia. November 24, 2003.

Palharya, J.P.; Siriah, V.K. and Malviya, S. (1993): In: Environmental impact of sewage and effluent disposal on the river system, *Ashish Pub. House*, New Delhi.

Panda, U. C.; Sunderay, S. K.; Rath, P.; Nayak, B. B. and Bhatta, D. (2006): Application of Factor and cluster analysis for characterization of river and estuarine water systems- A case study: Mahanadi River (India). *Journal of Hydrology*, 331: 434-445.

Pande, R.K. and Asha Mishra (2000): Water quality study of freshwaters of Dehradun (Sahastradhara stream and Mussoorie lake). *Aquacult.* Vol- (1): 57-62.

Parmar, K. and Parmar, V. (2010): Evaluation of water quality index for drinking purposes of river Subernarekha in Singhbhum District. *International Journal of Environmental Sciences*, 1(1): 77-81.

PAU (2005): Ken Betwa river link to submerge parts of Panna TR. In: Protected Area Update, October, 2005, (No. 57) Vol-XI, No-5, pp: 10.

Paul, D.K. and Verma, P.K. (1990): Hydorlogical status of a hill-stream of Santhal Pargna (Bihar). *J. Freshwater Biol.*, 2: 37-43.

Plummer, L.N. and Back, W. (1980): The mass balance approach: application to interpreting the chemical evolution of hydrologic systems. *Am. J. Sci.* 280: 130-142.

Prasad, N.R. and Patil, J.M. (2008): A study of physico-chemical parameters of Krishna river water particularly in western Maharashtra. *Rasayan J. Chem.*, 1(4): 943-958.

Prasanna, M.B. and Ranjan, P.C. (2010): Physico chemical properties of water collected from Dhamra Estuary. *International Journal of Environmental Sciences*, 1 (3): 334-342.

Psenner, R. (1989): Chemistry of high mountain lakes in siliceous catchments of central Alps. *Aquatic Sci.* 51: 108-128.

Puckeh. L.G. (1996): Identifying the major sources of nutrient water pollution. *Environmental science and technology*, 93:408A-414.

Quadri, M.Y. and Shah, G.M. (1984): Hydro-biological feature of Hoassar: A typical wetland of Kashmir-I, Biotope. *Indian J. Ecol.*, 2(2): 203-206.

Rani, N; Sinha, R.K.; Prasad, K and Kedia, D.K. (2011): Assessment of temporal variations in water quality of some important rivers in middle Gangtic plains, India. *Environmental Monitoring and Assessment*, 174 (1-4): 401-415.

Rao, D.S. and Govind, B.V. (1964): Hydrobiology of Tungbhadra reservoir. *Indian J. Fish*, 2(1): 321-344.

Rao, S.M. and Mamtha, P. (2004): Water quality in sustainable water management, Current Science, 87(7):942-947.

Rasmussen P, (1996): Monitoring shallow groundwater quality in agricultural watersheds in Denmark. *Environmental Geology*, 42: 309-319.

Resende, P.C.; Resende, P.; Pardal, M.; Almeida, S. and Ullisses, A. (2010): Use of biological indicators to assess water quality of the Ul river (Portugal). *Environmental Monitoring and Assessment*, 170 (1-4): 535-544.

Reuss, J.O and Johanson. D. W. (1986): Acidic deposition and acidification of soil and surface waters. *Ecological studies no. 59, Springer-Verlag, New York, U.S.A.*

Reza, T.;Bakar,A.; Islam, S. and Bhuiyan, H.R. (2010): Pollution level and monthly fluctuation of pollution -a study of wastewater of Chittagong city, Bangladesh. *Electronic Journal of Environmental, Agriculture and Food Chemistry*, 9 (1):234-238.

Richardson, R.F. (1921): Changes in bottom and shore fauna of the middle Illinois River and its connecting lakes since 1913-1915, as a result of the increased southward of sewage pollution Illinois Nat, *Hist. Surv. Bull.* 14:33-75.

Rocchini, R. and L.G. Swain (1995): The British Columbia Water Quality Index. Water Quality Branch, Environmental Protection Department, British Columbia Ministry of Environment, Land and Parks. pp: 13.

Ross, R.M.; Long, E.S. and Dropkin, D.S. (2008): Response of macroinvertibrate communities to remediation stimulating conditions in Pennsylvania streams influenced by acid mine drainage. *Environmental Monitoring and Assessment*, 145 (1-3): 323-338.

Round, F.E. (1991): Use of diatoms for monitoring rivers. In Whitton, B.A. Rott, E, and Friedrich, G. (eds), Use of algae for monitoring rivers. In: Proceedings of an international symposium 25-32. Dusseldorf: Landesant fur Wasser und Abfall Nordrhein –Westfalen.

Rundle, S.D., Jenkins, A. and Ormerod, S.J. (1993): Macroinvertebrate communities in streams in the Himalayas, Nepal. *Freshwater Biol.* 30: 169-180.

Saksena, D.N.; Garg, R.K. and Rao, R.J. (2008): Water quality and pollution status of Chambal river in National Chambal sanctuary, Madhya Pradesh. *Journal of Environmental Biology*, 29(5): 701-710.

Samantray, P.; Mishra, B.K.; Panda, C.R. and Rout, S.P. (2009): Assessment of Water Quality Index in Mahanadi and Atharabanki Rivers and Taldanda Canal in Paradip Area, India. *J. Hum. Ecol.*, 26(3): 153-161.

Santhanam, R.; Velayntham, p. and Jegatheesan, G; (1989): A manual of freshwater ecology". *Daya publishing house Delhi*-110006: 3-17, 53-92.

Sarin, M.M., Kishanaswamy. S., Dilli. K., Somyajulu. B.L.K. and Moore, W.S. (1989): Major ion chemistry of the Ganga Brahmaputra river system: withering processes and fluxes of the Bay of Bengal. *Geochim. Cosmochim. Acta.* 53: 997-1009.

Sarin, M.M., Krishnaswamy, S.K., Trivedi, J.R. and Sharma, K.K. (1992): Major ion chemistry of the Ganga source waters: weathering in high altitude Himalaya. In: *Proc, Indian acad. Sci.* (*Earth Planet Sci.*) 1, 89-98.

Schwoerbel, J. (1991): Handbook of Limnology, *Ellis Horwood Limited, Chichester, England:* pp- 95-114.

Sharma, (2003): Dams, Rivers and People, SANDRP MAY-JUNE 2003, pp: 44.

Shrama, R.C. (1986): Effect of physico-chemical factors on benthic fauna of Bhargirathi River Garhwal Himalaya. *Indian J. Ecol.* 13(1): 133-137.

Sikoki, F. D. and Zabbey, N. (2006): Environment gradients and benthic community of the middle reaches of Imo River, South Eastern Nigeria. *Environment and Ecology*, 24 (1): 32-36.

Singh, H.R. (2001): Introduction to animal ecology and Environmental Biology'. *S. Nagin and Co, Jalandhar.* pp-150-165, 348-357.

Singh, A.K., Hasnain, S.I. (1998): Major ion chemistry and weathering control in a high altitude basin: Alaknanda river, Garhwal Himalaya, India, *Hydrological science- Journal*, Vol-43 (4-6): 825-843.

Singh, S.N.;Gupta,M.L.; and Prakash, P. (1998): Hydro-biological studies of some eutrophic ponds of Rohtash, Bihar. *Environment and Ecology*, 16 (2): 457-462.

Sinha, D.K, Saxena Shilpi and Saxena Ritesh.2004.Water quality Index for Ram Ganga river at Mordabad. *Poll. Res.*, 23(3): 527-531.

Smith, A.J.; Turner JV, Herne DE, Hick W.P. (2003): Quantifying submarine dishcharge and nutrient discharge into Cockburn Sound, Western Australia. *Centre for Groundwater Studies Report* No. 104, pp: 185.

Solai, A.; Gandhi, M.S.; Sriram, E. (2010): Implications of physical parameters and trace elements in surface water off Pondicherry, Bay of Bengal, South East Coast of India. *International Journal of Environmental Sciences*, 1(4): 529-542.

Sparrevik, M.; Ellan, G.J. and Duijn, M. (2011): Evaluation of Factors Affecting Stakeholder Risk Perception of Contaminated Sediment Disposal in Oslo Harbor. *Environ. Sci. Technol.*, 45: 118–124.

Sridhar, R.; Thangaradjou, T.; Senthil Kumar, S. and Kannan, L. (2006): Water quality and phytoplankton characteristics in the Palk Bay, southeast coast of India. *J. Environ. Biol.*, 27:561-566.

Stottlemyer, R. (1997): Stream water chemistry in watersheds receiving different atmospheric inputs of H^{+}, NH_4^{+} and NO_3^{-} and SO_4^{-2}, *Journal of American water resources Association (JAWRA)* Vol-33 (4): 767-779.

Stottlemyer, R. and C.A., Troendle, (1992): Nutrient concentration patterns in stream draining alpine and sub alpine catchments, Fraser experimental forest, Colourado. *J. Of Hydrol*, 140: 179-208.

Stottlemyer, R. and D. Toczydlowski, (1991): Stream chemistry and hydrologic pathways during snowmelt in a small watershed adjacent lake superior. *Biogeochemistry* 13:177-197.

Subramanian, V. (1979): Chemical and suspended sediment characteristics of river of India. *J. Hydrol*, 44: 37-55.

Sunderay, S. K.; Panda, U. C.; Nayak, B. B. and Bhatta, D. (2006): Multivariate statistical techniques for the evaluation of spatial and temporal variation in water quality of Mahanadi riverestuarine system (India)- a case study. *Environmental Geochemistry and Health*, 28: 317-330.

Tessitore, U.S. (2010): Effects of Eutrophication on benthic life within the littoral zone of freshwater lakes. *International Journal of Environmental Sciences*, 1(4): 684-696.

Tiwari, T.N. and Ali. M. (1987): River pollution in Kathmandu valley- variations of water quality index. *Int. J. Environ. Pollut.* 7: 347-351.

Tranter, M., Tsiouris. S., Davis. T.D. and Jones H.G. (1992): A laboratory investigation of leaching of solute from snow peak by rainfall *Hydorl. Processes* 6: 169-178.

Trivedi, P.; Bajpai, A. and Thareja1, S. (2009): Evaluation of Water Quality: Physico – Chemical Characteristics of Ganga River at Kanpur by using Correlation Study. *Nature and Science*, 1(6): 91-94.

Trivedi, R.K. and Goel, P.K. (1984): Chemical and biological methods for water pollution studies Karad: *Environmental publication*, pp.1-251.

Upadhyaya, N.P. and Roy, N.N. (1982): Studies in river pollution Kathmandu valley, *Indian. J. Environ. Health.* 24: 124-135.

Vahrenkamp, H. (1979): Metalle in Lebensprozessen: Chemie in Unserer Zeit, 7: 97–105.

Varunprasath, K. and Daniel, N.A. (2010): Physico-Chemical Parameters of River Bhavani in Three Stations, Tamilnadu, India. *Iranica Journal of Energy and Environment*, 1 (4): 321-325.

Vasanthkumar, B. and Vijaykumar, K. (2011): Diurnal variation of physico-chemical properties and primary productivity of phytoplankton in Bheema river. *Recent Research in Science and Technology*, 3(4): 39-42.

Vashney, P.K.; R. Vijayalakshmi, Nair and S.H.H. Abid (1983): Primary productivity in near shore water of Thai Maharashtra coast, India. *J.Mar. Sci.* 12:27-30.

Vohra, C.P. (1993): Himalayan glaciers In: Harnessing the eastern Himalayan rivers, regional co-operation in South Asia (ed by B.G. Verghese and Ramaswamy R, lyer). *Kenark, New Delhi, India.*

Wang, L.; Wang, Y.; Xu, C.; An Z. and Wang, S. (2011): Analysis and evaluation of the sources of heavy metals in the water of the river Changjiang. *Environmental Monitoring and Assessment*, 173 (1-4): 301-313.

Wang, Y.; Yang, Z.; Shen, Z.; Tang, Z. and Niu, J. (2010): Assessment of heavy metals in sediments from a typical catchment of the Yangtze river, China. *Environmental Monitoring and Assessment*, 172 (1-4): 407-417.

Weier, K. (1999): The quality of groundwater beneath Australian sugarcane fields. *Australian Sugarcane*, pp: 54.

Weingberg, A.C. (1990): Low input agriculture reduces non-point source pollution. *J.Soil Wat. Conserv.* 45(1): 48-50.

Whitfield, P.H. (1983): Regionalization of water quality in the upper Fraser River basin, British Columbia. *Water Res.*, 17:1053-1066.

William, M.W., Brown, A. and Melack, J.M. (1993): Geochemical and hydrologic controls on the composition of surface water in the high elevation basin, *Sierra Navada. Limnol. Oceanogr*, 38: 775-797.

www.appliedhydrology.org

Xue, H.B. and Schooner, J.L. (1994): Acid deposition and lake chemistry in southwest China. *Wat. Air, Soil Pollut.* 75: 61-78.

Yeragi, S.G. and Nisar Shaikh (2003): Studies on primary productivity of Tansa River. *J. Natcon* 15 (1): 125-130.

Yu, J.; Ho, W.; Lu, H. and Yang, Y. (2011): Study on water quality and senotoxicity of surface microlayer and subsurface water in Guangzhou section of Pearl river. *Environmental Monitoring and Assessment*, 174 (1-4): 681-692.

Zabbey, N.; Sikoki, F.D. and Edoghotu, J. (2008): Plankton assemblages and environmental gradients in the middle reaches of the Imo River, Niger Delta, Nigeria. *African J. of Aquatic Science*, 33(2): 241-248.

Zhang, J., Huang, W.W., Letolle, R., Jusserand C. (1995): Major element chemistry of the Huanghe (yellow river), China- weathering processes and chemical fluxes. *'Journal of hydrology'* Vol-168 (1-4): 173-203.

Index